Praise for *Shift*

"*Shift into Freedom* is a gift to us all. I wholeheartedly recommend this inspiring and profound book. This is one of the finest contemporary meditation manuals that takes mindfulness to the next level. In Loch Kelly you've found a wonderful guide for the journey of awakening, which our endangered world is so hungry for."   LAMA SURYA DAS
Author of *Make Me One with Everything*
and *Awakening the Buddha Within*

"I am so happy that Loch Kelly's groundbreaking teachings are finally available to the general public. This wonderful book translates and updates what used to be only available to a select few who were willing to spend years in a monastery. Whether you are new to meditation or are a seasoned practitioner, *Shift into Freedom* will change you. It will revolutionize your life, giving you immediate access to the freeing awareness that makes it possible to go beyond our small self."

ADAM BUCKO
Co-author of *Occupy Spirituality* and *The New Monasticism*

"Practicing under Loch Kelly's guidance is mind-blowing. You shift out of your chattering mind, and awareness emerges—clear, fearless, unconditionally accepting. This is the 'shift' Loch is writing about, having found the words that point to the wordless. I'm keeping his book close."   AMY GROSS
Former editor-in-chief, *O, The Oprah Magazine*

"Many assume that genuine spiritual realization is either out of reach—'I'm too wounded . . . life's too stressful'—or way down the road. *Shift into Freedom* is a rare and invaluable book that awakens trust in what is possible in this very life, right now. With wisdom, clarity, and care, Loch Kelly offers teachings and practices that directly evolve consciousness and liberate the heart."   TARA BRACH, PHD
Author of *Radical Acceptance* and *True Refuge*

"*Shift into Freedom* offers the reader a remarkable synthesis of practical wisdom from across contemporary meditation, psychology, and neuroscience disciplines. Loch Kelly provides us with a direct and accessible taste of more profound and subtle experiences of effortless mindfulness and heart mindfulness."   DAVID VAGO, PHD
Meditation researcher, Harvard Medical School

"*Shift into Freedom* is a well-written and important contribution. An essential read for anyone interested in learning about this great meditation program of openhearted awareness."

ANDREW NEWBERG, MD
Author of *How God Changes Your Brain*

"This is one of best contemporary books on the integration of meditation and nonduality. Personally, I'm thankful to Loch for offering this gift to humanity at this crucial time when so many people are looking for living spirituality free from outdated paradigms. Read this if you want to wake up to the beautiful mystery of life."

ANAM THUBTEN
Author of *No Self, No Problem* and *The Magic of Awareness*

"*Shift into Freedom* is both a practical and inspirational guide for understanding and accessing what Loch calls 'openhearted awareness.' The book's power comes from decades of experiences accumulated by its author, one of America's most beloved teachers. By reading his words, one's awareness seems to quietly soften and expand into much larger space."   CATHERINE INGRAM
Author of *Passionate Presence* and *In the Footsteps of Gandhi*

"Loch is the best, or among the best, 'pointing-within' teachers in the world right now. By 'pointing-within,' I mean someone who can experientially introduce—and then continue to mentor—folks into authentic higher consciousness and heart. Since his book is about sustaining and maturing this process, it's likely that it will be a major 'threshold' book, just like Eckhart Tolle's *Power of Now* was at the time it was published."
KURT JOHNSON, PHD
Author of *The Coming Interspiritual Age* and *Nabokov's Blues*

"Loch shares his practice experience freely, links it to the similar experiences of many other traditions, and clarifies how these practices work with the science of the day. *Shift into Freedom* will be a great help to many people."
SHARON SALZBERG
Author of *Real Happiness*

"Awakening begins with a shift of identity. It's moving your inner center of gravity from your protective parts to your magnificent essence. Loch has condensed his decades of personal and teaching experience into this wonderful book, which not only makes you realize that such a shift is possible, it also provides exercises to help it happen."
RICHARD C. SCHWARTZ, PHD
Developer of the Internal Family Systems model of psychotherapy

"In this personal and practical call to awaken, Loch Kelly has synthesized decades of Eastern and Western studies and practice into a path that can change your life."
MICHAEL KATZ, PHD
Editor of *Dream Yoga and the Practice of Natural Light*
by Chogyal Namkhai Norbu

"*Shift into Freedom* is a clear and articulate map that combines the finest wisdom of nondual practice with modern psychology and neuroscience on meditation. It is a deep inquiry and wellspring of excellent and most helpful tools that guide us on our path of awakening. It provides us with a practical step-by-step process of deep open-hearted awakening. It will warm your heart, touch your soul, and may deliver you to a lasting, embodied freedom."

RONALD A. ALEXANDER, PHD
Author of *Wise Mind Open Mind*

"*Shift into Freedom* offers the heart-essence of Loch's deep integration of simple yet advanced meditation practices, neuroscience, and psychology. Loch Kelly is one of the very few people who are authorized teachers of mindfulness, Sutra Mahamudra, and nondual traditions. Loch presents simple methods for awakening to, and living from, open-hearted awareness in the midst of your daily life. I highly recommend this wonderfully clear book." PETER FENNER, PHD
Author of *Natural Awakening*

"*Shift into Freedom* is a clear, potent, and liberating guide for our journey from ego centeredness to open-hearted awareness. Drawing from wisdom teachings, neuroscience, and contemporary psychology, Loch Kelly offers a finely detailed, sophisticated set of maps and practices for waking up, waking in, and waking out—all so that we may fully actualize who we really are in our daily lives. Highly recommended!"

JOHN J. PRENDERGAST, PHD
Author of *In Touch: How to Tune in to the Inner Guidance of Your Body and Trust Yourself*

To Paula,

Enjoy the discovery and beautiful unfolding.

Josh

SHIFT
INTO
FREEDOM

Audio Program by Loch Kelly

*Shift into Freedom: A Training in the Science
and Practice of Open-Hearted Awareness*

SHIFT
INTO
FREEDOM

THE SCIENCE AND PRACTICE OF
OPEN-HEARTED AWARENESS

LOCH KELLY

sounds true
BOULDER, COLORADO

Sounds True
Boulder, CO 80306

This work is solely for personal growth and education. It should not be treated as
a substitute for professional assistance, therapeutic activities such as psychotherapy
or counseling, or medical advice. In the event of physical or mental distress,
please consult with appropriate health professionals. The application of protocols
and information in this book is the choice of each reader, who assumes full
responsibility for his or her understandings, interpretations, and results. The author
and publisher assume no responsibility for the actions or choices of any reader.

Published 2015

Cover design by Rachael Murray
Book design by Beth Skelley

Printed in the United States of America

Library of Congress Cataloging-in-Publication Data
Kelly, Loch.
  Shift into freedom : the science and practice of open-hearted awareness /
Loch Kelly ; foreword by Adyashanti.
      pages cm
  Includes bibliographical references and index.
  ISBN 978-1-62203-350-8
  1. Awareness. 2. Consciousness. 3. Mind and body. I. Title.
  BF311.K376 2015
  155.2—dc23
                              2015005862

Ebook ISBN 978-1-62203-389-8

10 9 8 7 6 5 4 3 2 1

To Paige, for all her love,
support, and inspiration

A human being is part of the whole, called by us 'universe,' a part limited in time and space. He experiences himself, his thoughts and feelings, as something separate from the rest— a kind of optical delusion of consciousness. This delusion is a kind of prison for us, restricting us to our personal desires and to affection for a few persons nearest to us. Our task must be to free ourselves from this prison by widening our circle of compassion to embrace all living creatures and the whole of nature in its beauty. The true value of a human being is determined primarily by the measure and the sense in which he has attained liberation from the self. We shall require a substantially new manner of thinking if humanity is to survive.

ALBERT EINSTEIN, *THE WORLD AS I SEE IT,* 1934

CONTENTS

FOREWORD
BY ADYASHANTI

Anew spirituality is dawning in which old ideologies are being reexamined, familiar assumptions are being challenged, and a new birth of teachings and teachers is flowering. At times such as these, when there is a flourishing of spiritual teachings, we need great clarity and discrimination in order to navigate the changing waters and to remain oriented toward what is authentic and mature.

In so many ways our modern life is characterized by change, insecurity, and the opening of new and creative possibilities. Amidst all of this flux and change, our hearts reach out in yearning for deeper forms of connection and wisdom that speak to the human desire for awakening to the sacred dimension of life, not only in the form of transcendence, but also in the form of embodying the sacred within our own humanity as well as in the creative expression of our lives.

Awakening is no longer seen as the exclusive purview of cloistered religious adepts; it is now seen as available to every human being regardless of background, social class, or religious persuasion. And while this new open-mindedness is a great blessing for us all, we need to remain mindful of the challenges and demands that any authentic form of spirituality presents us with. The evolution of the old forms of spiritual practice into new forms is an extremely important matter that requires great spiritual insight and dedication to retaining the profound wisdom of the old traditions while embracing the ever-changing context of secular life. The possibility of democratizing spiritual freedom is upon us, but it is we who must remain faithful to assuring that this new opening of possibilities be grounded in authentic and mature spiritual insight.

We are in need of straightforward, direct, and approachable forms of spirituality that are firmly grounded in the ancient wisdom traditions of our ancestors, while at the same time fully embracing the modern wisdom of both psychology and science. And while good and useful maps of this inclusive terrain of liberation are important, we also need wise and loving guides and mentors who themselves embody the road ahead—lest we end up staring at the map instead of taking the journey ourselves. This is no small task, but it is a necessary task if we are to continue to evolve our experiential knowledge of who and what we are, and to embody ever greater vistas of freedom and love in this ever-changing world of ours. For our human heart cries out for freedom, just as the heart of the world cries out for our wise and loving participation within it.

The book you now hold in your hands is, I believe, a great treasure of ancient, modern, and creatively new spiritual teachings uniquely suited to the challenges of awakening, embodying, and expressing in one's daily life, the deepest revelations of our true nature. In my many years of knowing and working with Loch Kelly, I feel that he is one of the clearest expressions of authentic awakened freedom and love that I know. His laughter and warmth always fill me with good cheer, and his vast experience and inclusiveness of all the dimensions of our shared humanity is a rare and welcomed aspect of his buoyant personality. This book is a shining gem in the modern spiritual landscape. One that invites you, challenges you, and requires you to fully participate in your awakening to truth and the embodiment of love.

The title of this book, *Shift Into Freedom,* hints at the immediacy and practicality of the teachings within it, as well as Loch Kelly's desire to present these teachings in the most available and useful form possible. *Shift Into Freedom* is wise and loving medicine for anyone who is ready to take responsibility for their own liberation here and now, for the teachings in this book put all the tools for liberating yourself in body, mind, and spirit into your own hands. There is no teacher worshiping here, no belief required, no theology to ascribe to—just direct, immediate, and practical guidance that evolved from Loch's vast experience and deep commitment to the whole spectrum of human potential and his desire to awaken to spiritual freedom. The intricate commitment to clarity and practicality that went into writing this book is a gift to us all and I, for one, am grateful for Loch's lifelong commitment to the dharma and to his dedication to presenting these powerful teachings in such a contemporary and approachable way.

INTRODUCTION

Tell me, what is it you plan to do
with your one wild and precious life?

MARY OLIVER, FROM "THE SUMMER DAY"¹

I remember it was one of those cold, clear winter nights. As my college library closed its doors, I began to trudge up the steep hill to my dorm. My body was exhausted; my heart was heavy with grief as my mind pored over the events of the past year. I'd lost my father, who'd been battling brain cancer for two years. My grandmother, who had been living with our family for twelve years, had recently passed on. And then a month later, one of my best friends died in a tragic car accident. I'd been plunged deep into the river of old age, sickness, and death—and I was trying to swim or at least stay afloat.

Halfway up the hill, I heard a loud thought in my mind: *I don't know if you can take this much pain.* I stopped and stood still. Who was talking and who couldn't take the pain? I turned within and looked for who was talking, but to my surprise found open space. My thoughts quieted and my heart broke wide open. The weight of my despair lifted, and I felt not only relief but also pervasive joy, wellbeing, and love streaming through my being. Tears ran down my cheeks, and I laughed and cried at the same time. I looked up at the stars sparkling in the boundless night sky, feeling connected and supported.

As I stood there, breathing deeply, I noticed that my usual sense of self was gone, yet I felt fully embodied and alive. From that night onward I could feel the grief, but there was more space and compassion to help me feel my emotions without being overwhelmed. I even remember thinking that I, too, would die one day—but even that seemed okay. Something had changed and a new process had begun. I realized that I had the freedom to choose to do anything with my life.

The experience showed me the possibility that consciousness can shift unintentionally, but at that time I didn't yet know how to let go and shift into it intentionally. Now, my motivation for writing this book is to provide a clear guide to awakening, written in modern language—a guide I would have liked to read myself in the midst of my own journey. Writing has been a labor of love underlied by the intention to share these tools with you.

Back then, I shared my experience with a few close friends, but no one could relate. So I began to seek understanding by reading about other peoples' similar experiences. At the time, I'd just finished *The Varieties of Religious Experience* by William James, a psychologist during the turn of the twentieth century, who talked about these experiences by understanding them in spiritual, psychological, and consciousness terms rather than only in religious language. He included reports from ordinary people who described awakenings and shifts of consciousness that seemed natural and deeper than our ordinary, egoic self-consciousness.

I'd experienced small, spontaneous shifts earlier in my life, but after that night I began trying to find ways to intentionally shift my consciousness. This exploration proved to be a long and winding road, where I often stumbled toward the light. Eventually I came to realize that the most important and common aspect is relief from the burden of an anxious and dissatisfied "self." I wondered, is this relief a temporary state? Or is it possible that the sense of love, wellbeing, and unity is the potential foundation of who we are, always present underneath our chattering mind?

Wanting to learn from those who had explored similar questions, I went to graduate school and was offered a traveling fellowship to Sri Lanka, India, and Nepal. There I had time to meditate and meet remarkable people who discussed their experiences and journeys freely. When I returned, I trained to become a psychotherapist who combines meditation with psychology, and I worked in community mental health for many years. I started seeing a psychotherapist for myself, got sober, and married the most amazing woman, who is the love of my life.

I had also fallen in love with inquiring into the play of consciousness and the potential for anyone to awaken. In 2002 a friend gave me a book and told me that the author and I shared the same way of talking about awakening and embodiment. I went to meet and sit with the American-born meditation teacher Adyashanti, who soon after invited me to join him in teaching a modern, nondual approach to awakening. This approach emphasized the possibility of awakening in the midst of everyday life. I had studied this type of approach with my first teacher, Tulku Urgyen Rinpoche, in Nepal. Since then, I studied for many years with his sons, Tsoknyi Rinpoche and Mingyur Rinpoche. In 2004, during a meeting with Mingyur Rinpoche after a retreat, I told him about the awareness approach I was developing to teach meditation. After a long, in-depth discussion during which Rinpoche interviewed me about my view and experience, he said, "I would like you to teach Sutra Mahamudra." When he authorized me to teach, he emphasized how important it was to include contemporary science and to find ways to make awakening more available to people.

Mahamudra is taught mainly in Tibetan Buddhism today, but its roots come from the Indian Buddhism of the second century. Mahamudra was primarily a movement of lay practitioners who developed a style of practice to facilitate awakening in the midst of their daily lives. The practice of Mahamudra flourished because it was simple, direct, and did not include complicated physical or energetic practices. One of my teachers, Dzogchen Ponlop Rinpoche, says, "The meditation of Sutra Mahamudra essentially consists of resting one's mind, free of mental activity, in the state of nonconceptual wisdom. . . . [Sutra Mahamudra] is seen as a very profound method because it does not require any of the sophisticated and complex tantric rituals, deity yoga visualization practices, or *samayas*. . . . Sutra Mahamudra has a tradition of skillful means that contains profound methods of directly pointing out the selfless and luminous nature of mind."[2]

A modern Sutra Mahamudra approach starts with mindfulness meditation, which has been proven to reduce stress, and then continues to the next levels of meditation, including effortless mindfulness and heart mindfulness, which relieve deeper levels of suffering. Today, I draw on examples from these and many other meditation traditions in my teaching, in what I consider a modern *human being lineage*.

Where Are We Now?

Humanity has made rapid progress during recent years in areas such as technology, medicine, and communications. Yet parts of our brain and consciousness still operate as if we're living in primitive times. If we're going to survive and thrive in the twenty-first century, we must consciously participate in evolving and upgrading our own operating system. Effective tools of awareness are very much needed now, if we want to preserve our planet and create a sustainable quality of life for all people. The good news is we can learn how to intentionally shift our awareness in order to grow into the next stage of human development.

We are very fortunate that many ancient, rare meditation manuals have recently been brought out of their native countries, translated, published, and made available to the public. However, these ancient manuals often use archaic or esoteric language. This book is an attempt to translate these practices into modern, simple, and experiential language. In order to understand awakening, we cannot look only at the physical, mental, emotional, or psychological levels of experience. This is why it may initially seem difficult to understand.

We can learn a new way of using the tools of awareness to examine the levels of consciousness within us. This is a new way of looking, but it is no more difficult than looking at our mental or psychological experience. There really are no words in English that accurately describe the subtle states of consciousness discovered in the process of awakening. The subtler levels of consciousness can be very difficult to articulate or understand without experiencing them for yourself. Although awakening may be beyond precise description, living from open-hearted awareness is a palpable experience—and therefore learnable and teachable.

Shift into Freedom is a synthesis of ancient wisdom, modern psychology, and current neuroscience research. This is not a psychological or religious approach but an adult-education way of learning the map and tools to transform your own consciousness. The intention is to bring the process of awakening into our modern culture so that it can be studied, discussed, and included in the same way psychology and, more recently, mindfulness meditation have been. My focus is not on the psychological work that helps you prepare for awakening, but on how to welcome and detox your thoughts and emotions after you start awakening. It offers unique awareness practices for the body, mind, and emotions that can be done in the midst of your daily life. The result of these practices is the discovery of a deeper sense of wellbeing and peace of mind, along with a feeling of loving connection. The unique premise of this book is that wellbeing is not found by calming the mind, changing our thoughts, or adjusting our attitudes, but by actually shifting into a level of mind that is already calm and alert.

Shift into Freedom begins where many books on spiritual growth, meditation, and psychology leave off. It expands the definition of awakening. Awakening has been deemed a rare occurrence because its principles have not yet been understood in a modern way. One view holds that you can't awaken because it's too hard without living in a monastery or cave. The other view is that there is nothing to do—that there are no meditations, steps, or stages. In this view, you can't awaken intentionally; it happens only by luck or grace—and then you remain awake. The middle way is that a series of direct recognitions can lead to a gradual unfolding with steps and stages. Awakening is not too difficult if you're interested and motivated. It's like learning to read and write: we all have the capacity to awaken.

We start by learning how to wake up from our mistaken identity, continue by "waking-in" to our body and emotions, and then "waking-out" to relationships with others and seeing that we are part of a greater whole. The book presents living from open-hearted awareness as the next stage of human development.

The tools in this book enable us grow beyond our current small, self-centered viewpoint to live from a more open-hearted, interconnected, and embodied ground of Being. Many meditation descriptions and talks have been updated with modern metaphors. The emphasis here is to modernize the practices so that they're more available to everyone. The open-hearted awareness approach updates what are considered advanced meditations. However, these methods are just as easy to learn as beginning meditation practices.

The goal of the open-hearted awareness approach to awakening and growing up is not showing you how to transcend or escape the human condition, but helping you discover how to live a fully intimate human life. To do this, you'll first develop the capacity to see things as they really are. This includes both the positive qualities as well as the capacity to see the truth of how we have been creating suffering for ourselves and others.

Learning how to employ awareness to navigate, shift, and reconfigure your consciousness is the key to your freedom and happiness. Instead of using meditation only to enjoy brief periods of relief and stress reduction, you can learn how to develop into a stable stage of honest, clear, compassionate expression and how to awaken to your full potential as a human being. *Shift into Freedom* is designed to help you shift out of the separate, small sense of self that makes you feel alienated, alone, anxious, and fearful and into the support of awake awareness that is already calm, alert, loving, and wise. Once you shift into freedom, your true nature spontaneously emerges as a vast, interconnected ground of being.

Guideposts along the Journey

Part I of this book, The View, provides an overview of the open-hearted awareness approach and how it synthesizes science, psychology, and meditation. The first chapter describes awake awareness as a natural human capacity, while the second chapter illustrates the primary method of directly recognizing awake awareness and focusing on the unfolding. Chapter 3 introduces the unique tool of local awareness, which is what allows us to shift, and chapter 4 offers a map of the levels of mind that we shift through. The View section ends with a chapter on recent scientific research and a modern context for awakening that's available to all people.

Part II focuses on shifts in our way of knowing and identity. It begins with two chapters that describe a shift from thought-based, conceptual knowing to awareness-based, nonconceptual knowing. Then it goes on to describe the root cause of our mistaken identity. The second section ends with a description of the anatomy of awareness and a chapter that defines living from embodied, open-hearted awareness.

The book's final section focuses on "waking-up," "waking-in," and "waking-out" as the next stages of human development. I discuss effortless mindfulness as a way of practicing in order to stabilize and live from open-hearted awareness. This section concludes with a discussion of the process of unfolding, detoxing, and rewiring in order to live from the new awareness-based operating system.

Throughout this book, you'll find practices at the end of each chapter designed to help you experience the material directly for yourself. You'll encounter some repetition of themes and definitions throughout this book because it is a practice book. This is done to introduce new material and build new habits. There's reinforcement in saying some of the same things in different ways. I often first give you a simple definition and basic principle but then later go into more depth and show how it relates to new themes and practices. I also present several different metaphors for the same topic so that people of all learning styles can relate. I liken this approach to walking around an object to look at it from all sides. The words in this book are pointers to help you experience shifting into freedom and living from there.

The Experiential Map

Shift into Freedom will show you the anatomy of awareness, a useful map that allows you to navigate your journey. This book uniquely focuses on the journey after initial awakening and how to develop emotional intelligence to support the unfolding. Even if you choose not to travel the full journey available in this book, there are tools that you can use right away, and even one small glimpse of what I call "awake awareness" may change your life. You will read about how to shift immediately into open-hearted awareness, using small glimpses many times. These glimpses retrain your brain and can lead you into a new stage of development.

It's one thing to sit on the beach and read a book about the ocean; it's another thing to jump into the water! I'm pointing you toward the ocean, but you won't fully understand until you've jumped in. You won't need to intellectually comprehend your new consciousness before glimpsing it directly. The descriptions are meant to reframe the way you look at things. I encourage you to keep reading even if you don't understand all the new terms right away. Later, after you've tried some of the practices, you can come back and reread the descriptions to compare them to your experience. Awakening is more like learning to ride a bicycle, type on a keyboard, or drive a car than studying for an exam. Once you directly experience these states and stages of consciousness, they will become second nature to you, and you will be able to shift easily.

This book is a user's manual for your consciousness that can be adapted to your individual learning style. I give you the map, show you the direction to travel, and offer descriptions of the territory you may find. The pointers are to help find your own inner GPS so you can navigate your own way. But you won't know what it's really like until you've been there yourself. Don't take my words, pointers, or impressionistic map too literally. Read initially to get the gist of the approach, but trust what you learn from your own experience.

While a detailed map of awakening can be helpful to many, it's not meant to guide you through a mandatory, step-by-step process. There is no right or wrong way to experience the unfolding of awakening. Although I break down awakening into levels of mind, please remember that these levels are nested within one another. People have shifted levels of mind in many different ways and accessed awakening through various doorways. For example, where I have described four small, distinctive steps, some people arrive at open-hearted awareness in a single movement without breaking it down into steps. If some of the instructions puzzle you, don't worry. This book presents a variety of ways to learn about and navigate the territory of awakening. There are general principles, of course, but each person has his or her own way of living them.

The open-hearted awareness practices provide pointers to guide you back to the living truth that's already within you. My intention here is to present you with a hypothesis and a set of experiments. It will be up to you to try out these experiments and observe the results. My hope is that this experience will shift you into a new way of knowing and being. To learn the open-hearted awareness approach to awakening, you'll enter a new way of learning and unlearning, and you'll need to make this a daily habit to gain the most benefits. If you enter with a beginner's mind and open heart, I trust you will find that the experience of freedom and love will become your motivation.

THE VIEW

1

BEING HOME
WHILE RETURNING HOME

*Don't go to the tangled jungle looking for the great awakened elephant
that is already resting quietly at home in front of your own hearth.*

LAMA GENDUN RINPOCHE[1]

Once there was a fish who had heard tales of the Source of Life, which would bring whoever found it their heart's desires. The fish swam to every corner of the ocean, asking: "Where is the Source of Life? How can I find it?" She kept getting pointed toward different tasks and to more remote parts of the sea—farther, deeper, higher.

After many years of seeking, the fish arrived back at the place where she had first started. Entering her home waters, she encountered an older fish who asked, "What is going on with you, my friend? Why do you look so worried and dejected?"

"I've spent years looking for the Source of Life," the fish explained. "I can't even begin to tell you how many things I've tried or the number of places I've searched—all in vain. I don't suppose you know where I could find it?"

The old fish smiled and said, "I've heard many names for the Source of Life in my day, but the simplest is 'water.'"

Just like the fish, we have been searching for an amazing life source. Although this essential source is beyond our ability to accurately describe in words, we have given it many names: Truth, God, Peace, Source, Love, True Nature, Enlightenment, Unity, or Spirit, but the simplest name is *awareness*. Like the fish, we may have looked high and low, inside and outside, for this source of life and freedom. But what if that which we seek is closer than our own breath? What if the source of life already surrounds and permeates us?

Meeting thousands of people from many cultures and all walks of life, I've found that most have tasted the "water of life." Many have glimpsed the depth and essential quality of our being: an experience of peace and love, free from our limited mind. Like the fish, we long to find and live from that level of awareness, but because most of us have stumbled upon it unintentionally, we don't know how to find it intentionally.

Awareness is the foundation of living a human life. We cannot know anything without it. Yet, although awareness is so essential, we know very little about it. Mostly we take it for granted and focus on content: things we are aware *of* rather than awareness itself. The awareness we seek is right here, right now, and equally available to each of us. Similar to functions of the autonomic nervous system such as breathing, awake awareness is already happening by itself. However, awareness usually remains elusive because we don't know how to recognize it. Awareness is not something we need to create or develop. We will need to find a way to discover, uncover, or recover this awareness. Discovering awareness involves as much unlearning as learning, but I'm convinced there is a way for each of us to shift into awareness, feel the freedom it offers, and learn to live from here. You can glimpse this freedom of awareness and shift into it as easily as you can now shift from being aware of reading to being aware of the sensations in your right hand.

Awareness Is Awake

When our basic awareness is revealed to be the foundation of both how we know and who we are, we can call it "awake awareness." Discovering awake awareness is key to the transformation of consciousness called *awakening* that leads to our ability to live from freedom, wellbeing, and loving connection. Awakening is a shift of our identity and also a shift of our way of knowing. Awake awareness is the essence of both our ground of Being and the source of our mind. This transformation is a simple shift of awake awareness from the background of our consciousness to the foreground.

Because we're in the habit of focusing on fast-moving thoughts and strong emotions, and of seeking happiness outside ourselves, we don't notice awake awareness. Our current constellation of consciousness restricts our perception of our wholeness. Awakening does not begin by changing our belief system or improving our external circumstances. Awakening begins with shifting out of the way we organize our current mind and identity, which is creating ignorance and confusion. We can learn how to shift out of our thought-based mind and into an awareness-based way of knowing. Then, from awareness-based knowing, we can embody, connect, and welcome all experience. The feeling of embodied, awareness-based knowing is similar to being in a flow state, being in the zone, being in love, doing selfless service, or laughing with close friends. It is being so fully alive in the now that you "forget yourself." Living from awareness-based knowing gives us true freedom of choice.

Awake awareness is invisible, contentless, formless, boundless, and timeless, but it is the ground of our being. When you shift out of your conventional sense of self, there is a gap of not-knowing. Awake awareness is who we *are* prior to the personal conditioning we usually turn to for our identity. Rather than looking to our thoughts, memories, personality, or roles to identify ourselves, we learn to know awake awareness as the primary dimension of who we are, the ground of Being. Then, with unconditioned awake awareness as the foundation of identity, we can include our conditioned thoughts, emotions, and sensations as waves of the ocean of our life. When people feel awake awareness as their primary dimension of consciousness, they report feeling an essential wellbeing that is free, loving, and safe. Awake awareness, as the ground of being, is the same in all of us, and our individuality arises out of it.

Awake awareness is sometimes called "pure awareness," but it's also inherent within all forms of our consciousness. At other times, the term "awakened awareness" is used, but awareness is always awake and so has not awakened. Awake awareness is always already here, and it is only a matter of learning how to directly access it. One of the most important things to learn is how to separate awareness from thinking, and then we can see that thoughts and emotions are not the center of who we are. We then discover that awareness is the source of mind that brings the peace that passes understanding. One student said, "This is what it feels like to be open-minded." It is our natural wisdom mind, both prior to and beyond conceptual thinking. Awake awareness can "know" something without referring overtly to thoughts, but it can also use thought when needed.

When we discover the important ability to step back into awake awareness, we are no longer identified with our worried thoughts and fearful emotions. That which is aware of fear is not fearful. When awake awareness is then experienced as inherent within everything, we feel unity with all life. We begin to move from open-mindedness to *open-hearted awareness,* the expression of awake awareness that knows unconditional love and interconnectedness with all things. Recognition of awake awareness as the ground of Being is like "returning home" and resting as who you have always been.

Shifting into awake awareness is not like putting on rose-colored glasses; it's more like taking away our blinders. In the open-hearted awareness approach, instead of trying to tame the wild horses of thoughts and emotions inside a too-small corral, we simply open the gates, discovering the larger field of awareness in which the thoughts can move freely. The most helpful way to be free of disturbing emotional states is not by attempting to "break" or get rid of them, but by realizing that these states are made of awareness itself. Awake awareness, as the primary source of how we know and who we are, can't be harmed by any strong emotional state. You will discover that essential wellbeing is not found by calming our minds or by changing our thoughts or attitudes, but actually by shifting out of our chattering minds and into a freedom that is already available.

The journey of awakening is a series of shifts and small glimpses. Awake awareness can be glimpsed and directly experienced in an instant, bringing great relief. A man who helped me with my computer one day asked for an experiential pointer to awake awareness before he left. I showed him one similar to the "glimpse" practices at the end of this chapter. He emailed me back, saying, "When I came to see you, I had been anxious, overwhelmed, and stressed for weeks. All of that seemed to drop away in minutes and didn't start up again. I probably had the best week of my life this week." This is an example of why awake awareness is often called the "ultimate medicine." The discovery and uncovering of awake awareness immediately opens us to natural qualities of peace, joy, love, and courage.

Why We Don't Recognize Awake Awareness

If awake awareness is something we've all experienced, and if it's so close and accessible, why isn't it more familiar to us? How could we have we missed it? Why haven't we been able to access it intentionally? If awake awareness has so many benefits, why isn't it primary on our psychological maps?

The Shangpa Kagyü Tibetan Buddhist tradition gives us a poetic response to the question of why we don't recognize awake awareness. We don't recognize awake awareness because it is:

> So close you can't see it
> So subtle your mind can't understand it
> So simple you can't believe it
> So good you can't accept it

We are so smart, and our lives are so complex, that it's hard to believe that simply discovering awake awareness could be the solution to our suffering. It's also hard to believe that the most important discovery is already here within us; we don't have to go on an odyssey to find it, earn it, or develop it. We are so used to knowing ourselves through our troubles, our dramas, and our obsessions that awake awareness, which is our true nature and our basic goodness, is hard to accept as our true identity.

The main obstacle to relief from suffering is our current identity, what Einstein called our "optical delusion of consciousness." Paradoxically, this same identity is trying to solve the problem of our suffering. This identity seems very real, as if it is a separate self that feels located in our heads. Both ancient wisdom and modern neuroscience now agree that there is no physical location of a separate self that can be found in the brain. Living as if there were a separate self inside your head is considered having a mistaken identity, and this is the root of suffering. We will call this mental self-referencing process *ego-identification.*

Shame-based core stories of being unlovable and worthless are held together by our mistaken identity, but we can be liberated from feeling worthless by shifting into awake awareness. Ego-identification is only one limited way of organizing your identity. Ego-identification is not "you" identifying with "your ego"; it is a pattern of consciousness made up of thinking and ego functions (such as seeking and protection) that form during our early biological development. Once this ego-identification pattern begins to generate the feeling that it has a physical boundary, a central seat of identity is created.

Ego-identification is not our personality, our personal history, or our ego functions. The simple confusion of ego functions (what we do) and self-awareness (the ability to think about thinking) with our identity (who we are) is at the root of this type of existential suffering. Ego-identification is a mental pattern of consciousness that creates the feeling of a "mini-me" inside our heads. It doesn't have to be fought, repressed, extinguished, denied, or killed. We don't become a nobody, an angel, or a couch potato. Instead, when we discover awake awareness as our true nature, our ego functions can return to their natural roles and semi-retire from their second job as identity.

One woman said her life had transformed because of these practices. "The panic attacks I had are gone," she said. "I laugh more, and mostly at myself!" She brought her husband to an introductory class I was teaching, and he sat at the back of the room with his arms crossed, looking half-asleep during my initial talk. After the second experiential exercise, when I asked everyone what the shift into awake awareness revealed, he suddenly brightened and said, "It's me! The *real* me I haven't felt since childhood."

When we shift out of ego-identification and subsequently know awake awareness as our true ground of being, we feel that there's nothing we need to gain or get rid of in order to feel okay on the level of identity. We will not discover freedom and love by restricting our physical needs; by creating a stronger, calmer, more focused mind; or by trying to create security and success in the world. Moving pieces on the chessboard of our minds will not clear up our confusion or end our suffering. For that, we need to shift out of ego-identification and into awake awareness.

By deconstructing, or shifting out of ego-identification, we won't necessarily discover awake awareness. We can end up being spaced out, blissed-in, or lost in our unconscious mind. We can even become caught in meditation states such as being "comfortably numb" or in a detached "witness-protection program." It is not enough to have an insight into the absence of a separate self. We must also discover the presence of awareness-based knowing so that we can live from here.

Awake awareness might seem like a new experience; however, it's not an altered state, a transcendent state, or even a meditative state. It's our innate, true nature that is always here. When we have shifted into awake awareness, we realize that ego-identification is actually the altered state. By recognizing awake awareness, we are dehypnotizing ourselves from the trance of ego-identification.

HAVE WE MET BEFORE?

Many of us have unwittingly glimpsed awake awareness throughout our lives. In fact, we often seek its enjoyable qualities without realizing that awake awareness is their source. From our current level of mind we cannot experience our ground of Being, deep wisdom or open-hearted awareness. Although we may not have known it, whenever we experienced love and wisdom, it has always been because we shifted levels of mind.

Many of us have unknowingly dropped into awake awareness while walking in nature, being creative, making love, or playing sports; some of us have experienced it through crisis that became opportunity. Although activities like nature walks are pleasurable in themselves, they also relax the dominance of ego-identification, allowing awake awareness to emerge from the background.

When we go hiking and get to the top of a hill, our seeking to reach a goal stops. We relax fully, and our identity as the seeker drops away, revealing the awake awareness that was naturally there all along. At times like these, natural qualities of awake awareness show up—among them clarity, boundless freedom, peace of mind, joy, connection, and a sense of wellbeing. Because we don't know that the source of our joy and freedom is already within us, we might say later, "I feel miserable these days. I'll just have to wait until I can go back to the top of that hill again next year."

There is an old wisdom saying: "Silence is not the absence of sound but the absence of self."[2] In other words, we don't need to go to a physically quiet place. We can experience both the deep stillness and the dancing aliveness that arise simultaneously. Silence and stillness are here now within you as you are reading this book. Awake awareness and its natural qualities are not connected to any specific place, person, or activity—nor is awake awareness dependent on any internal thoughts or external conditions. If we try to re-create our experience by going back up that hill, our expectant state may keep us from letting go of the seeking mind long enough to allow awake awareness to be revealed again.

Many of us have tried to find awake awareness. We've tried to earn it through good deeds, achieve it through meditation, or pray that it will be granted. Some believe that it is available only to the highly evolved. Others believe it only appears through luck or a kind of grace that is either given to us or absent from our lives. When the obscuration of ego-identification dissolves, it can seem as if grace or awake awareness had been absent and then newly arrives from somewhere else. What if awake awareness is not earned by good deeds or given only to a fortunate few? What if awake awareness is not missing and does not come and go? What if awake awareness is *always* already here, inherent within each of us? We can learn to become grace prone by becoming familiar with opening to the grace that's always here within and around us.

Many people get caught in the trap of focusing only on manifestations of the invisible awareness. These kinds of manifestations include light, energy, rapture, bliss, external success, charisma, an inner voice, visions, or stillness. These manifestations are real, but they are only transitional meditation effects. They are not awake awareness itself. Positive energetic expressions can be preliminary stepping-stones or doorways to awake awareness.

We can also get caught up in focusing on positive manifestations in the world as our goal. But if we don't recognize awake awareness as the unmanifest source of all manifestations, the positive manifestations can seduce us into believing external things that come and go are the source of our happiness. When we are happy without a cause, we are free to make choices that benefit ourselves and others.

Many who have longed and strived to know awake awareness have missed it, not because they lacked desire or commitment, but because they didn't know where to look or what to look with. One reason we *can't find it, see it,* or *understand it* is because awake awareness is not an "it." Awake awareness is not an object or thing that can be seen, heard, touched, smelled, or tasted. It isn't a thought, an emotion, image, belief, sensation, or even energy. The Zen tradition says, "To seek Mind with the discriminating mind is the greatest of all mistakes."[3] Neither the five senses, the thinking mind, the ego, the will, the imagination, nor attention can know awake awareness. Just as the eye cannot hear sounds, thinking and attention cannot know awake awareness. The one who is reading these words and trying to experience awake awareness cannot do so until you let go of the way of knowing that you use in other areas of life. Only awake awareness can know awake awareness.

The Power of How: Local Awareness

One of the main reasons we don't awaken is because we have not yet solved this paradox of how *only awareness can know awareness.* The question arises: If we are not operating from awareness now, how do we access the awareness that can know awake awareness?

The most common answer is to sit in meditation for long periods of time so the chattering mind will settle and eventually allow awake awareness to be revealed. This usually requires a full-time commitment. However, with the discovery of local awareness, we can immediately access awake awareness in any place at any time. *Local awareness* is the expression of awake awareness that can unhook from thinking and know itself. Although you may not understand what local awareness is or how to find it, once you are introduced to local awareness in the glimpse practices at the end of this chapter, you will discover that using it is as easy as tying your shoes.

The open-hearted awareness approach first introduces you to local awareness, and then local awareness will introduce you to all levels of mind and locations of identity. Then you can begin to navigate through your own consciousness and become able to live from fully embodied, open-hearted awareness. Local awareness, the primary tool of the open-hearted awareness approach, is the mode or expression of awake awareness that is able to move to different levels of mind.

Normally, local awareness is obscured by our faster-moving thoughts and stronger emotions. However, we find that local awareness can easily detach from thinking and shift into awake awareness, which is then our new ground of being. This process of local awareness detaching from thought and then joining awake awareness is called *unhooking* and *recognizing.* We learn a simple set of practices for unhooking local awareness from ego-identification and using it to directly recognize awake awareness. Local awareness is able to know awareness that is already effortlessly awake because it is never separate from it. As soon as we are looking from awake awareness, we have shifted into an awareness-based operating system from which we can live.

CHANGING THE CHANNEL

Local awareness is like a radio tuner or TV remote that can intentionally shift us to different bandwidths of consciousness. Local awareness can tune away from the narrow, mental, ego-identified station that is the everyday mind and tune in to the station of the body's senses. Local awareness can also tune in to *spacious awareness,* the expression of awake awareness that is unconditioned, boundless, pure awareness.

Your mind is like a TV or radio with lots of stations playing all at once. Many of us are tuned in to the Thinking Channel all day long, and most of these programs are talk shows. We don't realize that there is a tuner that will allow us to change the channel. However, when we learn to use local awareness, then talk shows on the Thinking Channel no longer need to be our regularly scheduled programs. There are other dimensions of mind and identity that are always available and can be accessed with local awareness.

There's initial relief when we're able to tune away from the Thinking Channel, but if we don't know what to tune in to next, we may land on Negative-Mood Music Channel or the Unconscious Nightmare Station. Some people might subscribe to the Too-Serious Satellite Channel or You're No Good FM or the Fear-and-Worry News Network. In fact, we might become identified with one voice in our heads and believe this single, small bandwidth is who we are. This loud I-AM radio station is preset to override the other bandwidths of our lives.

You might be seeing old episodes from your early life playing in your mind's eye. Whether these are soap operas or horror shows, you're likely seeing them from the point of view of a character inside the story rather than that of an outside viewer. It's easy to get involved with chase scenes, revenge plotlines, or romantic tragedies if you don't know that they're only recordings being played over and over again. We think these regularly scheduled programs are the place to look for solutions to our dissatisfaction with our lives, so we channel-surf through them constantly. But reruns, reality shows, or game shows that offer cash and prizes are the wrong place to find satisfaction.

We can shift out of being located in ego-identification, which is looking through our eyes as if the world is virtual reality or reality TV. Fortunately, with local awareness, we can learn to intentionally tune away from chattering bandwidths and tune in to the silent music of the awake awareness that is always in the background. When we shift into awake awareness and awake awareness is embodied, we are in real contact with the world and ourselves.

The Paradox of Awakening

Moving from glimpsing awake awareness to knowing and living from awake awareness is called *awakening*. Awakening is not about simply believing that all is well; it's about shifting into the level of mind that knows and feels all is well. We cannot understand awakening if we consider only behavior, thinking, and psychology. To understand awakening, we need to look at the level of experience of consciousness and awareness. This may be new, but it's not difficult once you learn the basics of how to look, where to look, and what to look for. Intellectually understanding awakening is like having a strand of Christmas lights; directly experiencing awakening is like plugging them in.

Even though we are already home, we don't know it—so we need to learn to return. We begin by glimpsing the end goal. The goal is our path. There's a Tibetan Dzogchen saying that the journey of awakening is like climbing up a mountain while simultaneously swooping down from above. We're getting here while being here. Here is the paradox of being home while returning home: 1) Ultimately, you are already home in awake awareness, and all is well as it is. 2) However, usually we do not experience this from our everyday mind. 3) Awake awareness is like the sun: it's never gone, only covered by clouds. 4) Not knowing that we are home is the cause of suffering. 5) We can shift out of our thought-based, everyday mind and return home to awake awareness. 6) On the level of identity there is nothing to be improved. 7) On the level of mind we can glimpse awake awareness and then know and live from awake awareness.

Awakening will let you know that you are not who you think you are and will introduce you to your true nature. In order to live from a new view, we must first let go of the old. What feels like leaving home, with the fear of homelessness, is eventually discovered to be returning to the home you never left.

THE PROCESS OF AWAKENING

Awakening is possible for you. It may sound like a big, esoteric thing—especially when you are having a bad day. We are all imperfect. That is not going to change, but neither is the fact that we can realize who we are is already unconditional love itself. Today there is a potential for a new stage of human development that combines awakening and growing up. It's clear you can only grow up to a certain level unless you awaken, and it's also important to mature psychologically while awakening. No matter how advanced we get spiritually, the goal is not to transcend being human.

In order to awaken, you don't have to leave your life, go to a cave, become an Olympic-level meditator, or take on any set of religious beliefs. Regardless of your belief system or your spiritual affiliation (or nonaffiliation), you can begin awakening in the midst of your daily life. You don't even have to wait until you've gotten your life together. In fact, if you're looking from ego-identification, you'll never feel good enough or prepared enough. Most adults are ready. Chances are if you're reading this book, you're ready. If you've had practice concentrating, completing tasks in school and at work, and forming relationships, you've grown up enough to wake up and learn to live from open-hearted awareness.

Awakening is about relieving suffering and increasing wellbeing through a shift of identity and knowing. We all have frustrations and sufferings at all levels of our physical, mental, and emotional life. There are different ways to approach these problems. However, the suffering addressed in awakening is a very particular type of suffering—a pervasive confusion and a perpetual dissatisfaction caused by ego-identification. Awakening addresses the root cause—not just the symptoms of craving and aversion. Although physical and emotional pain are legitimate suffering and normal parts of human life, suffering from our mistaken identity is optional.

In this approach, awakening begins with a direct recognition but then has a gradual unfolding. It is not instant enlightenment or an escape from the human condition. Ultimately, who you are is always awake awareness—and yet realizing this begins an unfolding into human form. Just glimpsing your basic nature can be a profound shift in itself.

The awakening process often begins with an initial *waking-up* from ego-identification and into awake awareness. Then it continues with *waking-in* to include and know our body, thoughts, and emotions from nonconceptual knowing and abiding. The third stage, *waking-out,* involves creating and relating from open-hearted awareness. Each stage brings its own liberation. Waking-up leads to freedom from the fear of death. Waking-in leads to freedom from the fear of life. And waking-out leads to freedom from the fear of love.

Waking-up, the initial stage of awakening, can be divided into two important movements. The first of these is waking-up *out of* ego-identification, the normal way of organizing our identity that creates suffering. The second is waking-up *into* awake awareness as an alternative to our mistaken identity, and recognizing that awareness is already awake and intelligent. Realizing that we can shift out of ego-identification and into awake awareness is as revolutionary today as the recognition that the Earth revolves around the sun was in the seventeenth century.

In many wisdom traditions, the term *awakening* is often used because people report that their experience resembles waking from a dream. We are currently in an altered, dreamlike state, which creates suffering and confusion that disappear when we awaken. When we're dreaming at night, we are fully identified with the dream world and experience it as real and complete. But as soon as we wake up, we know for sure: "Oh, that was only a dream!"

When we come out of a dream, the entire dream world disappears. When we wake up out of ego-identification, our fearful and craving thoughts and projections disappear, leaving the physical world simpler and clearer. When we wake from a dream, we realize that whoever we mistook ourselves to be in the dream isn't who we really are. Our ego-identification's dreamlike perception disappears, and we stop sleepwalking through our lives. When we awaken and are grounded in awareness, our ego-identification is no longer the center of who we are. We may feel as if there had been a dream figure with our name that was trying to live our life.

Upon waking-up out of ego-identification, we may be surprised to discover that our limited perspective is only a small part of a much vaster reality. Awakening is like coming out of a movie theater after an engrossing drama. What seemed to be a real danger to the "mini-me" of ego-identification before, we now see as a story. When we awaken, we're no longer worried and scared about imaginary situations that had once seemed so troubling. We realize that we are the vast consciousness that has been acting out a small part.

Most of us assume that our ego-identification is who we are, and so we live our lives from its viewpoint. We think that our best opportunity for a safe, sane life is to strengthen this ego-identity. Looking from the lens of ego-identification, the subtler dimensions of reality are blurry, and we feel distinctly separate from everything. Awakening is the shift into the direct experience of a fuller reality that had previously been obscured by ignorance and delusion.

If we just wake up by deconstructing or transcending the mini-me, we can end up in a gap that feels like negative emptiness. This can seem like a scary transition, and there can be a rebound effect that sends us back to the mini-me. There is naturally a magnetic pull of habit to have consciousness reconstitute by identifying with thought-based knowing. We may feel like our thinking mind is our home. For many of us, in fact, it's the only home we know. We also may have learned to tell ourselves, "Don't go out of your mind," or, "Avoid the void." As soon as we return to our thinking mind for a second opinion, we reidentify with our contracted sense of self. By immediately recognizing awake awareness, we discover a positive emptiness that is not just an absence but a living presence, an open mind, a safe space, our new ground of being. We can only know who we truly are from awake awareness–based knowing. We can then welcome the fear of negative emptiness as a feeling.

As we wake in, we feel grounded, centered, and more in our bodies. As we wake out, we feel more creative and connected to others than ever before. Most of us have spent much of our lives working on the project of improving and developing our separate sense of self in order to succeed, win approval, and find happiness. We must have the willingness to go through the gap of not knowing, non-ego, and not being in control. By recognizing awake awareness immediately, we have the support to begin our new phase of life. Awakening may seem like a daunting challenge, but it's not any more difficult than other stages of learning and growth you've already been through, and it's more rewarding. In fact, in order for our awakening to be embodied, we need to show up and include all aspects of human growth, relationships, and development.

Awakening begins by discovering the awareness that is already free, awake, and connected, regardless of whether our thoughts are positive or negative. Awakening is not a one-time event, but a series of shifts and a process of unfolding that moves us away from the habit of trying to maintain a center, a point of view, and the primacy of a separate sense of self. The process of awakening and embodying has common principles, but it unfolds uniquely for each individual. We can begin our process by having small glimpses of awake awareness and repeating these glimpses many times.

The practice of small glimpses will begin to rewire our whole operating system and further support the unfolding process of awakening. Our entire mind-body system has been tied in knots by our attempts to defend against the pain caused by our mistaken identity. For this reason, most of us go through a process of thawing out, detoxing, and gradually rewiring our neural networks. The journey of awakening welcomes and liberates our deepest doubts and fears. The core stories—*I'm not good enough . . . Something's wrong with me . . . I'm unlovable*—are no longer convincing. We learn to return to awake awareness as our ground of being, and we train to remain in it.

The shift to a new perception, knowing, and identity generates a new kind of vitality. As a result, we discover a renewed level of motivation and creative expression.

You have to begin where you are, but the one who starts the journey is not the one who awakens. "You" do not awaken, and awareness does not awaken. Awake awareness, which is contentless and unconditioned, realizes that it has always been awake and is the primary foundation of your conditioning and human life. Many people call this *realization,* or *remembering who we truly are.* One person said: "This is the feeling of who I've been at all ages in my life, which hasn't changed." It is so ordinary that it is extraordinary. When you awaken, you awaken from a looping thought pattern that has been called "me" and feels located behind your eyes, in the middle of your head. But awakening doesn't make you become a nobody, a bliss-ninny, or a vacant robot. You are simply not the particular identity that you formerly took yourself to be. This journey starts with freedom from identification with our bodies and minds, but it ends up including and embracing everything from open-hearted awareness.

It may be hard for you to accept that shifting into freedom is really possible for you. But the natural, loving awareness that I am talking about is the source of your mind and identity. It is our natural condition; we can glimpse it at any moment, and it is the potential new operating system to which we can upgrade. Once we discover open-hearted awareness, we no longer have to live in the office cubicle of our head. Instead, we can stay at home in our heart and be connected to the information we need in our brain through open-hearted awareness Wi-Fi.

I suggest you do your first glimpse practice early in the day for five to twenty minutes. Once you've shifted into a new, stable ground of Being, you are done and ready to enjoy the day. One way to do this is to begin your glimpse practice first thing upon waking in the morning, while still in bed. Another way is to find a place to sit that feels comfortable and, with your eyes open or closed, settle in to do a glimpse practice that works for you. It is important to alternate and integrate sitting practice with glimpsing a number of times throughout your day. By doing this, you become able to unhook local awareness, shift, recognize, tune in, familiarize, marinate, and then see and do from Being.

When the habit of ego-identification arises, which is no big surprise, simply do a small glimpse practice and re-recognize your true nature. You can do the same one or try different ones, as you are learning how to navigate the territory of your own consciousness. Experiment and discover which glimpse practices work best in different situations.

The glimpse practices are designed to be read or listened to until you familiarize yourself with them enough to do them on your own during a break at work or while standing in line at a store. It can be difficult to do the practice while reading it, so you can either record your own voice speaking the practice or you can find video or audio versions of me guiding these practices online.

GLIMPSE 1 **No Problem**

This exercise is a direct pointer for shifting out of ego-identification and into awake awareness as your ground of Being. Most people feel a sense of underlying dissatisfaction that leads to craving and aversion, which is created by ego-identification. From ego-identification, we then try to solve the problem of mistaken identity by changing things in our personality or our environment. This creation of a problem-solver identity is what binds us and blinds us to the freedom that's already here. It creates a frantic continual search, like looking for your glasses when they're on your head.

In this practice, you'll discover that you can shift out of your mistaken identity in a moment. The goal is not to escape the normal issues and choices in your daily life, but to shift out of the mistaken problem-solver identity. When you make that shift and discover awake awareness as the ground of Being, you'll have fewer troubles and can more easily solve daily challenges.

1. When you're ready, put the book down and, with open or closed eyes, say this question to yourself internally: *What is here now if there is no problem to solve?*

2. Rest and remain alert to who or what is experiencing.

3. Who is here? What is aware? What is here when there is nowhere to go and nothing to do? Nothing to know or create or become? What is here, just now, when you are not the problem solver?

4. Feel into whatever shows up here and now. Who or what is aware? What is here when there is no referencing the past, no going one moment into the future, when you're not settling into sleep and not going up to thought? What's here now? *What's it like when there's no problem to solve just now?* What do you notice? What is absent? What essential qualities are revealed?

5. Again put your reading down. Take a breath and pause. Then ask with a beginner's mind and curiosity: *What is here now if there is no problem to solve?*

GLIMPSE 2 **Awake Awareness Is Aware without Using Thought**

The everyday mind needs an object to remain central. When awareness looks to space, we are free of the everyday mind. Ego-identification needs to look to thought, and from thought, to create a subject. When awareness makes awareness its subject and object, there is no longer a subject (self) that is made of thoughts. Awake awareness has become the primary way of knowing and the ground of Being.

1. Simply close your eyes while allowing your awareness to remain open and be within. Begin to feel your breath from within your body. Feel your whole body from within while breathing is happening by itself for three breaths.

2. Take a moment to see what is here now. Notice how your body is feeling. Is it uncomfortable, comfortable, agitated, relaxed, tired, or neutral? Just let your body be as it is without changing anything.

3. Now simply notice the awareness that is already accepting your body as it is. Feel the awareness in which these sensations are happening.

4. Become interested in activity of your mind and thoughts. Just be aware of whether your thoughts are agitated, calm, tired, emotional, anxious, or neutral. Without changing anything, allow your mind and thoughts to be as they are.

5. Now notice the space in which thoughts are moving. Be interested in the awareness instead of the thoughts. Notice how awareness allows your mind to be as it is without changing anything.

6. Begin to notice that awake awareness is alert, clear, and nonjudgmental. See also that awareness is not tired, anxious, or in pain. Notice that awake awareness is all around and inherent within your body and within your mind. Instead of being identified with the states of your body or mind or trying to accept or change them, simply become interested in *what* is aware and accepting.

7. What is awareness like that is already accepting of things as they are—right here and now? Notice the awareness of the next sound you hear. Does awareness have a location or size? What is it like to be aware of experiences from this pain- and thought-free awareness?

8. Now simply be aware of the awareness that is free from the contents of your mind and the sensations in your

body. Hang out as awareness without going up to thought or down to sleep. Be the awareness that welcomes your sensations and thoughts. Notice that awareness is not separate from thoughts, feelings, and sensations.

9. Just let go of focusing on any one thing. See everything without particularizing. Rest as the awareness that is aware without using thought. Can you see how no thought or feeling is solid? Can you see that awareness does not come and go?

10. Simply let be and remain uncontracted and undistracted without effort.

GLIMPSE 3 **Mind, the Gap**

This glimpse, "Mind, the Gap," is about finding awake awareness in the gap between thoughts. You may know a meditation practice where you repeat a word or a sacred phrase, known as a *mantra.* Here, you'll focus not on the word or its meaning but on the space—and awareness—between words. The intention is to give the thinking mind the simple task of repeating a word to occupy it while you become aware of the gap between your thoughts. As you explore the presence of awareness in space, you may begin to notice that the space between and around the words is the same continuous field of awareness that you are aware from.

1. Begin by silently and slowly repeating in your mind, "Blah," with some space in between. "Blah . . . blah . . . blah." Allow the word "blah" to float through the space of your mind like a feather. Don't create any other thoughts or be interested in any thoughts that arise. Let "blah" occupy all the interest and activity of thinking.

2. Begin to be aware of the thought-free space between the words, "blah" . . . space . . . "blah."

3. Next, become more interested in the quality of the
    space between the words. See if you notice that the
    space is not just a gap, but that the space itself is aware.
    "Blah" . . . aware space . . . "blah" . . . aware space . . .
    "blah" . . . aware space.

4. Feel the spacious awareness in between the words and all
    around them as a field of awake awareness in which the
    word "blah" and other thoughts now appear. Feel your
    mind not as a solid thing but as clear, open, and aware.

5. Feel and be awareness that is awake and alert without
    needing to go to thought for a second opinion. Be aware
    of the feeling of thought-free, alert clarity. Notice the ease
    and natural welcoming of all experiences that arise.

While doing this practice, you may have noticed that there are
two kinds of space. One is the physical space in the room—the
absence of objects and content. The other space is *presence* that
is aware and awake. What you've just experienced shows that
you can be aware, knowing, and intelligent—without relying
on thinking. Whether there are thoughts or no thoughts on the
screen of your mind, there is a background knowing that can
move to the foreground and then become the ground of your
Being. This silent, spacious awareness doesn't use thought to look
to other thoughts to confirm that you know what you know.

2

DIRECT RECOGNITION, GRADUAL UNFOLDING

Realization involves a process called recognizing, training,
and attaining stability. It's similar to planting the seed of a flower.
You plant it, nurture it, and finally it grows up and blossoms.

TULKU URGYEN RINPOCHE[1]

When I was a young kid, school was hard for me. I knew I was smart, but I couldn't get what I knew in my mind onto the written page. I had a hard time focusing and keeping things in order. Although I didn't know it at the time, I had some form of Attention Deficit Disorder (ADD) and dyslexia. In fifth grade, I studied hard for a spelling test, telling myself: "Remember the word 'Europe' begins with *E-u* and ends with *p-e*." When I got my test back, I couldn't understand why I had gotten it wrong. My friend Tim, looking over my shoulder, laughed out loud and said, "You wrote *Eupe.*"

As a kid, I loved playing sports. You name it, I loved it—from neighborhood tag and catch with friends to playing on organized teams. I could stay focused, calm, and connected with others while engaged in sports. In high school, I was the goalie for the ice hockey team. During my sophomore year, I played particularly well during one game and helped my team shut out the opposing team.

In the locker room after the game, my good friend Bruce sat down next to me. "Man, you made some amazing saves," he said. "How did you do that?"

"Well, if you really want to know . . . " I hesitated, wondering whether I dared describe my experience out loud, or if I could even put it into words. "I do this thing I call 'eyes in the back of my head,'" I began. "I open my peripheral vision to the sides of my head, and then I let it keep going—all the way around to the back of my head. Then an amazing change happens: Time slows down. I feel open and connected to everything around me. It gets real quiet inside me, and outside seems strangely quiet too. I feel like a cat: calm, alert, and ready to move when necessary. Instead of my eyes staring at one thing, all of my senses seem wide open, and I feel plugged into everything."

I was excited to be explaining this out loud to someone else, rather than mulling it over by myself. "It's like this," I continued with enthusiasm. "A guy hits a slap shot from the blue line, and I see the puck travel in a line for the first foot or two. But then I lose sight of it in the scramble of legs and sticks. After that, without thinking about it, my hand naturally shoots out, and the puck lands in my glove."

Bruce gave me a blank stare. "Oh, that's cool," he finally said before walking away.

The captain of the team, a senior, must have overheard me, because he came up after the next game and handed me a copy of *Zen in the Art of Archery.* "Here, kid," he said. "Read this. It's just what you were talking about last week."

I went home and read the whole short book that night. It blew me away that others had experiences similar to my own. Although I didn't understand everything in the book, I was amazed at the similarities between the Zen approach to archery and my own experience playing sports. The author wrote, "In the case of archery, the hitter and the hit are no longer two opposing objects, but are one reality."[2] Not only does the Zen method help you improve your skill, it also turns a sport into the training ground for a new way of living based on an effortlessly aware flow state.

The book went on to say that this kind of Zen practice brings with it the feeling of being "completely empty and rid of the self."[3] This phrase felt strangely familiar, but curious. When I opened my awareness and let go of thinking about what I was doing, I became more alert, relaxed, and successful. I felt emptied of one sense of self, and yet more like my true self. I knew exactly what was going on, but I wasn't thinking! Thoughts like "Am I making a mistake?" or "Try harder!" were absent. I wanted to know more about how to experience this way of being more often. It seemed so important that I wondered why we didn't study this in school. I eventually ended up going to graduate school in psychology and comparative religions, though I didn't find what I was looking for in the classroom.

One year during graduate school, I had a lingering cold, and a fellow student suggested I visit Dr. Chan, who'd been a physician in China before escaping during the Cultural Revolution. Dr. Chan lived and worked out of a fourth-floor walkup in New York City's Chinatown. After examining me, he mixed a bag of herbs, leaves, and sticks for a tea that I would take home. Dr. Chan was interested when I told him I was studying comparative spirituality and psychology.

"Do you want to treat the cold and the root cause of suffering?" he asked me, and laughed.

"The root cause of the cold?" I responded, uncertain I'd understood him.

"Yes, that," he agreed, and then clarified, "but also the root cause of suffering."

I told him I was interested.

Along with the bag of herbs, he gave me a Taoist book, *The Secret of the Golden Flower*. "Take this tea every morning and evening," he instructed. "Read this book each day until you finish, and come back in one week."

When I returned the next week, I was feeling better. That day, Dr. Chan taught me how to do a practice from *The Secret of the Golden Flower* called "turning the light of awareness around." He explained that in China this practice is often confused with a circulation-of-energy practice. Dr. Chan appreciated energy-circulating practices, but he emphasized that these practices were not the same as turning around awareness.

I recorded what he said in my diary: "Awareness is prior to energy, and awareness is within energy. First we see what awareness is and then what awareness knows."

Although I didn't really understand exactly what I was supposed to do when Dr. Chan gave the first pointing-out instruction, I gave it a try anyway. My awareness seemed to go out into the room, then turn around to look back *through* my mind and thoughts. Awareness moved through what I felt was "me"—or at least through the "me" that previously seemed to be located in my head. The result was an immediate experience of freedom from my small sense of self and a boundless awareness from which I was now looking. I felt such clarity, love, and connection that I actually laughed out loud. This wasn't a calm meditation state; it was a simple, alert, joyful, loving, and wise innocence—and it was happening by itself. I also felt sweet sadness, as though I were reuniting with a loved one upon returning home. Tears of joy began to well up in my eyes at the intimacy and beauty of everything.

I told Dr. Chan about my childhood experience of "eyes in the back of my head." That made him happy. He explained how this was one of the simplest, but most precious ancient teachings. Dr. Chan felt these teachings should be shared with everyone. He added that the word "transmission" had been misunderstood to mean the special energy or powers of a tradition or teacher. He talked about institutions and gurus who tried to keep secret these simple, ancient teachings or who confused these practices with energy (*chi* or *prana*), calm meditation, or intellectual beliefs. Energy could be transmitted from person to person, but the light of awareness is already equally inherent within everyone and therefore cannot travel from one person to another. All a teacher can do is offer others pointing instructions. The student must find awareness within himself or herself; it was even possible to stumble upon awareness without a teacher or tradition.

After I left Dr. Chan's office that day, the foundation of awake awareness effortlessly maintained itself through the night and into the next afternoon before the old way of being "me" began to return. That glimpse of my true nature was so simple that it inspired me with confidence. The unique thing was that awake awareness could be accessed intentionally and immediately. Once I learned how to make the simple movement of awareness, I was able to repeat the shift to awake awareness on my own.

The next year, I went on a traveling fellowship. I studied insight meditation in Sri Lanka, then studied with teachers in India. I ended up in Nepal, where I met Tibetan Buddhist teacher Tulku Urgyen Rinpoche. He gave simple, yet profound pointing-out instructions freely to anyone at retreats, and even during public talks.

In the Tibetan Buddhist Dzogchen and Mahamudra traditions, *rigpa* or "awake awareness" is the empty, yet active, awareness–based operating system from which we can learn how to live. Currently, we are living from a thought-based operating system, called *sem*. Sem creates confusion that leads to dualistic perception. Pointing-out instructions are often called an "introduction to awareness." Pointing-out instructions are hints on how and where to look for awake awareness as the source of your mind. Pointing-out instructions are pragmatic, simple ways of seeing through our mistaken identity by having our mind look at our mind, having awareness look at awareness.

I was particularly drawn to the Sutra Mahamudra style of Buddhism, which offers access to awake awareness and the ability to live from it in the midst of daily life. Early practitioners of Mahamudra were neither Tibetan nor monastic; they were a diverse group of men and women from India—artists, salespeople, healers, family members, politicians, nobility, and outcasts—all engaged in the world in a non-sectarian, nonrenunciated, nonelitist, noninstitutional, nonritualistic, and nondual way.

Sam Harris, a neuroscientist and author of *Waking Up,* who also studied with Tulku Urgyen Rinpoche, writes about how valuable this learning experience was for him: "Tulku Urgyen simply handed me the ability to cut through the illusion of the self directly, even in ordinary states of consciousness. This instruction was, without question, the most important thing I have ever been explicitly taught by another human being. It has given me a way to escape the usual tides of psychological suffering—fear, anger, shame—in an instant."[4]

What Is Direct Recognition and Gradual Unfolding?

In some traditions, there is a distinction made between gradual awakening and sudden awakening. Paradoxically, the open-hearted awareness approach is neither of these and both of these. Even in traditions that emphasize a gradual approach to awakening, there is an acknowledgment that the direct approach can be easier for some people. *The Attention Revolution,* by B. Alan Wallace, PhD, outlines ten stages of progressive meditation training from the Tibetan tradition. The first four stages develop one-pointed focus and train toward a mindful witness. Stages five through seven are called "settling the mind in its natural state," which means a resting and letting-be practice similar to the Zen approach of just sitting.[5] Wallace writes, "From the eighth stage onward, we move on to the still subtler practice of maintaining awareness of awareness itself." The practice of awareness of awareness "may be optimal from the beginning for those who are strongly drawn to it."[6]

Open-hearted awareness begins with awareness of awareness. It is an *essence* approach, also called the *direct* approach. The word *essence* comes from the Latin root *esse,* meaning "to be," but it doesn't imply that there's an unchanging substance at our core. Instead of doing, thinking, or believing, we begin by discovering our essential nature—and then we are able to act from there. *Direct* refers to the ability to access our essential nature immediately, knowing it's already fully here and doesn't need to be created or developed.

Some form of essence approach appears in most traditions and cultures around the world, including Christian mysticism, Sufism, Judaic Kabbalah, Zen Buddhism, Tibetan Dzogchen and Mahamudra, Chinese Taoism, Tantric yoga, Advaita Vedanta, and shamanism. It also seems important to acknowledge that throughout history, people have reported spontaneous awakenings outside of any religious or spiritual tradition.

Nineteenth-century poet Alfred Lord Tennyson wrote about his own experience with inquiry, as discovered during his childhood: "This has come upon me through repeating my own name to myself silently, till all at once, as it were out of the intensity of the consciousness of individuality, individuality itself seemed to dissolve and fade away into boundless being, and this was not a confused state but the clearest, the surest of the surest, utterly beyond words—where death was an almost laughable impossibility—the loss of personality (if so it were) seeming no extinction, but the only true life."[7]

Direct recognition is a kind of remembering, not a literal recollection of information, memories, or facts, but a deeper uncovering of our true nature. In Greek, the word for truth is *alethia,* and its opposite is *lethe,* which means "forgetfulness" or "oblivion." In Greek myths, if you drink the water of the River Lethe—which flows through Hades's underworld—you forget who you are and remain there, lost and wandering. Truth means remembering. The experience of direct recognition is like waking up from sleepwalking: it reveals who you have always been.

The open-hearted awareness approach focuses on uncovering or discovering our essential nature and then shifting our level of mind to live from open-hearted awareness. Because awake awareness is already here, there is no need to strive to earn it, create it, or develop it; nor is it effective to adopt the passive attitude of waiting for it to find us. Awake awareness, the ground of being, is equally available within each of us, as our essence. However, simply believing this—or intellectually understanding it—is not enough.

One new student lamented, "I don't get it; this is too intellectual for me!" I replied, "It may be hard to grasp because you don't need to use your intellect at all; it's not known through our usual, conceptual way of knowing." This approach is not intellectual, conceptual, or linear, so it may seem unusual, paradoxical, or initially hard to grasp. When this student directly glimpsed awake awareness, she remarked, "Now I see! This isn't too intellectual. It's so simple. How could I have missed it?"

Awakening means thought-based knowing no longer dominates our perception. We are shifting into an awareness-based way of knowing and being. There may a period of disorientation before we become reoriented at our new level of mind. We begin by glimpsing the end goal, which is already here. Rather than doing any technique to calm our chattering mind, we start with a direct glimpse of awake awareness, which is already calm, intelligent, loving, and inclusive.

The open-hearted awareness approach begins with methods designed to bring about a direct recognition of awake awareness. After direct recognition, there is a gradual unfolding as we reintegrate our emotions, thoughts, and ordinary functioning from awake awareness. The Mahamudra tradition has practices for *yoking* and *mixing* absolute awareness with our conventional physical life.

Awakening through this approach begins with encountering the selflessness of awareness. This initial direct recognition of awake awareness begins a process that continues with a gradual unfolding. Some traditions emphasize the need for preliminary practices as preparation for introducing awareness of awareness so that we won't minimize the recognition and return to the sleep of ignorance. The training of modern life brings emotional development as well as skills of concentration and discipline. People with and without an existing meditation practice are equally capable of beginning with awareness of awareness if they're motivated. In the open-hearted awareness approach, the emphasis is on post-recognition teachings and cultivating the process of unfolding.

One way to understand the process of direct recognition and gradual unfolding is to break it into stages: recognition, realization, stabilization, and expression. Recognition is our first glimpse of awake awareness. Realization is an identity shift, when we come to understand that we're looking *from* awake awareness, which has become our ground of being. Stabilization begins when awake awareness is our primary way of knowing. Expression occurs when we have discovered open-hearted awareness and rewired our brains to create and relate from here.

The open-hearted awareness approach goes directly to the root of our suffering and reveals the absence of self and the presence of natural, positive qualities. The shift into awake awareness is a shift into a whole new way of knowing and being. With the initial shift away from the everyday mind comes a not-knowing. With the first taste of not-knowing, there's tremendous freedom from controlling, resisting, judging, and checking in with thinking every moment. But not-knowing isn't the culmination of the process. Not-knowing is the gap or bridge that leads to a new way of knowing that's very different, a kind of not-knowing-that-knows.

The not-knowing is freedom from ego-identification, while the not-knowing-that-knows is perhaps the most important element for stabilization and expression. Learning how to shift into awake awareness is not an intellectual or conceptual learning process. You can only truly know awake awareness when you've shifted *into* it and know *from* it.

The most important thing is not just the initial pointing-out of awake awareness but to "train to remain." We start the process with recognizing selflessness and not-knowing, then we continue by realizing that awake awareness and nonconceptual knowing are our ground of being. Next we experience the already-embodied presence, then we shift into seeing and knowing from awake awareness, and finally we begin to function from embodied, open-hearted awareness.

The Tibetan word for meditation, *sgom,* is translated as "familiarization." In order to abide in awake awareness, we must glimpse it several times and become familiar with the view from this new level of mind. There's an ongoing dance of letting go and becoming acquainted with awake awareness as our ground of being. Familiarizing is a kind of tuning in, a marination in awake awareness, a rewiring of our bodies and minds to the new awake awareness–based operating system.

Our entire mind-body system has been tied in knots by our attempts to defend against the pain caused by our mistaken identity. For this reason, most of us go through a process of unfolding that includes thawing out, detoxing, and gradually rewiring our neural networks. We learn to move through growing pains and to welcome rejected feelings and subpersonalities—all while the tightly held knots of energy and belief gradually detox. We learn to return to our ground of being, and we train to remain here. The shift to a new perception, knowing, and identity leads to new vitality. As a result, we discover new motivation and creative expression.

It is important for you to discover which preliminary practices, if any, are most useful for you in preparing to shift. You may already know ways of settling your body and mind. You can begin with yoga, focusing on your breath, sound meditation, or deliberate mindfulness as an initial stepping-stone. However, you can only soothe the animal of your body and calm your mind for short periods before becoming agitated or stressed again.

Don't get caught in the trap of only doing preliminary practices; use them until they've served their purpose. For instance, do one-pointed meditation only until your chattering mind calms. Practice deliberate mindfulness until you see that you're not a thought-based, small self. Then take the next step that will enable you to glimpse awake awareness—the step you might call "letting go," "surrendering," "turning over," "unhooking," "shifting," or "dissolving."

Once we've shifted to an awareness–based way of knowing, an entirely new phase of growth begins—one that was impossible before. Each of us has different knots or types of resistance, so we each need to use different ways of preparation before we let go. As we awaken, it's important to continue our development in physical, emotional, mental, and relational areas. Growing up in other areas of life supports our unfolding. However, we can only mature to a certain level of development without the shift that identity awakening provides. From our new sense of identity, many of the problems and emotional binds we've been experiencing loosen spontaneously, and we open to a fresh perspective. There's no single right way to access awake awareness or to transition into living from it, but there are some common principles and doorways.

The Doorways of Direct Recognition

The two most common methods for directly recognizing our true nature are the *looking method* and the *resting method*. Christian mystical tradition calls these two approaches *Via Positiva* (the looking method) and *Via Negativa* (the resting method). Via Positiva suggests: "Seek and you will find." Via Negativa suggests: "Give up seeking, and you will find." Most meditation paths include aspects of both these styles. In addition, both Via Positiva and Via Negativa agree that ego-identification is the obstacle to awakening.

Via Negativa does not mean being negative. It is a way of negating all the many things that obscure the living truth of our being. It is the spiritual practice of deconstructing, dissolving, and letting go of what is *not* our true nature. We learn how to rest until what binds and blinds us finally relaxes. The search for who you are begins with letting go of everything and seeing who or what is left. The most common form of this experience is sitting meditation.

Via Positiva, or the looking method, is the way of seeking spirit, reality, awake awareness, or true nature as simply and directly as possible. The particular looking method we'll explore is a form of inquiry in which we intentionally and directly turn awareness around to find that awareness is the source of mind and our ground of being.

THE RESTING METHOD

Buddhism in its earliest Theravada tradition emphasizes the resting method—the most widely used direct method for accessing our true nature. In the four foundations of mindfulness, the goal is to see each of the mental processes that combine to create the feeling of a separate, solid self. Buddha avoided describing awakening or enlightenment in positive terms. Instead, he talked about freedom from suffering, fear, attachment, and hatred. There are even extreme forms of Via Negativa that regard all activity, including meditation, as egoic effort that obscures realization. This approach says, "There is no method. There is nothing to do. You are already awake; you just need to stop all effort. Be still." It is possible to awaken unintentionally; however, the saying "There is nothing to do" is actually a pointing-out instruction that requires a small, initial effort to stop egoic effort.

In the resting method, you sit and begin by withdrawing from all external tasks. You then let go of any internal identification with doing, monitoring, analyzing, judging, and controlling. The resting method is trying to go beyond the ego-doer by taking away its job. The resting method tries not to create an imaginary picture, philosophy, memory, or idea of awake awareness. Some resting methods ask us not to pay attention to thoughts; others direct us to simply let thoughts pass by.

Zen Buddhism uses two different Via Negativa approaches for letting go of your mistaken identity so that your true nature can appear: *koan* practice and "just sitting." The koan method presents students with what seems to be a looking method by posing a question like: "What is the sound of one hand clapping?" The intention is not for the meditator to find an answer, but to deconstruct both the seeker and the usual way of conceptually knowing. Koans short-circuit the conceptual mind with a problem it can't resolve, causing it to exhaust itself and release its claim on being the primary way of knowing. When pondering a koan, the student tries to find an answer until the everyday mind gives up and his or her true nature is revealed to be spontaneously there.

The "just sitting" method (*shikantaza* in Japanese) can be summed up by the Zen saying "Muddy water—let stand—becomes clear." In other words, we simply stop, rest, and let everything be as it is. Then the everyday mind is able to relax its perpetual agitation. Resting from the mental pattern of ego-identification, everyday mind releases its claim on the primary level of mind and identity. When the everyday mind calms and settles, the clarity of awake awareness is revealed.

Adyashanti, who uses both looking and resting methods in his teaching, gives a helpful modern description of the resting method, which he calls "true meditation":

> In true meditation, all objects (thoughts, feelings, emotions, memories, etc.) are left to their natural functioning. This means that no effort should be made to focus on, manipulate, control, or suppress any object of awareness. In true meditation, the emphasis is on being awareness; not on being aware of objects, but on resting as primordial awareness itself. Primordial awareness is the source in which all objects arise and subside.
>
> As you gently relax into awareness, into listening, the mind's compulsive contraction around objects will fade. Silence of being will come more clearly into consciousness as a welcoming to rest and abide. An attitude of open

receptivity, free of any goal or anticipation, will facilitate the presence of silence and stillness to be revealed as your natural condition.[8]

THE LOOKING METHOD

Directly seeing through our current, mistaken identity to find the foundation of freedom that's already here is what looking methods are about. When we discover that awake awareness is already awake and available without needing to be developed, we realize that, as Saint Francis of Assisi said, "What we are looking for is what is looking."[9]

The instructions that Dr. Chan and Tulku Urgyen gave me—turning my awareness to look back through what I assumed to be "me"—were looking methods. They pointed out where and how to look for my mind's true nature. When a teacher points out, his or her work is done. You need to look and find for yourself because the teacher cannot do this for you. Once you know where and how to look, you can do *pointing within* without a teacher.

Garab Dorje, the first teacher of Tibetan Dzogchen, gave a very simple description of direct recognition and gradual unfolding called The Three Vital Points. The first point is to directly recognize your own true nature. The second is to decide for yourself that this is true—meaning that you've recognized your true nature and are knowing from awake awareness. The third is to proceed with confidence in the unfolding liberation.

Once you've recognized awake awareness as your true nature, it's up to you to remain and then learn to return when you become identified. To become more familiar with awake awareness, you need to find the pointers that work best for you. Sutra Mahamudra–style practice uses a pointing within, in which you learn to look for yourself. When you practice pointing within daily to shift out of ego-identification, you engage in the practice of small glimpses many times. Different looking methods are taught in many traditions, including the inquiry practice of "Who am I?" in the Advaita tradition, or "Taking the backward step" in the Zen tradition.

As we turn the light of awareness toward the observer, an ego-identified observer cannot be found. We experience going beyond subject-versus-object duality. The observer that felt located in our head is experienced as lacking independent existence. Amazingly, there is not only emptiness as absence but an alive, spacious knowing without a specific location of observing. Egolessness or seeing through the illusion of a separate self is not the end. There has to be an awareness of what is here in its place as the new foundation of identity and base of operation. Some people get to this stage of awakening but do not know how to continue to unfold. During a phone consultation, a man named Eric told me: "I started reading online about enlightenment and then had a disorienting experience. The person 'Eric' was gone and seemingly nonexistent. There was no 'I am'—only an emptiness like a room full of furniture being emptied." Focusing on this transition of selflessness as if it were the goal can lead to stopping partway. It's like making a goal of driving from the East Coast to the Pacific Ocean but stopping at the Grand Canyon and living there. We can get stuck in stillness, an eddy along the way that Zen calls the "emptiness of emptiness."

The Tibetan phrase for *recognition* translates as "looking back at your own face." Awake awareness is as familiar and close as your own face. Many people report "it feels like returning home" when they first recognize awake awareness. Turning around to look and recognize awareness is not the physical process of looking with our eyes. The ability of awake awareness to know itself has been called *reflexive awareness*. The word *reflexive* means "directed or turned back on itself." Reflexive awareness emphasizes that our true nature is already here.

If we are to become aware of awareness, how do we find that first awareness that can turn back on itself? For reflexive awareness to work, we need a new way of looking, to know who or what turns around or steps back. Local awareness is the experiential answer to this inquiry, as it can move from being identified to being free. Since only awareness can recognize awareness, getting familiar with local awareness is a necessary first step. As children, many of us sang and danced "The Hokey Pokey": "You do the Hokey Pokey and you turn yourself around.

That's what it's all about." A clever bumper sticker reads: "What if the Hokey Pokey really *is* what it's all about?" However, my experience is that the "turning yourself around" is what it is all about.

The Two You-Turns of Awareness

Ramana Maharshi wrote regarding awakening: "Other than inquiry, there are no adequate means."[10] He said that inquiry was simple and direct. "If one inquires 'who am I,' the mind will go back to the Source . . . Not letting the mind go out, but retaining it in the Heart . . . "[11] In the first part of inquiry, the mind returns to its source and then, in order to live, a new location of mind gets established "in the Heart." This is a good description of open-hearted awareness.

Let's explore how this new looking method works. Inquiry instructions from different traditions say, "Mind will go back to the Source," "Take the backward step," "Turn the light around," and, "Let the mind look at the mind." The important question here is, what steps back? What turns around? Where is the mind or light that can turn and find the source? Our conceptual, everyday mind cannot know awake awareness. Even attention and our subtle mind, used for mindfulness, cannot find awake awareness. Nevertheless, we have to begin to inquire from where we are now. We will discover that local awareness is able to unhook from our thoughts and find spacious awareness.

The first step in awareness inquiry is to use your thinking mind to understand the words of the question you're trying to resolve. The next step is to understand how to look, where to look, and what you are looking with. If we use thought to look at thought, we re-create the ego-identification or mental pattern that we're trying to go beyond. In the open-hearted awareness approach, local awareness looks through or unhooks from the mental pattern of "I." We can then inquire: "Is there an 'I' here? What is its color? Shape? Size?" The result is that no separate looker can be found in any location. When we do not find anything or anyone who is a subject, we begin to experience the spacious awareness that is inherent within our thoughts and sensations.

In this step, we're discovering the ability of awareness to turn back to know itself rather than to look out and forward at objects in the world. Awareness has to look for itself—and find itself—to be truly liberated. This method of looking is about turning around to peer back through and beyond the observing position of the ego-identity. The location of the observer opens or dissolves as we do this. We cannot stop by looking at the absence of the ego-identity, or the space where the ego-identity used to be. Here, we need to find the awareness that's always been looking.

Awareness has to look for—and find—itself in order to live from a new ground of Being that's not ego centered or ego identified. Here, we step out of our everyday mind and discover the awareness that's always been looking. Spacious awareness has intelligence and intentionality; therefore we can focus, choose, and act from it.

Here's a short description of the awareness-inquiry process: You can start by unhooking local awareness from thinking, then shift to becoming aware of spacious awareness. You are making the first U-turn (or You-turn) in awareness and identity, in which you turn away from looking out at the world and have awareness turn around and look back through the looker to find itself. The result is that you may discover that awareness is already aware of itself, by itself. Once you're established in awake awareness, you can make the second You-turn to view and include the contents of your mind and body from the perspective of a transcendent, effortless, mindful witness. Next, awareness recognizes itself within our body as embodied presence, and then we can experience the one taste of the unity of all things. From open-hearted awareness, we can create and relate, feeling an unconditional loving connection to all.

We will need to find out where the awareness that can discover our essential nature is currently located. Consider the traditional metaphor of inquiry: dropping a pebble into a lake. If the pebble is made of conceptual thought, it is heavy and dense like a stone, so it cannot know the water. In small glimpses, the pebble is made of what it is seeking: water into water, awareness aware of awareness. Local awareness as a drop of water can recognize its source; when a drop of water goes into the lake, it is a homecoming.

Where, Oh Where, Is Awareness?

Let's look now at how awareness is normally hidden in the background, identified with thought, or caught in the middle of our way of perceiving. Awareness is commonly limited to a medium of knowing, a connection between you and what you're seeing. In many meditation systems, awareness, attention, and consciousness are treated as if they're the same. In Western psychology and even in our common speech, we often use the words "aware" and "conscious" as if they meant the same thing. For example, "I am aware of what I am reading," and, "I am conscious of what I am reading." We also use "awareness" and "attention" interchangeably: "Bring your attention to what you're hearing," and, "Bring your awareness to what you're hearing." In this way, we regard awareness as a limited type of consciousness that is "between" myself, as the subject, and an object, as in "I am aware of that cup." In this case, awareness is the medium, the link between you—the one who is looking—and the cup, which is the object being seen.

Awake awareness is not the medium *between* you and an object; it is the foundation of who you are and how you know. Awareness, as used here, is different from "conscious," "attention," and "consciousness." Even mindful attention cannot know awake awareness or the true nature of who you are.

Our current sense of "I" is built around self-reflective thinking, so awareness is caught in the middle and reduced to a function or tool of the mind and identity. This method shifts us from reflective thinking (thinking about thinking) to reflexive awareness (awareness of awareness). Instead of thought looking to thought, awareness looks to awareness—and then awareness can include thought.

Currently, awareness is not experienced as where we're observing *from,* but feels like it's in the middle: i.e., "I am aware of seeing the cup."

- Awareness begins as if it is a functional tool of "I," as in:
  I am → aware of → seeing the cup.

- "I" is a pattern of thought—ego-identification—that takes itself to be the subject.

- "Am" is currently connected to "I" instead of awareness.

- Awareness is reduced to attention as an intermediary tool of conscious focusing.

- "Seeing" is the particular sense that is being used here.

- The cup is the object of focus—"the seen."

When local awareness does a You-turn and looks back, it sees through ego-identification and discovers that awake awareness is now where "am" is located.

Local awareness goes out to the cup, then back from the cup to seeing, then back through the "I" to awake awareness.

The normal way of perceiving:
I am → aware → of seeing → the cup (seen).

The You-turn reverses the process:
Aware of the seen → aware of seeing → look back through the "I" pattern of ego-identification → to that which is aware of itself, seeing, and seen.

A simple version of a You-turn:
Aware of the seen → aware of seeing → rest as that which is aware of seeing.

Awake awareness can move from being stuck in the middle as a mode of perception to turning around and looking back through the mental pattern of "I" to find awake awareness. Awake awareness becomes the primary location of observing. The "am" is no longer located within thinking, but is now felt as a boundless field of awake awareness connecting through thinking, perception, and seeing to the cup and the space, all around.

GLIMPSE 1 **Seen, Seeing, and Awareness**

In this glimpse, you'll use your visual sense to become aware of awareness. You can use the words on this page as the object of focus while you're reading, or you can learn the exercise first and then try it with another object, like a cup.

1. Become aware of the words on this page as objects.

2. Notice your normal way of seeing the words on the page: looking outward from subject ("I") to object (words). Notice: "I am aware of seeing the words."

3. Now reverse the process. Notice the words as *the seen*.

4. Next, be aware of light reflecting off the page and coming to your eyes as *seeing*.

5. Now follow your awareness back to rest as *that which is aware of seeing*.

6. Let your awareness move backwards from the seen . . . to seeing . . . and then through the "I" to rest back as that which is aware of seeing.

7. Let awareness move back from the page to discover the awareness behind and within that is already aware and looking.

8. Allow awareness to rest back until it discovers the awake awareness that is effortlessly reading the words.

GLIMPSE 2 **Awareness of Awareness**

1. Look out at an object in the room. Notice being aware of that object.

2. Now notice being aware of seeing.

3. Now close your eyes and feel that the same awareness that was used to look outward can now be aware of awareness. Allow awareness to be interested and aware of itself: awareness resting back to become the subject and the object. Feel awareness as intimate, soft, spacious, and pervasive.

4. Let go of interest in thoughts, sentences, ideas, or points of view. Allow your awareness to be interested completely in awareness.

5. Let the awareness rest as the awareness that already knows itself and is aware of arising experiences.

6. Notice what it is like to be aware from awareness rather than from thinking or ego-identity.

GLIMPSE 3 **Awareness Yoga**

In a yoga class, you learn how to move your body to feel renewed, refreshed, balanced, and unified. In this practice, we're learning to move awareness for the same purposes. Use these four pointers one at a time to shift your view, pausing in between to experience what they point to. Instead of trying to understand the meaning of the statement, just be curious. Let your awareness look. Repeat each one as many times as you like. You can say these phrases with your eyes open or closed, as you prefer. The important thing is to shift awareness to look and to *feel* where you're looking from after you shift.

- Look from awareness to see what the next thought will be.

- Look from awareness to experience the space through which thoughts move.

- Look from awareness to see what is aware of space and moving thoughts.

- Look from awareness and rest as the field of spacious and pervasive awareness and aliveness.

GLIMPSE 4   **Making a You-Turn**

1. Unhook local awareness from thought and send local awareness up to a corner of the room.

2. Now have that local awareness look back to and through the one who sent it.

3. Notice that in true seeing, there is nothing to see.

4. Notice the absence of a local observer in your head. Neither an observer nor the observed—just observing. Notice the boundless space that you are aware from.

5. Feel from the continuous field of awareness that is aware of itself and that is now what is seeing. Rest as this spacious awareness that is aware of what is.

6. If you chose to send awareness to a corner of the room in front of you, now send awareness up to a corner behind you and repeat the other steps.

3

LOCAL AWARENESS

Just turn the light around; this is unexcelled sublime truth.

THE SECRET OF THE GOLDEN FLOWER[1]

We all long for freedom, but real freedom is not a quality you gain; it is who you already are. Freedom arises from a deep sense of wellbeing that does not depend on any life circumstances. However, even when we've tasted real freedom, most of us can't figure out how to intentionally return to it. What's missing from our approach is not willingness, intellectual understanding, or effort, but the means to shift out of the confusion that causes our suffering and into the new way of being.

A student of mine, who'd only recently learned to shift local awareness, was at dinner with some friends he hadn't seen for a while. He realized he was feeling anxious and self-conscious. He tried to calm himself, but nothing changed. Then he remembered that he'd learned a method of unhooking local awareness and shifting into his naturally peaceful mind. He'd only tried this method in the quiet solitude of his home before, but that night he decided to see if it worked at the dinner party.

While his companions placed their orders with the waiter, he discovered that only a short time was needed to unhook and shift his local awareness away from his painful, contracted state of self-consciousness and into a new way of seeing and being. He later told me, "I immediately noticed relief. My internal judge was gone—the critic of myself and others—and this allowed me to listen to my friends in a way that was much more engaged, heartfelt, and easygoing. Until the critic was gone, I hadn't even noticed how much this anxious judge ruled my world."

From the very first experience of shifting local awareness, many people report a kind of release or unburdening—like putting down a heavy backpack. Sometimes people experience an absence of negative qualities that have haunted them their whole lives; they feel relief from worry, agitation, fear, obsessive thinking, shame, and judgment. Others notice positive qualities like peace, spaciousness, unity, and love arising spontaneously. When you try unhooking local awareness from your thoughts, you'll discover that you can experience the benefits immediately. The next step is learning which dimension to intentionally shift into. You don't need to leave the room and meditate for half an hour in the middle of your workday or during a social gathering to discover the peace of mind that's already here within.

Four Expressions of Awake Awareness

Local awareness is one of awake awareness's four modes of expression, along with spacious awareness, awake awareness embodied, and open-hearted awareness. Local awareness is a vehicle that is already here and can take us home. Over the ages, people have tried many methods of going beyond the mind, including using the five senses, the conceptual mind, the ego, and our will or attention—none of which can find awake awareness. The five senses can only know what they're designed to know. Thinking is not designed to know awareness either. In order to find awake awareness, we must learn how to unhook local awareness from conceptual thought. In this way, we discover that local awareness can shift into and know awake awareness.

Local awareness is the dynamic, interactive dimension of awake awareness that can unhook from thought. It is the skillful means to immediately know our ground of being. Local awareness can *shift into and know* spacious awareness as itself. To understand local awareness, it's helpful to understand the other three modes of expression of awake awareness as well.

The second expression of awake awareness is *spacious awareness*, which is timeless, boundless, changeless, contentless, formless, and knowing. Spacious awareness is our ground of being, the source of our identity. Spacious awareness as pure awareness is the nature of mind like the clear, open sky that's behind and within the clouds of our body and mind.

The third expression is called *awake awareness embodied*, or *presence*, which is the realization of nonduality, when formless spacious awareness realizes that it is also form. Spacious awareness is innate within the body, the way atoms are within molecules and space is within every atom. Presence recognizes that the atoms, molecules, and our bodies are a unified expression of awake awareness. From presence, all energy patterns, forms, appearances, and matter are experienced as waves arising from the ocean of awake awareness.

The fourth expression of awake awareness is open-hearted awareness, which knows through unconditional love, interconnectedness with all things, and relationship with others. From open-hearted awareness, we have the capacity to be creative and compassionate.

It is important to remember that spacious awareness, local awareness, awake awareness embodied, and open-hearted awareness are *not* four separate things. *They are all different expressions of awake awareness.* When I say "spacious awareness," it always means "spacious awake awareness."

Local awareness is like an additional sense that can know the other three modes of awake awareness. Local awareness is nondual in that it can know and move between both formless awareness and forms of consciousness. Local awareness can shift into and know spacious awareness as itself. Then, when we shift into presence and open-hearted awareness, local awareness replaces attention as our way of focusing.

Once you have a sense of local awareness, you can experiment with the glimpse practices and make them your own. We will begin by learning to detach (or unhook) local awareness from your ego-identified everyday mind. Once you learn how to unhook and move local awareness, you will be able to navigate through the different levels of mind. Once you learn to shift, you will discover the positive, natural qualities that are always available within you.

Local awareness can be equally likened to a microscope that allows us to see the subtlest dimensions and to a telescope that allows us to experience the most immense ones. Although there are other ways to shift into freedom, local awareness—as the movable dimension of awake awareness—allows for fully unfolding into embodied, open-hearted awareness. Once we learn how to use local awareness, we can shift no matter where we are or what we're doing.

Local Awareness in Other Traditions

Although subtly covered by the stronger, faster dimensions of everyday consciousness, local awareness is always present. Inherent within us, it's a potential way of discovering spacious awareness, and it can eventually teach us how to focus from spacious awareness.

Local awareness is not subtle energy, not what Christianity calls a *soul* nor what Hinduism calls *atman.* Local awareness is one mode of awake awareness that's able to focus and move through dimensions of consciousness. This capacity for turning awareness around to see itself is revered in many wisdom traditions.

In Tibetan Buddhism, recognition of our true nature is sometimes called the meeting of "child" awareness with "mother" awareness. Local awareness can move away, sometimes getting lost in thought, like a toddler exploring the world. But child awareness can always return to its source, the mother field of spacious awareness, and be welcomed home. Once mother and child know they are the same family, they are always connected. One famous Mahamudra text points to what I am calling local awareness when it says, "As this is imperative, tighten your awareness and look [at your mind]."[2]

Unhooking

Local awareness is a vehicle that travels over the living bridge between formlessness and form; it helps us see unity in the seemingly separate domains of subject and object, human and divine, tangible and intangible, finite and infinite. Local awareness can carry us from one state of being to another. We don't have to alternate between ego-identification and spacious awareness, between "getting it" and "losing it." We can experience both relative and ultimate levels of reality simultaneously.

Normally, local awareness is identified, attached, or obscured within the thinking mind and ego function. Yet we cannot know awake awareness through thinking; our contracted, isolated sense of self prevents us from recognizing it. We may begin with a few preliminary practices such as reading, chanting, meditating, or yoga. We can begin the journey from our current level of mind by understanding instructions and starting toward the bridge. These initial practices are done by ego-identification with the goal of relaxing the grip of ego-identification. However, in order to cross the bridge, it is imperative to let go of any initial technique, level of mind, and doer. Some people call this movement "dropping," "releasing," "surrendering," "letting go," or "turning over." I call it "unhooking."

We don't have to change our minds first to unhook local awareness from thought. We unhook local awareness in order to change our level of mind. Unhooking is the ability of local awareness to detach from, tune out of, let go of, or disidentify from any state of mind. Not merely a change of attitude, it's an experiential movement away from enmeshment with the contents of our everyday minds. When local awareness is no longer identified, we are no longer caught in ego-identification.

So the fundamental question we need to answer is: how do I unhook? But "you" don't unhook. Local awareness unhooks from the "you" that plans to unhook. One of the reasons we have not been able to unhook easily is because the "I" can't do it. However, local awareness is already inherently within us as an expression of awake awareness. You have the capacity to move local awareness intentionally, even though you don't know it. Once you get a feel for it, you will be able to move local awareness from thinking to spacious awareness. It is like moving your awareness from seeing to hearing. The learning of it feels more physical than mental. As Dudjom Rinpoche says, the moment of unhooking and recognizing is "like taking a hood off your head. What boundless spaciousness and relief! This is the supreme seeing: seeing what was not seen before."[3]

Unhooking involves going beyond the "doer" who started the journey across the living bridge. The recognition of local awareness resolves an ancient question experientially: *If we go beyond the current ego-identified doer, how can we "do" anything?* We need to find an experiential answer to this question in order to live an awakened life. Ultimately, you will be able to answer this question with your own direct experience of shifting local awareness. When you unhook local awareness from the "me," a transfer of identity occurs, like a baton being passed between relay racers. The baton is local awareness; the ego-identified "doer" collapses like an exhausted runner. The baton is in the capable hands of spacious awareness, which can now focus using local awareness. Then, from awake awareness embodied we can begin to know and do from Being.

People often feel they must either meditate passively to discover spacious awareness or reengage the old doer in order to function in the world. When local awareness is discovered, there is now a new option of living from the unity of two worlds that have always been together. When local awareness unhooks from thinking and ego functioning, local awareness has intelligence and intention inherent within it. Thinking is returned to its natural function as the sixth sense; it's no longer the primary way of knowing. This means that the "doer," from the everyday mind, is no longer the actor initiating choice.

Unhooking can be the initial movement that takes us out of the ego-identified state, but it will not always lead to awake awareness. Just getting into a car doesn't get you to your destination.

You can shift into different dimensions of consciousness: daydreams, sleep, your personal unconscious, collective unconscious, hypnotic trance, or a restful, meditative state. There is nothing wrong with any of these states. However, our particular path right now is not interested in them. Instead, we are using local awareness in the most direct way to find the subtlest, most foundational level of mind and ground of being, while trying to avoid fascinations and distractions along the way. Some interesting and pleasant states can begin to arise, but until we abide in the ground of being, we can never establish the embodied open-hearted awareness that is our home.

Local awareness has to find spacious awareness and then get to know the feeling of seeing and being from spacious awareness. When local awareness discovers spacious awareness, its job is not done. Local awareness takes over the job previously done by intention and attention. Local awareness is the skillful means of focusing from spacious awareness that can intentionally focus while maintaining an open-hearted view.

The Sufi poet Rumi called the mind a "globe of awareness." Local awareness is like a clear bubble of intelligence that can travel and know directly from wherever it is within our bodies or from the field of spacious awareness. Local awareness knows from within its new location, instead of feeling the location of the perceiver behind our eyes, in our head. For instance, when local awareness travels to your hand, it knows directly from within your hand. When it moves to your emotions of sadness or joy, it knows from within those feelings. Like a spotlight, local awareness has the ability to focus in one area. Local awareness can become small or expand to a larger area. Local awareness can move, become identified, or disidentified. It lights up its location from within. When awake awareness is the primary operating system, we can remain spacious and open while simultaneously focusing on a particular task.

Some people do not experience the distinct separation of local awareness from the field of spacious awareness. Ultimately, it's true that there is no separation. Here is an image that helps us feel simultaneously spacious and focused in one area: Imagine local awareness as a wave that arises from the ocean of spacious awareness. We can see how the wave appears as a distinct movement of water. From one perspective, a wave arises, crests, and breaks. Yet it never really stops being ocean. Ocean is its essence. If we identify ourselves as solid, separate waves, we may feel frightened that we are about to crash. Once we realize that the wave is only the particular, local appearance of the ocean, there is no more fear.

Awake awareness is formlessness and also inherent within form. It is not one or the other; it merely displays diverse appearances. Local awareness can shift from a coarse level of mind to a subtle level. When we are located in our everyday mind and using our attention to focus on things, we can only experience a coarse level of reality. Local awareness has the ability to experience the subtle level of intelligence any place it looks. When we have shifted to the new operating system of awake awareness embodied, we will use local awareness to focus without having to go back to the everyday mind.

Even if you didn't know anything about unhooking local awareness before now, you can still do it. It's not done by understanding with thought or as an act of will through intense effort. In fact, you may not understand how to do it even when you do unhook and move local awareness. It's like balancing on a bicycle. You get a feel for it, and then you practice until you develop trust that you can do it again.

Deepening Your Experience of Local Awareness

Everything in the open-hearted awareness approach to awakening is built on the first step of unhooking awareness from thought. Unhooking may happen easily, or it may take a few tries. It may not even feel like unhooking to you. It may feel more like dissolving, sliding, releasing, or stepping back—like tuning out and tuning in. Or it may happen so quickly you don't feel the process. The key is for local awareness to completely disidentify, separate, or detach from thinking. However that happens is fine. I encourage you to experiment and find the pointers that work best for you.

The most important thing is this: You cannot do these exercises; only awareness can. Once local awareness unhooks from thought, the sense of "you" that began is no longer your current identity or location of knowing. You have unhooked from the ego-identity that started the journey, and now local awareness knows directly.

Our interest here is in directly experiencing and getting to know the different qualities of local awareness better. Let's experience how local awake awareness can:

- *unhook* from thinking and ego-identification

- *intentionally move* to different dimensions of consciousness

- *know directly from within* without using conceptual thinking

- *focus* without using attention

Even if local awareness sounds somewhat similar to other kinds of practices, remember that the invitation now is to approach the following exercises with a beginner's mind and an open heart. The following experiment offers a glimpse of how easily local awareness can move from one sense to another, such as from seeing to hearing.

Local Awareness Is Different from Attention

It's very important to recognize that attention is not the same as local awareness. "Attention," according to the Merriam-Webster dictionary, is the "act or state of applying the mind to something."[4] Attention is the way we focus when located in our everyday mind. Applying the mind is the experience of being a subject located in your head, perceiving an object (even a part of your own body) located elsewhere.

According to pioneering psychologist William James, "There is no such thing as voluntary attention sustained for more than a few seconds at a time. What is called 'sustained voluntary attention' is a repetition of successive efforts which bring back the topic to the mind."[5]

Maintaining continuous attention is difficult because the everyday mind is not a stable entity. Everyday mind, which is trying to pay attention, is made of a flowing stream of thoughts and feelings that come and go. You can begin with the thought: "Pay attention to your left hand." Then you apply your mind to your hand. As soon as your attention goes to your left hand, your thinking mind wanders away. The mind based in thought that started the task has already changed during those few moments. You have to remind yourself, re-creating a self in your mind. Then you have to give yourself the instruction again: "Pay attention to your hand." This all happens very quickly.

When using attention to focus, we always lag one second behind direct experience. This means that knowing through attention is always a past experience, a reflection, a picture, a memory, or an image of what just happened. Local awareness knows directly, without needing the mind to interpret, explain, or categorize. When we don't use thinking as our primary way of knowing, our everyday mind doesn't need to remind us to focus.

One detour that some people experience when they're initially learning to unhook from thought is the stretching of attention. You can remain in your everyday mind and register sensations and emotions in your body below your neck by intense-focusing from your mind, but this is not a true unhooking from the everyday mind.

Just as attention is the focusing aspect of the mind, local awareness is the focusing aspect of awake awareness. Local awareness resembles attention in that it is capable of selectively focusing, but local awareness is essentially different from attention. When paying attention, the mind is applied to an object, but local awareness knows directly from awake awareness, which is within your body.

GLIMPSE 1 **Experience Attention**

Take a moment right now to explore the experience of attention.

1. Look at one of your hands. Now move that hand out of your vision, and bring your attention to that hand. Try to continue applying your attention there for a short while.

2. What was your experience of attention like?

Initially, when you use attention to focus, you may feel that your head (where your brain and eyes are located) is your central place of perceiving. When you bring your attention to your hand, does it feel like "you" are in your head, looking down at your hand? Or does it seem as if "you" are shining a flashlight from your head to your hand? Or do you feel connected, as if a telephone cable is running from your head to your hand and sending signals back and forth? Do you feel how attention can wander?

Are you able to feel that maintaining attention is actually a continuous process of remembering and forgetting?

GLIMPSE 2 **Experience Local Awareness**

Now that we've experienced attention, let's see how local awareness differs. In order to experience local awareness, you need to unhook local awareness from thought and know your hand directly from within. Try this for yourself now:

1. Unhook local awareness from thought, and let local awareness begin to move down through your neck and know your shoulder from within.

2. Slowly move local awareness like a knowing, invisible bubble down your arm into your elbow. Feel the awareness of space and sensation directly from within.

3. Continue to let local awareness move down your forearm until it feels your hand from within.

4. Experience this new type of knowing that is happening directly, from within your hand.

5. Notice that when awareness knows your hand from within, it does not refer to a mental image of your hand. It feels the space and aliveness of the sensations so there is not a clear boundary of inside and out.

Notice the way in which awake awareness knows itself and your body through local awareness. Once local awareness has unhooked, thought is no longer the primary mode of knowing, yet thought is available as needed. If you do not reference a memory or image of your hand, your experience of your hand shifts into direct knowing. Direct knowing is spacious, alive, and much more fluid in feeling than attention.

You've just experienced how local awareness moves from thinking in your head to being able to directly know from within your hand. Now you can begin to get a sense of the feeling of local awareness unhooking and moving to other senses. The important thing here is feeling how local awareness moves. This next series, Glimpse 3 through Glimpse 6, will give you step-by-step training to unhook local awareness and begin to feel how it moves to different levels of mind.

GLIMPSE 3 **Coming Back to Your Senses**

In this exercise, you'll feel how local awareness unhooks before it moves.

1. As you look at this page, feel local awareness unhook from thinking about the words to seeing the printed words as objects being seen.

2. Next, unhook local awareness from seeing, and shift to hearing. Notice the dramatic difference in your experience resulting from this small shift of awareness: from seeing to hearing.

3. As local awareness shifts back from hearing to seeing, take your time and feel local awareness as it moves from one sense to the other.

4. Now local awareness unhooks from seeing and thinking, and feels down through your neck into your upper body.

5. Notice that local awareness within your body is not looking down from thought, nor is it looking up to thought in order to know.

6. What is it like when local awareness feels and knows both awareness and the alive sensations directly from within your upper body?

7. Let's do the previous six steps again when you're ready, using a different object. Before you move, say to yourself: "Awareness is about to shift from thinking to seeing, then shift from seeing to hearing." Then go slowly and feel the process of awareness moving as it tunes out of seeing and into hearing. In order to feel local awareness moving, you can take your time now: pause, look up from reading, and experience the ability to shift local awareness intentionally. First, feel local awareness unhook from seeing and move to join with hearing. Second, feel local awareness unhook from hearing and move down through your neck to know your body directly from within. Feel what it's like for awareness to come back to your senses and know directly, from within your body, without referring to thought.

GLIMPSE 4 **Awareness of Space**

Local awareness is malleable: it can focus and join with one of the senses. In this next glimpse, local awareness can let go and move to be aware of objectless space.

1. Unhook local awareness from thought, and let it focus on hearing the sounds coming to one of your ears.

2. Focus neither on who is hearing or what is heard, just the sensation of hearing.

3. Notice how awareness is able to focus on the vibration of sound in this one small area.

4. Now, unhook local awareness from hearing, and open to the space outside your body in which sound is coming and going.

5. Notice the movement of sounds through space, but then become interested in the objectless space through which the sounds are moving.

6. Notice the effects of awareness of space.

GLIMPSE 5　**Awareness of Awareness**

In this next glimpse, local awareness moves to space and then discovers spacious awareness. Here, we will let awareness mingle with space and become aware of itself. When local awareness opens to spacious awareness, you can focus on spacious awareness within your body or go to the space outside your body. Because our senses are so oriented to the front of our bodies, it might be easier to discover spacious awareness on one side of your body or behind your body.

1. Unhook local awareness from thought, and have awareness focus on hearing the sounds coming to one of your ears.

2. Don't focus on who is hearing or what is heard, just the sensation of hearing.

3. Notice how local awareness is able to focus on the vibration of sound at one ear.

4. Just as local awareness can focus on a very small area, notice how local awareness can now open to be interested in the space in which sound is coming and going.

5. Rather than focusing on the movement of sounds through space, let local awareness rest in the open space.

6. Local awareness opens to space until it discovers that open space is aware.

7. Feel that local awareness is like an air bubble blending into thin air and mingling with the field of spacious awareness that is already aware.

8. Let awareness palpably know and feel itself, without looking to thought or sensation.

9. Stay with this contentless, timeless, boundless awareness itself. Remain undistracted, without effort. Take as long as you need to get a feel for spacious awareness being aware of itself without any physical or mental references. It can be like tuning into a radio station of pure awareness. Only the knowing from awake awareness can confirm when you're there.

10. For a minute or two, relax into abiding as this field aware of itself without subject or object.

11. Rest as awareness: rest in the spacious field that is nonphysical, thought free, timeless, boundless, contentless, yet fully alert and aware.

12. When awake awareness is primary, include everything and notice that you are aware of thoughts, feelings, and sensations from sky-like spacious awareness.

4

LOCATION, LOCATION, LOCATION

Now every great meditative tradition the world over has major maps
of the significant steps or stages in meditation as their tradition has
come to understand and practice them. And what significant research
has demonstrated is that, although the surface features of each of these
traditions and their stages differ considerably from culture to culture, the
deep features of all of them are in many ways significantly similar. In
fact, virtually all of them follow the four or five major natural states of
consciousness given cross-culturally and universally to all human beings.

KEN WILBER[1]

In the open-hearted awareness approach to awakening and growing
up, the simplest way to answer all questions about how to relieve
the root of suffering is the same: shift. This includes questions like:
What should I do about this issue or situation in my life? How do I
deal with this difficult relationship? How do I become more accepting,
peaceful, and loving? Any time you mistake a self-image, an emotion,
or a belief for who you are, you need to shift and relocate your identity.
You're not just shifting out of the problem, you're shifting into that
which sees the situation differently. Once you shift, the answer will
come from within you.

The most-asked question in meditation classes is: How do I deal
with my disturbing emotions? Having spent thirty years as a psychotherapist, I know the value of good psychological and common-sense
advice. However, we need to separate awakening from psychological

improvement so that we can do both. Thinking positive thoughts or being more accepting may help us temporarily deal with difficult emotions, but we're still working in the realm of ego-identification and the everyday mind.

We have all heard the saying "seeing is believing." But our beliefs create how we see. In other words, our perspectives influence our perceptions. This is why we need to shift out of the limited location of our everyday mind and its conditioning.

Swiss psychiatrist Carl Jung called neurosis the avoidance of legitimate suffering. We avoid suffering related to loss, disappointment, or growing pains because we don't have the capacity to bear it if we're operating from ego-identification. Our sense of self is just too small to deal with more powerful emotions. How do we remain vulnerable, sensitive, and intimate with life without being overwhelmed? Tulku Urgyen Rinpoche says, "Everyone is overcome by disturbing emotions unless they are stable in nondual [awake] awareness."[2] We begin by immediately shifting our location into awake awareness rather than working first with our emotions or external situations from ego-identification.

What if your difficult feelings, your sensitive emotional make-up, or the memories of your traumas never go away? What I'm getting at is that instead of focusing on what emotions are arising, the real question is who or what are the feelings arising to? From what level of consciousness are you viewing and feeling? From awareness-based knowing, you can be sensitive, vulnerable, and courageous.

Of course, it's important to know *what* does the shifting, *how* to shift, and *where* to shift. All human beings have the same structure of consciousness. In this book, we'll learn to shift our awareness through five major, natural dimensions of consciousness. Each level of consciousness and its contents can be observed. However, when we *know from* any of the five levels of consciousness rather than look at them, we will call them the *five levels of mind.* When we look from a particular level of mind, we experience its unique way of perceiving and knowing. We have very distinct experiences of the same situations depending on which level of mind we're located in.

Most adults throughout the world have a similar way of locating their identity and way of knowing within these levels of mind. We are most often located in the first level, called *everyday mind,* with its fast-moving thoughts, physical instinctual impulses, and strong emotions, while the subtlest dimensions of consciousness are harder to access. In themselves, even the denser and faster-moving dimensions of consciousness aren't a problem. It is when we locate our identity in these dimensions that we create suffering. Albert Einstein famously said, "You can't solve the problem on the level of consciousness that created it." We'll learn how to use local awareness to make the shift to locate our identities within the subtler and more pervasive levels of mind.

What Does a Shift Feel Like?

Look at figure 1. What is this a picture of?

Did you think, "It's a picture of birds"? That's what most people say. What if you were to look at this picture again, in a fresh way, as a picture of the sky through which birds are passing. Rather than focusing on the objects, how does it feel when you shift to looking at space as your primary interest?

What is your experience now? This is how a shift might feel.

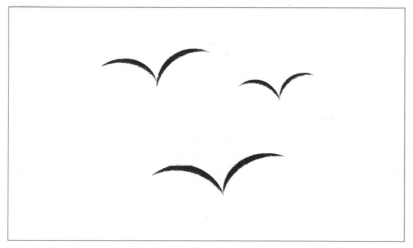

FIGURE 1. A picture of birds? Or of sky?

This exercise can give you a sense of the perspective change that can happen in a moment. We're not only shifting our way of perceiving, but we're also shifting the location of the perceiver.

What Is the Cause of Suffering?

According to Buddhism, suffering is created by ignorance, craving, and aversion. There are two common ways to alleviate suffering. The first approach focuses on reducing craving and aversion; the second aims to clear up ignorance. Each begins with a different starting point.

The first approach tries to decrease cravings that "I" feel attached to and reduce aversions to what "I" don't like. "I" can become attached to and identified with various roles, places, and things such as money, status, or objects of desire as "mine." "I" try to decrease or renounce desire and aversion, while increasing loving-kindness, acceptance, and compassion. Or "I" try to transform the disturbing emotions that accompany craving and aversion. These types of practices can lead to temporary relief of suffering; they can also end up supporting a less stressed, but still separate, sense of self.

The second approach goes right to the root of suffering: the creation of a sufferer. Rather than focusing on what "I" am attached to or repelled by, this approach goes directly to the source of identification that creates an "I" in the first place. Ultimately, the cause of suffering is always ignorance. Here, however, ignorance does not mean lack of information or knowledge.

What are we ignorant about? In Tibetan, the word for "ignorance" is *ma-rigpa*, which simply means not recognizing *rigpa* (awake awareness). When awareness does not recognize itself but identifies instead as a thinker, the small separate "I" forms. Immediately, the separate "I" has insatiable desires and aversions and, because it is made of thought, nothing can satisfy or threaten it. Desires and aversions can be understood as symptoms we can resolve merely by shifting our identity into awake awareness as our ground of being. Ultimately, there is nothing to reject or transform.

During meditation, five hindrances are named as obstacles to peaceful abiding and can hinder your ability to be mindful. From this second approach, the five hindrances—craving, aversion, apathy, worry, and doubt—are simply signs that you're looking and feeling from everyday mind. The doubt "I am not going to get this" is correct, on one level, because the "I" of the everyday mind cannot know awake awareness. Rather than trying to counteract these hindrances, simply recognize them as a sign you're caught and shift into awake awareness, which by its nature is never identified with these hindrances.

What Are We Shifting Out Of?

The open-hearted awareness approach helps us shift our perception, our sense of identity, and our way of knowing. On the level of perception, we are shifting out of ego-identification's dualistic perspective that sees everything as either a potential threat or object of satisfaction. On the level of identity, we are shifting out of ego-identification, away from the sense of being a separate, small entity that co-opts our physical-boundary program and feels perpetually dissatisfied. On the level of knowing, we are shifting out of the noise of the chattering, everyday mind. We often use words related to location to describe this condition: "stuck," "hooked," "trapped," "isolated," "lost," "contracted," or "distracted."

The type of thinking that co-opts the boundary-survival program is called *self-awareness.* Psychologists define self-awareness as the "psychological state in which one takes oneself as an object of attention."[3] Self-awareness allows us to objectify ourselves for the purpose of introspection, ethical behavior, and planning for the future. In order to do this, we have to split our identity into two parts. Self-awareness creates a separate sense of self, a mini-me, out of thought, which can then observe "me" as an object—as in, "I'm so upset with myself." The process of self-awareness uses the physical body's survival programs to create the feeling of a mini-me within us that mistakenly perceives it has a physical boundary. It is not able to be aware of itself because "you" are looking out from it. It is looking out of your eyes and you feel like it is you. Self-awareness, as a form of mindfulness, can be aware of thoughts, feelings, and sensations, and of your body and personality as a separate object, "me," but it cannot see itself.

This is why mindfulness has to reach a level of being able to observe not just thoughts, but self-awareness. You can be mindful from self-awareness, and then you can be mindful from awake awareness of the process of self-awareness. Only when you are looking from awake awareness can you see that what you took to be a solid self is a flurry of changing content arising within your mind.

Our current address is ego-identification, the habitual looping pattern of ego functions and thinking that has created the sense of "I." Ego-identification is not just a belief, story, thought, or attitude, but a habitual way of organizing consciousness that we can shift out of. The reason we want to shift out of it is that this thought-based creation of an illusory sense of self leaves us feeling alienated, as if something is always wrong with who we are or what is happening to us. Shifting into awake awareness can relieve us of the bondage of a self.

What Are We Shifting Into?

In the simplest sense, we are shifting into a new awareness-based operating system. The first step is to shift out of ego-identification and our current level of everyday mind. When we shift, there are many different dimensions of consciousness that we may access, but not all of them are useful in this approach. We will need to learn how to shift into awake awareness specifically, instead of landing in other types of consciousness and unconsciousness, such as daydreaming, calm meditation states, or personal or collective unconscious.

When we shift into awake awareness, our perception returns to its natural way of seeing people and the world, without projecting onto them. Instead of trying to calm our chattering mind, to redecorate the rut we're stuck in, or to improve our ego-identification, we can learn to use local awareness to immediately shift out of this mental bandwidth, just as if we were changing the channel.

We are shifting from everyday mind and ego-identification into awake awareness as our ground of being. When awake awareness is the new foundation, we include our body and thoughts as we discover embodied open-hearted awareness as our way of knowing and relating.

We can get to open-hearted awareness in one shift, or we can get there through a series of smaller shifts. With every shift, we access a new view from a new level of mind. When we shift, we need to become more comfortable with going through a gap of not-knowing. When we discover awake awareness, we need to become familiar with feeling more spacious, fluid, and open—without referring to thought for orienting ourselves as to who we are. We become free from alienation, anxiety, fear, and shame.

With awake awareness as our ground of being, we begin to have an entirely new relationship with our issues, subpersonalities, thoughts, and emotions. We can see them more clearly. Over time, emotions that have been repressed or frozen will detox spontaneously. The subpersonalities we took to be ourselves—our mistaken identities—are now recognizable as patterns of thought and emotion. With repeated glimpses of awake awareness, achieved by practicing open-hearted awareness, we begin to rewire our neural networks to create the new normal: the awareness-based operating system.

Where Am I?

"Location, location, location" is a phrase used by real-estate agents to emphasize that identical homes have different values based on where they're located. If a building has two apartments—one with windows looking out at brick walls and the other, three floors higher, with panoramic views—the upstairs apartment is much more valuable. The open-hearted awareness approach helps you shift into your best location with a spacious view from which you can realize how valuable you already are.

The small sense of self feels separate, and this location makes us feel contracted, isolated, and in our heads. The experience of opening up during the process of awakening first brings spaciousness, emptiness, and freedom; these qualities can then be followed by embodiment, oneness, fullness, unity, and flow. In our journey of awaking the sense of no-self is a freedom from a specific place of viewing. We can feel infinite, everywhere, nowhere, here, and now.

Location matters: *Where* are you viewing from? From which level of mind are you looking? Contrary to popular belief, relief from suffering is not achieved by changing the thoughts, emotions, and situations that arise. Instead, relief is directly related to the level of mind from which we experience these. Ask yourself this question about any thoughts, feelings, beliefs, judgments, worries, and fears that arise:

Who or what are these experiences arising to?

This focus on location may seem like a new way to do meditation or inquiry. However, I've found that working with our identity shift in the context of location makes awakening more visceral and easier to learn.

You may not have previously thought about meditation as a way of shifting location. Our sense of self and our way of knowing is "normally" located within our thoughts. We can learn to shift the location of the observer out of identification with thinking. When you become *aware of* your thoughts—instead of remaining located *within* them—you begin to feel some relief from stress. Research showing that meditation reduces stress demonstrates that the stress is not caused by the external situations we usually blame, but is generated instead by the previous location of identity in our thoughts.

We all know what it's like to be located in a bad mood, a daydream, a righteous point of view, or a fantasy. When we're self-centered, our location is clearly the problem. When we put ourselves into another person's shoes, we're changing our location to feel empathy and compassion.

In the open-hearted awareness approach, we learn to use local awareness for shifting our location. When we shift location, we change the way our brain works. When we use local awareness to shift our level of mind, our perception of the whole world changes. We are no longer confined to a small self in our heads, looking out from behind our eyes. We can learn how to move local awareness to a new location that generates a profound change in our sense of identity. This change takes us out of the emotional turmoil perpetuated by our current location. When we shift to a new level of mind, we find more capacity, space, and the ability to relate without fear or shame.

The movement of local awareness occurs on an invisible level within our physical body. Once we get the hang of it, moving local awareness feels very palpable. As we shift locations, our point of view changes to a new level of mind. The felt sense of each level of mind can be slightly different for each person.

The most common inquiry used to shift out of the current location of your identity is not "*Who* am I?" or "*What* am I?" but "*Where* am I?" Asking *where* leads to an experiential, felt-sense pointer for shifting from a small, separate sense of self into the boundless ground of being.

Let's use local awareness to look back now and inquire: *Where is the hearer?*

When no hearer can be found, notice how it feels to have a more spacious view.

When Am I?

Contrary to popular belief, you can't be in the present moment. However, you are always here now. It is only a matter of whether you know it or not. The Now is often confused with our understanding of the present time or the present moment. In Tibetan Buddhism, the Now is considered the "timeless time" that includes the three relative times of past, present, and future. We know not to get caught in the past or the future, but in order to be in the Now, we also have to let go of the present. The Now is not confined by relative clock time, yet it is also not only pure timelessness. The Now is the meeting place of timeless spacious awareness with the relative world and its conventional time. The Now does not come and go, but includes everything all at once. When we're aware of being in the Now, present moments come and go, like ripples and waves in the ocean of awake awareness.

When we don't know the alternative to the three relative times, we create an imitation of the Now and call it "the moment" or "the present." Here's how Merriam-Webster defines *moment*.

> a: a minute portion or point of time: INSTANT
> b: a comparatively brief period of time[4]

Clearly, we can't live in the moment, because moments come and go like the tick-tock of a clock. Moment . . . gone . . . new moment . . . gone . . . new moment . . . gone. You can't stop moments or be quick enough to be in any moment of time. Physicist Max Planck recognized that moments are flashes in relative time. He divided moments into small measures known as Planck units, which are 10^{-43} seconds long. No matter how hard we try, we can never slice time thin enough to enter the moment.

Our perceived experience is made up of mind moments that appear continuous, like movies. Films project twenty-four still frames every second in order to make the movement of their images appear lifelike to the brain. A moment is like a single frame that we can look at but cannot remain in. Even if we took one still frame from a movie, we would see a frozen moment, not the dynamic living Now.

Trying to be in the Now by entering the present moment is also like sitting at the edge of a river, looking at the water flowing over one rock. As soon as you focus on one moment in the flow of water, that portion of water has already moved downstream. We cannot enter present moments because they move too fast and change continuously. Contemporary Tibetan Buddhist teacher Mingyur Rinpoche says, "If you examine even the present moment carefully, you find that it also is made up of earlier and later moments. In the end, if you keep examining the present moment, you find that there is no present moment that exists either."[5]

Interestingly, mindfulness meditation begins with the opposite approach to trying to be in the moment; it asks us to actually notice moment-to-moment change. One of the great insights we can get from mindfulness meditation practice is that each moment of experience arises and passes. Having a direct experience of this impermanence, from observing awareness, helps us to let go of the attempt to calcify any single moment of time, to try to make something stable that is not. When we really get a feeling for the coming and going of moments, it helps us break the illusion of a solid, separate self, which gives us relief from suffering.

The present time is not the Now. When Gampopa, an eleventh-century Buddhist teacher, said, "Don't invite the future. Don't pursue the past. Let go of the present. Relax right now,"[6] he was pointing to the fact that trying to locate yourself in any of the three relative times, including the present, can cause suffering. It's not always a benefit to strive to be in the present. While working as a psychotherapist, I saw that the distinguishing feature of clinical depression is feeling stuck in the present. As one client said, "It feels like there is only this present, unbearable pain and no hope of it changing." Being depressed is like being in a prison where you're cut off from positive memories of the past and from the potential to change in the future. Part of the treatment for depression is to have people remember how they got through sad periods in the past and realize there's a positive future. In terms of the present, it's helpful to realize "This too shall pass."

It is true that our attention can be negatively obsessed with remembering the past. However, most of us would agree on an everyday level with poet and philosopher George Santayana, who said, "Those who cannot remember the past are condemned to repeat it."[7] We can also be preoccupied with fearing the future. The ability to imagine the future has helped all of us survive and thrive, for instance by being able to prepare for the coming winter or spring. You can plan for the future and recall the past while being in the Now.

The most important thing to know is that we are always already in the Now—however, we are not always *aware* of being in the Now. You can only know the Now from awake awareness. Many of us have experienced being in the Now when we were "in the zone" or in a panoramic flow state.

When we learn to shift into directly being aware of being in the Now, our whole sense of reality changes for the better. We can't be aware of being in the Now from our everyday, ego-identified state of mind. We can shift through the door of the Now into awake awareness, or when abiding in awake awareness, we can begin to notice the feeling of being in the Now. The purpose of clarifying and distinguishing the Now from the present and present moment is for us to be able to shift into being in the Now and know we are here.

What Are the Five Levels of Mind?

Most of us have spent a lot of time trying to reduce suffering by changing our thoughts, beliefs, attitudes, or circumstances. This is the basis for behavioral, cognitive, or analytic approaches to reduced suffering. Now, instead of adding or subtracting thoughts, emotions, and behaviors, we will learn to shift our awareness into another level of mind that has a completely different view of the same conditions. We are relocating our view—decentering from ego-identification, where we'd previously been located—to the foundation of awake awareness.

Each level of consciousness and its contents can be observed, and we can observe from each level of consciousness. When we look out from a particular level of consciousness, we experience its unique way of perceiving and knowing. When we are *knowing from* the five levels of consciousness rather than looking at them, we will call them the *five levels of mind.*

In this open-hearted awareness approach, we will relocate our identity in five different levels of mind and their associated types of awareness. We can look at each of these levels of mind from the event perspective or the mind perspective. The *event perspective* is when we *look at* and experience the contents and capabilities of any level of mind. The *mind perspective* is when we are located in and *look from* that level of mind. The lower levels cannot know the higher levels, but each new level of mind can know and include the previous ones.

1. **Everyday mind** is experienced as sense perceptions, thoughts, and emotions. Everyday mind *looks from* thoughts and ego functions to create ego-identification and a subject-versus-object dualistic split that obscures the subtler levels of mind. Everyday mind uses attention and self-awareness to focus.

2. **Subtle mind** is experienced as the ability to step back from everyday mind and be located in mindful awareness, the meditator, or an observing ego. Subtle mind *looks from* a mindful witness of thoughts, feelings, and sensations as the

contents of our experience arise and pass. Subtle mind uses mindful awareness and subtle-body awareness to focus.

3. **Awake-aware mind** knows itself as timeless, formless, changeless, contentless, spacious awareness. Awake-aware mind *looks from* a big-sky witness of spacious awareness to see subtle mind and everyday mind, as well as the world. Awake-aware mind is already here and aware by itself, so when we look from it, we are using effortless mindfulness.

4. **Simultaneous mind** experiences ultimate reality and relative reality at the same time. The ocean of awake awareness experiences all energy and form as its own waves. We feel spacious and pervasive boundless freedom, and awake awareness is embodied as an interconnected presence while being capable of perceiving each previous level of consciousness. Simultaneous mind *looks from* unity consciousness, where nondual awareness is knowing from within our consciousness while not becoming ego-identified.

5. **Heart mind** is free of the location of any particular witnessing self. In this level of mind, we feel connected and protected, vulnerable and courageous, and motivated to create and relate. Heart mindfulness *looks from* our ground of being, which is now operating from open-hearted awareness, a wisdom-based loving intelligence that feels boundless, interconnected, and fully human.

Mindfulness is the connection from the level of mind we are perceiving from, to what is perceived. The perceiver is different from each level of mind. So mindfulness is the connection and relating from your level of mind to objects and tasks on the relative level.

When located in everyday mind, you can use concentration to be mindful of thinking and performing tasks. From subtle mind, you can look from the meditator, aware of the contents of your mind, realizing you are not your thoughts. Then you can be ego-less when awareness is aware of itself as spacious awake awareness. Local awareness steps back and discovers the awareness that is leaning in, including and welcoming. Effortless mindfulness begins when we are located in spacious awareness. Then awareness is embodied as presence, knowing from innate simultaneous mindfulness. Then heart-mind uses heart mindfulness to feel interconnection, creativity, and compassion.

What Are the Three Shifts of Identity?

We begin our journey of awakening by being ego-identified. This is when the thought-based operating system creates a small, separate sense of a "mini-me" located in the center of the head. As we shift the location of our identity, we won't have to get rid of our ego functions (like knowing how to do our tasks at work) or our basic ego personality (like our sense of humor). What we let go of is our ego-identification. Our ego functions and ego personality become less stressed, defensive, and constricted; ego-identification is no longer experienced as the center of who we are. We will go through a gap of egolessness—the dropping away of the illusory sense of ego-identification—before discovering awake awareness to be the true foundation of our identity.

When we wake up, we shift into an awareness-based identity called the witnessing self, which is a skylike, detached observer of the contents of our consciousness. We are no longer ego-identified, as from this self we are able to observe from outside. This self is a mindful witness that uses nonconceptual awareness as the primary way of knowing. You will learn to observe from a big-sky view, a witness consciousness looking from spacious awareness. With this shift, our identity will be located in the awake-aware level of mind. We don't want to get stuck here in the "witness-protection program."

The next shift is waking-in, when spacious awareness, which is formless and boundless, recognizes that it is energy and form as well as space. From the witnessing self, you feel as though you are the sky, in which thoughts and feelings are objects that come and go. When awake awareness becomes embodied, you feel at first as though you are a wave in the ocean of awareness. There can be a transition here—a feeling of no-self, the experience of perceiving without a perceiver located in any one point of view. Awake awareness is not a new, separate, individual identity because we now correctly perceive ourselves as always interconnected. Awake awareness is the ground of Being that we all have in common. Being is the discovery or rediscovery of your identity based in okay-ness, basic trust, basic goodness, and the coming together of the ultimate level of reality with our relative humanity. Seeing from Being uses simultaneous mind to perceive formlessness as awake awareness within form. We begin waking-out by discovering open-hearted awareness, which is the fabric of love, connected to all.

At this point, we are no longer centered in our head, but are knowing from heart-mind. Most of us have not been taught how to access open-hearted awareness. It's not that it's so esoteric or difficult to find. Mainly we don't access it because we haven't known it was possible and natural. The truth is that even if you haven't known anything about shifting via local awareness, you can do it. No matter how long a room has been dark, the minute you flip the switch, the room is completely filled with light.

What Is the Relationship between Mind, Identity, and Awakening?

LEVELS OF MIND	STAGES OF AWAKENING	SHIFTS OF IDENTITY
Everyday Mind	Normal, everyday life	Ego-identification
Subtle Mind		
Awake-Aware Mind	Waking-up	Self
Simultaneous Mind	Waking-in	Being
Open-Hearted Awareness	Waking-out	

What Is a Glimpse?

A glimpse is not a spiritual experience happening to our current identity and conceptual mind. A glimpse begins as if we were knowing awake awareness as an object, but we realize awake awareness knows itself—and then we shift into knowing *from* awake awareness. A glimpse is a shift into seeing and being from a new level of mind and identity. In other words, a glimpse is a not always a peak experience, one that's a euphoric state. Instead, it could be called a "peek" experience because the underlying ground of our Being is now the location of seeing.

You could say that a glimpse is an insight. In this context, *insight* means seeing from within or discovering a new way of seeing and being. This insight is not information that you get from a new level of mind, but the way that nonconceptual awareness sees. Our goal is to get a full glimpse of our natural awakeness and its positive qualities. When local awareness shifts, it glimpses from a new way of being. We let go of any effort and let everything be. Once we glimpse, we can immediately go about our daily activities or we can sit quietly, but rather than meditating, we can let our system *marinate* in awake awareness. Awake awareness can be marinating, saturating, and detoxing your body. We are resting as awake awareness, and from awake awareness we can be active.

Small Glimpses Many Times

The main practice is small glimpses many times, but sometimes one small glimpse changes everything. These shifts can be done in the midst of our daily life.

The reason the glimpses are small is that when we shift into awake awareness, we let go of efforting and allow the new knowing to know on its own. We can't use the effort of the egoic doer to help in any way. It can be helpful to begin our day with a twenty-minute session of awareness inquiry in order to tune into awareness-based knowing. We can finish this initial session by marinating in a new mode of perception, knowing, and identity, and by familiarizing ourselves with this way of being and seeing.

The practice of small glimpses many times during the day is what builds the new habit of knowing from awake awareness. This trains our brain to remain in it for longer periods of time. Eventually, we are able to glimpse even while standing in line at the grocery store. When the inertia of old habits returns you to ego-identification, you can say to yourself, "No big surprise, just re-recognize." We realize that our quality of life is not dependent on the experiences arising in the world or our minds, but on the level of mind they are rising to. We can feel good even when we do not feel good.

Remember to Remember

No matter what you do, no matter what situation you are in—whether walking, sitting, eating, or lying down—always return your awareness within the nature of awake awareness. That's it!

TULKU URGYEN RINPOCHE, WHEN ASKED ABOUT HIS DAILY PRACTICE[8]

In order not to get pulled back to identification, you can do the following process of recognizing your true nature:

- Recognize that you are caught, attached, or identified.

- Realize there is another way to be.

- Remember a method of returning or recognizing that has worked for you.

- Choose a glimpse practice that works for you.

- Do it! Surrender local awareness back to spacious awareness. Look from spacious awareness. Allow awareness to embody.

- Feel the dance between formlessness and form, without landing in either one.

- Know with your new heart-knowing—without going back to thought for a second opinion or allowing a subpersonality to take over.

- Let be and rest in the ground of being. Be this safety, live from this, as this. Invite all experience to this new, centerless center.

- Live from open-hearted awareness. Allow the knowing from unconditioned awareness and unconditional love to connect outward to all.

- Do from being. Trust in the new knowing and begin to rewire your brain and ego functions by going about your daily tasks from this new view.

- Detox, welcome, liberate. Open-hearted awareness welcomes and liberates unpleasant feelings, detoxing, rewiring, and working with emotions and subpersonalities.

- Remain undistracted without effort.

- When you get re-identified and caught, no big surprise . . . just re-recognize.

Glimpsing All the Way Home

Being located in everyday mind is like living in a storm cloud: chaotic, turbulent, and filled with fog, wind, and lightning. You may feel that "who you are" is located in this cloud, and everything outside is "other." In the cloud, it's a struggle to see clearly. No matter where you move or what you do, as long as you're confined to the cloud, your feelings will be stormy and your vision foggy. When local awareness makes its first shift, it simply steps out of the cloud and recognizes the wide-open sky of awake awareness. You feel free and spacious. You're now the witness, aware *of* the sky and aware *from* the sky. You're now located in spacious awareness with a new perspective on the cloud of your mind and body. Then, as the open sky, you can include the stormy contents of the cloud, while remaining open. The ground of being is able to welcome and embrace all thoughts and feelings without becoming reidentified with them.

In other words, when you feel anxious, fearful, lonely, depressed, or upset, your awareness is obscured by the habit of looking to your small, conceptual mind. Local awareness deliberately shifts out of identification with the cloud to a skylike view from awake awareness. From the sky of awake awareness, any thought patterns or emotional storms are included. By recognizing the spacious dimension of awake awareness as the source of mind, you have discovered that you are both the sky of awake awareness and your particular body and mind. Everything that happens is just weather.

After all, no storm ever hurts the sky, and the sky permeates even the thickest, darkest clouds. If you go all the way with this, to the point where awake awareness recognizes itself as both the sky and the cloud, then you will feel a compassionate, open-hearted response to your own stormy feelings and those of others. Ultimately, our wellbeing is not based on the changing weather conditions, but on what level of mind we are aware from.

The Simple Steps: Unhook, Drop, Open, See, Include, Know, Let Be

This is one of the full practices in the open-hearted awareness approach, which uses local awareness to shift through each of the five levels of mind. Let me give you a sense of the steps, and then you can do the experiment for yourself. Once you learn these simple steps, you can do it anywhere, at any time of the day.

1. **Unhook.** You will step off the train of thought you're on. Once unhooked, local awareness will become the primary source and location of intelligence. Local awareness

will know directly from within your body rather than looking down from your everyday mind. The key of this step is to unhook awareness so that you're not looking from your thoughts, not looking up to your thoughts, and not applying your mind by using attention. Local awareness can completely detach, unhook, or step away from thinking. You can discover local awareness without knowing what it is. Just give it a try.

2. **Drop.** What will drop is not your everyday mind, not your ego, and not your attention; it will be local awareness. Local awareness will move like an invisible globe of awareness below your neck and will know awareness and aliveness directly from within your body. You will come back to your senses and know directly with thought-free awareness. This is the experience of *subtle mind and body* or inner-body presence.

3. **Open.** Local awareness will open to space and then mingle with spacious awareness all around your body. You become aware of open space, then open space is aware.

4. **See.** Local awareness will become aware of spacious awareness, then spacious awareness becomes aware of itself as a field: boundless, formless, timeless, contentless, continuous, and awake. Spacious awareness is nonconceptually knowing and seeing.

5. **Include.** Begin by witnessing the contents of your body and mind from spacious awareness. Spacious awareness that knows itself as formless will now also know itself as form. Spacious awareness will remain boundless as it includes aliveness within your body. This natural, embodied awake awareness will be effortlessly aware and include energy, thoughts, feelings, and sensations

without becoming reidentified with an egoic point of view. Embodied awake awareness does not resist anything, but welcomes everything that's arising.

6. **Know.** When awake awareness is embodied it will not need to go back to thought to know or to create an ego manager. Local awareness will search through the contents of body and mind for an object called "self," and when it is not findable then awareness will be free. A new kind of knowing will arise that has no thoughts on the screen of the mind, but it has access to all information instantly as needed. This new heart-knowing does not have to orient by going up to thought, going down to sleep, going one moment forward into the future, referring to past memory, or holding on to the experience of the present moment. You will notice the shift as nonconceptual awareness takes on the flavor of heart-knowing; feeling connected, curious, loving, safe, creative, and response-able; and knowing that all is well.

7. **Let be.** During this step, notice that open-hearted awareness is already awake and aware and does not require thought or effort. At this point, you can remain undistracted without effort. You can let go of controlling and let be. Rest like a child who was lost and has returned to the loving arms of a mother.

GLIMPSE 1 **Shift into Freedom**

We are going to do a simple series of shifts. These begin with unhooking local awareness from thought and having local awareness be the location of knowing. You do not need to understand how to unhook local awareness from thinking. Just assume you will be able to do it intuitively. If it helps, you can let awareness ride your in-breath below your neck to be aware from within.

1. Sit comfortably with your eyes open or closed, and simply be aware of your senses. Notice the activity of thinking in your head.

2. Now, **unhook** local awareness from thinking and let it **drop** down through your neck and into your upper body.

3. Feel local awareness knowing sensations and awareness directly from within your body. Stay with this for a while.

4. With awareness knowing the aliveness and awareness directly within your upper body, don't go back up to thought or down to sleep.

5. Now, let local awareness **open** to the space outside your body.

6. Simply be aware of space.

7. Let awareness mingle with space.

8. Be aware of open space and then notice that open space is aware.

9. Feel the awareness aware of itself as a boundless, contentless, changeless field of spacious awareness. Stay here for a while.

10. Now shift from being aware of spacious awareness to **see** from spacious awareness. Ask: "Am I noticing spacious awareness or is spacious awareness aware of the thoughts, feelings, and sensations that I formerly took to be me?"

11. Notice that the spacious awareness outside is the same as the awareness and aliveness within your body. The field of awareness is spacious and pervasive.

12. Feel how the formless spacious awareness **includes** all appearances and aliveness within as one continuous ocean of awareness with waves of experience arising.

13. Notice how you can be simultaneously aware outside and within.

14. Let local awareness search the contents of the body and mind for the location of a witnessing self. When no self can be found, notice the awareness that's knowing from everywhere, nowhere, and here.

15. Rather than going back up to thought for words, wait and feel the potential to **know** from open-hearted awareness. Inquire: "What does open-hearted awareness know?"

16. Feel the boundless, embodied, alert, and interconnected sense of knowing, safety, and wellbeing.

17. Inquire: "What is here now if there is no problem to solve?" Rather than going back to thought to know the answer, allow open-hearted awareness to know.

18. Remain undistracted without effort.

19. Let be.

The following table shows the shifts you made into and through each of the five levels of mind.

FIVE LEVELS OF MIND	GLIMPSE SERIES
Level 1: Everyday Mind The everyday mind is identified with the contents of our mind looking to thought and looking from thought.	**Start Where You Are** We start by noticing the activity of our everyday mind centered in our head.
Moving from Level 1 to Level 2 Local awareness is identified with the everyday mind. It is able to unhook from thought and know directly, moving through all the other levels of mind.	**Unhook** We unhook local awareness from identification with everyday mind. Local awareness then drops and moves below our neck to experience awareness and aliveness within the body.
Level 2: Subtle Mind & Subtle Body Subtle mind is the nonjudgmental, mindful witness of contents of mind and body. Subtle body is when local awareness experiences our body and energy directly from within.	Unhooking brings us to the level of subtle mind and subtle body that knows awareness and sensation directly from within.
Level 3: Awake-Aware Mind Local awareness knows spacious awareness as itself through awareness of awareness. The awake-aware mind level can be called spacious awareness. The experience is contentless, boundless, and timeless. Spacious awareness then can witness from this open sky of awareness back to our contents of mind through effortless mindfulness.	**Open** Local awareness opens to directly experience spacious awareness, the very subtle mind, within and all around our body. **See** Spacious awareness first knows and sees itself through awareness of awareness. Then spacious awareness, as the witnessing self, sees the contents of our minds and bodies from the field of spacious awareness.

FIVE LEVELS OF MIND	GLIMPSE SERIES
Level 4: Simultaneous Mind Awake awareness embodied is when spacious awake awareness remains spacious and primary but also knows itself as inherently within, including the alive energy in the body and seeing from the very subtle mind. The simultaneous mind is able to experience emptiness, fullness, boundlessness, and distinction.	**Include** Spacious awareness first knows itself as formless awareness, then knows itself also equally as form. Awake awareness becomes embodied as presence and is discovered to be the new source of intelligence and identity as simultaneous mind, which experiences both ultimate reality and relative reality.
Level 5: Open-Hearted Awareness Open-hearted awareness is the knowing from heart mindfulness. The feeling of not being a separate self leads to wellbeing and interconnectedness with all people and all things as a field of love and wisdom, in the flow of ordinary life.	**Know** Open-hearted awareness arises as the new way of knowing, creating and relating to others and the world from a loving presence. **Let Be** There is a sense of resting as who you truly are and a whole new way of doing from being.

5

THE ART AND SCIENCE
OF AWAKENING

All of humanity's problems stem from man's inability
to sit quietly in a room alone.

BLAISE PASCAL[1]

The results are in: meditation is one of the best things you can do for yourself. Its benefits have recently become accepted in mainstream culture. In the very near future, regular meditation will be considered as important for your brain as regular exercise is for your body. My hope is that, following the acceptance of regular meditation, awakening will also become a common, intentional stage of growth—much like going to college.

For centuries, spiritual practitioners and meditators have reported positive changes in their lives as a result of meditation, prayer, inquiry, and spiritual practice. These accounts of increased compassion, peace of mind, and improved focusing ability are now being scientifically verified. Over the past twenty years, research has shown that meditation has beneficial effects on the body, mind, and emotions. Since meditation has been recognized for reducing stress-related symptoms, many health professionals and psychotherapists now recommend it. It is documented that meditation reduces anxiety, depression, and chronic pain; improves cognitive function; boosts immunity; and lowers blood pressure.[2] Furthermore, mindfulness practices are effective ways to train people in interpersonal and social qualities like ethics, empathy, emotional communication, and compassion.

However, most types of meditation currently studied are only the introductory practices from traditions in which awakening is the goal. These preliminary practices—like one-pointed concentration and deliberate mindfulness—relieve stress and improve focus. Why stop there? We can start with the current neuroscience research that confirms the absence of a separate self that's centered in the brain, then explore the presence of awake awareness and its benefits.

The open-hearted awareness approach presents the next levels of practice, which are just as easy to learn as the preliminary practices. Though these next-level practices—*awareness of awareness, effortless mindfulness, and heart mindfulness*—offer similar benefits in terms of stress relief and focus, they're primarily designed to relieve the root of suffering caused by ego-identification and to help us access our natural potential for joy, wellbeing, and living from an embodied flow state.

Experts in the fields of science and spirituality, who have been mostly at odds with each other for centuries, are now joining in public dialogues and even common ventures (in spite of fundamentalists in both camps). Some scientists are changing their long-held assumptions about the human mind as a result of research on meditation and brain scans of spiritual practitioners. At the same time, some spiritual practitioners are beginning to go beyond the insular beliefs of their doctrines to open their minds and practices to recent scientific studies; some even participate in research. On a number of occasions when the Dalai Lama was asked what he would do if scientific studies invalidated his beliefs, he replied that he would simply change his beliefs.

Scientific research operates through a three-part method. The first part is to objectively observe items of study, the second is to create a thesis and conclusions based on these observable phenomena, and the third is to develop a hypothesis and experiments that test these conclusions. Meditation research unites scientific, third-person observation with first-person reports of meditation experiences. Subjective experience can't be thrown out just because a third party cannot observe it.

Those of us in the meditative field need to separate superstition and pseudoscience from the repeatable and beneficial effects of meditation.

Awareness is invisible, and it can't be seen by an outside observer, but the effects of intentionally applying awareness can be seen in the brain. Modern technology has provided amazing advances in our ability to observe brain functions. Instruments like the SPECT scan (which measures blood flow in the brain) and the fMRI (which uses a magnet about seven times stronger than the magnets that pick up cars) can give precise images of brain activity and the changes brought about by different meditation practices.

Neuroscience is still in its early stages. We cannot make any exact correlation between current brain studies and occurrences in our consciousness. We still don't know what consciousness is or where it comes from. The research we're interested in is primarily the clinical applications: whether meditation practices reduce suffering and increase wellbeing. Even early in this field of study, we can say that meditation reliably offers relief from suffering at many different levels.

Old Brains Can Learn New Tricks

Recently, a commonly held belief has changed dramatically: the assumption that the adult brain has little capacity for growth. We've all heard the saying "You can't teach an old dog new tricks." But old brains *can* learn new habits. The brain has more plasticity, the ability to change and grow, during adulthood than anyone had realized. Repeated activities—mental or physical—can create neural networks that strengthen with use. Pioneering neuropsychologist Donald O. Hebb, PhD, states, "Neurons that fire together wire together."[3] One basic premise of neural plasticity is the now-observable ability of the brain to create new neuronal habits through intentional exercises. The collaboration of modern science with ancient methods of meditation has made meditation available to many people who'd previously shied away from it because of its religious associations.

No one can say for sure whether awareness comes from the brain or the brain comes from awareness. But we do know that awareness can change the brain. Awareness practices not only rest your brain, they change its way of functioning. Intentionally moving awareness within your consciousness will upgrade your brain. Scientific observations now validate the positive brain changes that meditators have been experiencing as a result of intentional training through meditation and awareness practices for centuries.

In all traditions and lineages, meditation has progressive steps, but training styles differ. The open-hearted awareness approach offers a few different ways to begin—each geared toward a different learning style. The Glimpse practices can be considered advanced forms of meditation that are as easy to learn as most beginner-level meditations.

Using the open-hearted awareness approach, which includes practices like effortless mindfulness, you will get the same physical and emotional benefits as people pursuing other mindfulness-meditation techniques. However, by shifting levels of mind, you can also receive additional benefits, which come from the relief of deep existential suffering. In some forms of meditation, you try to calm your everyday mind, but in this approach, you will learn how to shift out of the thinking mind and discover another level of mind that is already calm and alert: awake awareness. Awake awareness has been called the ultimate medicine because it helps relieve suffering and offers us access to a profound sense of wellbeing—no matter what's happening in our lives.

The Default Mode Network: Waking from the Daydream

We have seen how ego-identification is the way most people organize their identities and operate throughout daily life. The creation of ego-identification is so ingrained in our brain that it even occurs unconsciously during our daydreams. A recent discovery in neuroscience has important implications for our ability to live an awakened life. In 2001, Marcus Raichle, MD, coined the term *default mode network* after conducting an fMRI brain-scanning study. In between taking measurements for an education study, he left the fMRI on.

He found that certain areas of his subjects' brains became activated when they were told to rest or do nothing.[4] The default mode network is a system of brain regions that engages in self-referential thoughts when not focusing on a task or the outside world. His first discovery was that our brains are never quiet. Even when we're trying to rest and do nothing, our brains remain active, usually with a particular kind of conscious activity, such as chattering thoughts and to-do lists. When we look closer, we find a perpetually dissatisfied mini-me is operating unconsciously.

During goal-oriented activity, the default mode network is deactivated, and another network, the *task-positive network*, is activated. Our brains continuously and rhythmically alternate between the external, goal-directed, task-positive mode and the internal, self-referencing, default mode. If you have ever tried to meditate by focusing on one task like watching your breath, you know how your mind wanders into a kind of daydreaming state. The mind wandering is a particular kind of daydream—one in which ego-identification is the subject. The internally focused default mode is primarily experienced as self-referencing thoughts with the mini-me as the main character. This daydream tells the story of ego-identification's illusory and impossible search for satisfaction in current dramas or future hopes, and the resulting continual sense of unfulfilled longing and unhappiness.

Psychologists Matthew A. Killingsworth and Daniel T. Gilbert conducted a study on the effects of the default mode network with 2,250 students at Harvard University. Using a smartphone app, researchers contacted the students at random intervals to question them about "how happy they were, what they were currently doing, and whether they were thinking about their current activity or thinking about something else that was pleasant, neutral, or unpleasant."[5] From the enormous amount of data collected, Killingsworth and Gilbert gleaned that 49.6 percent of students' waking hours were spent thinking about something other than what they were doing. Research further revealed that this kind of thinking made the students unhappy. The study concluded: "The human mind is a wandering mind, and a wandering mind is an unhappy mind."[6]

Many people try to stay busy, even becoming workaholics, as a strategy for maintaining a task-positive mode that avoids the unhappiness of mind-wandering. But staying busy is not a solution for the problem of unhappiness. Evidence shows that only 10 percent of our happiness is based on external success. According to Killingsworth and Gilbert, as little as 4.6 percent of our happiness is derived from the specific activity that we're doing.[7]

Even if we're very mindful during our everyday tasks, we still need to learn how to address the unhappiness caused by the mind-wandering of the default mode network. Is the default mode's self-referencing activity a fixed biological condition? Or is it plastic and able to change? Research shows that the default mode network does undergo developmental change. The infant brain exhibits limited evidence of the default mode network, but in children aged nine to twelve years, default mode network activity has already become more active.[8]

One potential way to reduce default mode network activity is through the practice of mindfulness meditation. There have been a number of studies showing that the neural activity in a core region of the default mode network—the posterior cingulate cortex—becomes less activated during mindfulness practices.[9] Mindfulness meditation practices such as open monitoring, insight meditation, and choiceless awareness reduce the activity of the default mode network, but they do so by observing internal content only. Meditations such as mindful walking and eating, one-pointed concentration, *shamatha,* and focused attention also reduce the activity of the default mode network, but they do so by focusing only externally, therefore activating the task-positive network. In so doing, these mindfulness meditation practices successfully reduce the default mode network, but they also support a continued dualistic alternating of the two networks. I had an experience of this early in my meditation training.

While I was in graduate school, I traveled to Sri Lanka, India, and Nepal on a fellowship. I studied in the University of Kandy in Sri Lanka and learned mindfulness meditation in monasteries and meditation centers. Being in a different culture and studying meditation was transformational on so many levels. During my first long, twenty-one-day retreat, I felt a continuous state of calm abiding for the entire last week. When the retreat ended, I walked down the mountain in a blissful, peaceful state believing that I might remain there forever.

I got on the local bus at the bottom of the hill, which was packed with people at rush hour. As the local bus continued, more and more people got on until at one point a heavyset man who seemed drunk pushed his way in. He knocked people aside and kicked me square in the ankle. As the pain shot to my brain, my calmness disappeared and I was filled with hurt and anger. I said to him, "Hey, man, watch what you're doing!" He turned, looked at me, and just laughed. It seemed like the laugh of the universe: "Oh, I thought you had transcended disturbing feelings? Not so easy, eh? Ha ha." The calm state that took such a long time to develop was gone in minutes.

We don't want to completely shut down the default mode network because it has positive aspects, including giving us the ability to imagine, free-associate, and think creatively. These cognitive capacities distinguish us from other creatures, as they enable us to imagine future outcomes and plan for them—an evolutionary advantage. If we were to repress the default mode network entirely in an attempt to make ourselves happy, we would lose out on creativity. Is it possible to keep the positive aspects and yet not be hijacked into unhappiness by the default mode network all day long?

One clinical study, in which I participated as a subject, showed that during nondual awareness practices, meditators were able to be simultaneously aware of their internal and external experience while synchronizing intrinsic and extrinsic networks. Nondual awareness meditation "enables an atypical state of mind in which extrinsic and intrinsic experiences are increasingly synergistic rather than competing."[10]

The nondual, embodied awareness practices you will learn as part of the open-hearted awareness approach are designed to help you balance the default mode network and the task-positive network, and will help you disengage from self-referencing mind-wandering, which clears up the state of unhappiness and the unconscious hold of ego-identification. Nondual awareness—also called *presence, unity consciousness,* or *one taste*—is the experience of awake awareness embodied, where you are aware both outside and inside your body simultaneously. This experience seems to synchronize the default mode network. Your inner world and creativity are still available to you.

We can retrain the brain intentionally to remain synchronized so that we can be effortlessly focused, undistracted, connected, and calm while functioning in the world. When we discover that open-hearted awareness is already naturally unified, we can learn to live from its compassionate view. The power of the default mode network, which unconsciously reinforces ego-identification, can be reduced. At the same time, the positive and creative aspects of the default mode network can also remain available through open-hearted awareness practices.

Self-Liberation Reveals Natural Positive Qualities

Andrew Newberg, MD, director of research at the Myrna Brind Center of Integrative Medicine at Thomas Jefferson University, has long been fascinated with the science of brain changes as related to spiritual practices. In one study, Newberg used a SPECT (single-photon emission computed tomography) scan to look at activity in the brains of meditating Tibetan Buddhists and praying Franciscan nuns. Many meditation studies have focused on the frontal lobes of the brain, which are related to attention. Newberg was particularly interested in the superior parietal lobes, located toward the back part of the brain. These lobes, which he called the orientation association area (OAA), are responsible for orienting us in time and space, among other things. When the parietal lobes are at their normal level of activity, they create a strong sense of a physical boundary and separation from others. The co-opting of the physical-boundary program by ego-identification creates the feeling of being a solid, separate self. Ego-identification uses the OAA to help create the feeling of a bounded self on the level of identity.

From his research, Newberg concluded: "If you could consciously decrease activity in your parietal lobes, you would probably feel a brief loss or suspension of self-awareness. You might also experience a loss of your sense of space and time. We discovered that both the nuns and the Buddhists did just that—they were able to deliberately reduce activity in their parietal lobes while meditating."[11]

During meditation or prayer practices, the SPECT scan showed significant reductions of activity in the OAA of participants. At the same time, these meditators reported feeling less ego-centered while experiencing a boundless unity. The changes observed on their brain scans were similar, and participants reported similar experiences of losing the sense of a separate self. Along with the absence of a small self, there was an increase in the positive qualities of unity, alertness, clarity, boundlessness, freedom, joy, love, and connection.

Therefore, when we use spiritual practices that decrease parietal lobe activity, our sense of identity becomes untied from the physical-boundary program and begins to experience our true nature's boundless condition. It is important to learn meditations and awareness practices that slightly reduce the activity in this brain area in order to facilitate decoupling the normal physical sense of our bodies from our boundless ground of being.

Our brains are wired to focus on the particular content of what is happening and not the context. By opening and looking from spacious awareness, we retrain our brain to open beyond the hypervigilant scanning for potential danger—focusing on each particular movement inside or outside. When you are resting as spacious awareness, one famous pointer simply says, "Don't particularize."

In fact, we can experience this sense of egoless-ness and boundless interconnection as a highly functional *flow state,* like we are in "the zone." In this way, we shift from feeling that our identity is located in our heads behind our eyes to a more spacious, yet embodied and interconnected experience. As we train in open-hearted awareness, we can learn to feel boundlessness and interconnectedness as our identity, and yet remain embodied and responsive to our physical environment. With the open-hearted awareness approach, this slightly reduced parietal lobe activity does not lead to being spaced out. Instead we feel even safer, and more relaxed, sensitive, open, and responsive—like a tai chi master.

What Is the Common Experience?

It is important to note that in Newberg's meditation study, three aspects of experience were the same for both the participating nuns and Buddhists, while one area was different. The three aspects in common were: 1) SPECT scan images during meditation, 2) immediate subjective changes in perception and increased positive qualities, 3) the reported capacity to intentionally access these changes during daily life.

The one major difference among participants was their interpretation of the primary cause of their experiences. Although both groups articulated similar qualities, each used the language of their own tradition to report and interpret their experiences. For example, Buddhist meditators might say, "It feels like I am part of everyone and everything in existence."[12] In contrast, one of the Catholic nuns described having a "tangible sense of closeness with God and mingling with Him."[13] Each person viewed and described their experience through the lens of the belief systems of their religious traditions.

Interestingly, after Dr. Newberg published the results of his study, he received letters from scientists who claimed his research proved their belief in materialism, confirming that all spiritual experience could be reduced to brain activity. But, he also received numerous letters from religious practitioners proclaiming that his study was proof that human beings are biologically "hardwired for God."

Instead of engaging in discourse about the differences between meditative paths or philosophical interpretations, in this book we're going to focus on effective practices that lead to common benefits. It has been said that when the Buddha had his initial awakening, he despaired over putting his realization into words and teaching it to others. When he finally decided to try communicating what he'd realized, he used the medical model of his time instead of religious language. He spoke about the way to relieve suffering by asking: 1) What is the illness? The diagnosis identified the illness and the nature of the illness; 2) What is the cause? The etiology identified the causes of the illness; 3) What is the cure? The prognosis identified a cure for the illness; 4) What is the treatment? The prescription offered a treatment for the illness that could bring about a cure.

The Buddhist parable that best illustrates this practical approach posits a person who has been shot with a poisoned arrow. The person could be focused on who made the arrow, what its origins were, or even who shot it; or he could get treatment for his wound first. If he insists upon asking questions about the origin of the arrow before getting treatment, he may die before he receives any answers. In fact, it is said that the Buddha would never enter theological discussions. Instead he said, "I teach one thing and one thing only: suffering and the end of suffering." The most advanced awareness practices seem to work regardless of belief about ultimate causes. If we can learn the intricacies of our human consciousness the way we have learned human biology, we can reduce suffering and increase individual and societal wellbeing.

Awakening in Contemporary Times

Most of the early explorers of awakening were associated with a particular religious tradition. Upon awakening, these inner astronauts described their experiences in their own cultural or religious languages. Because similar discoveries were made in many cultures and religions, it seems clear that something common in human consciousness is being explored. The differences we see expressed are the result of the different languages, cultures, lineages, and worldviews through which our experience is filtered. Awakening is not part of any one tradition and does not reveal any specific religious doctrine. Awakening and awake awareness are part of the human lineage we all share. Everyone can experience awakening and awake awareness while maintaining his or her own beliefs, philosophy, and theology. You don't have to join any religion, or leave your current one, in order to awaken.

Awakening is part art, part science, and a good deal of mystery. Once we learn the principles of upgrading our common human consciousness, we see that awakening has observable principles and patterns, and is both teachable and learnable. Awake awareness may seem new, but it has been recognized by meditation masters for millennia and given names like *spirit, grace, true nature, source,* and *the ground of being.* In the twenty-first century, there may be opportunities to describe this dimension of reality in a new, common language.

It's been notoriously difficult to describe the nature of awake awareness in language. This does not mean that it is less real or less important. Invisible forces like gravity are difficult to describe, and yet we need to understand our relationship to them. The world-renowned quantum physicist David Bohm suggests that rather than throwing out the word "spirit," we should redefine it for modern times by going back to the original definition to see why it's so important. "What is spirit? The word is derived from the Latin word meaning 'breath' or 'wind' (like *respiration* or *inspiration*). It is suggested by the trees moving with the invisible force of the wind. We must then think of spirit as an invisible force—a life-giving essence that moves us deeply, or as a source that moves everything from within. Spirit is, therefore, not manifest. Although unseen and ungraspable, it is of key importance."[14]

The awareness that is naturally available to you is dynamic and yet invisibly inherent in all experience. Paradoxically, awake awareness may seem much vaster than you are, and yet it is not "other" than you. Some people have defined the direct experience of awake awareness as completely "other," by projecting it outward onto the image of a deity or spiritual teacher. Some people mistake it for a quality of their own unique personality. Some people may have missed seeing that awake awareness is equally available *to* each of us and *as* each of us. Our most revered wisdom teachers have pointed to this deep understanding by saying things like: "The kingdom of heaven is within you." Here, "within" does not mean "inside of you" personally. It means, "within you and all of us," like space is within all atoms.

However, in most institutionalized religions, the main taboo is experiencing that we are inseparable from spirit, God, Buddha nature, Christ consciousness, the ground of being, or universal reality. Many meditation masters and mystics were excommunicated or burned at the stake for sharing insights about how to connect directly with the spiritual dimension within us, rather than relying on a religious institution. The Protestant Reformation (which led to modern concepts of democracy) made sacred texts available to ordinary people by translating those texts from Latin into their native languages. However, it often happens that the teachings of one era's innovator evolve into the orthodoxy of the next era's institutionalized religious dogma. It always struck me as funny that so many reformers who critiqued and split off from the traditions in which they were raised ended up becoming fundamentalists about their new belief systems instead of being more open to innovation. It seems counterintuitive to discover boundless love for everyone without wanting to share it. Why retain for a small group something so beneficial for the relief of suffering? It doesn't make sense, especially in these times when helping more people to awaken would so greatly benefit our planet. The challenge now is to find a way to experience these truths directly and to build community while respecting diversity.

Some people who have experience with awakening focus on teaching a few students in their own traditions. Others have spoken in favor of making awakening available to anyone, and have been thrown out of their traditions. Others became innovators inside or outside of their original traditions by creating new models and methods of helping others to awaken. Most religious traditions have kept the higher levels of consciousness to themselves, keeping esoteric knowledge in the fold and feeling reticent to share it with outsiders. Some religious traditions take the perspective that it is dangerous to awaken without joining and going through traditional training.

I was fortunate enough to study with teachers from many different backgrounds who were willing to offer these direct methods freely and who encouraged me to teach in a modern way. My teachers Tulku Urgyen Rinpoche, Tsoknyi Rinpoche, and Mingyur Rinpoche gave direct teachings at public talks and to those who were sincerely interested. Open-hearted awareness practices do not have strong energy and physical practices and are not any more dangerous than introductory mindfulness practices. Another of my teachers, Khenchen Thrangu Rinpoche, writes: "The practice of Mahamudra is free from such dangers and complications. It is simply a matter of looking at our mind, recognizing its nature, and remaining within that recognition.

The Mahamudra instructions penetrate right to the essence of the teachings, and if they are followed there is no risk to body or mind."[15]

Awake awareness training introduces you to the support necessary to deal with changes in your consciousness, and today many people are spontaneously awakening outside of any tradition. It may be more dangerous at this crucial time in our human history to withhold these simple and profound pointers from people than to offer them teachings and risk that they might be misunderstood or intellectualized. One reason often given for why more people do not awaken is that most people have limited capacity. I have seen many people of different backgrounds begin to awaken, and it seems the limitations are not in the student but in the teaching methods.

Recently, many meditation talks have been updated with contemporary metaphors and explanations that speak to contemporary people. My interest has been to adapt meditation and inquiry practices for people in these new times without changing the basic principles. For example, one woman was able to shift into awake awareness—and began to live from there—after many years of meditation study and practice. She remarked, "I thought I had tried everything and that I was dense. This is just a different doorway that was here all along." It is important to point out awake awareness as the nature of mind, but then there are equally important pointers for the unfolding from recognition to realization, to stabilization, to expression.

These teachings are not just interesting philosophical concepts or wise poetic sayings. They are ways of transforming our consciousness, our motivations, and our interactions with the world. We cannot develop our full human potential if we do not awaken as well as grow up. Today we are in much need of the clarity and love that become available through learning to live from open-hearted awareness.

There are many movements and dialogues between science and spirituality today, including conferences on contemplative science. Books like *The Coming Interspiritual Age* by Kurt Johnson and David Robert Ord describe how interspiritual dialogues are happening more often. You may be part of a specific religion, or you may consider yourself "spiritual but not religious." You may believe that awakening is a matter of human consciousness and choose not to use the word *spiritual* in relation to these matters. I've seen this work for people of all faiths and no faith. The effectiveness of this awakening process is based on working with your human consciousness, not on your belief system.

The open-hearted awareness approach overlaps spirituality and psychology, but it is an awareness approach. Changing your physical body, your mental thoughts, your personal psychological inner life, or your consciousness are each different levels of experience and require different approaches. This is an experiential approach that focuses on exploring the subtlest dimensions of consciousness, using tools of awareness. Most of the ancient meditation systems were practiced in religious traditions so we can honor them as containers for the flourishing of inner exploration. Some people benefit from joining and staying with one particular tradition. The advantage of studying and practicing in one tradition is consistency in language and system, making it easier to be clear about subtle distinctions. However, you can be at a disadvantage if the methods of practice don't fit your learning style.

The main role of a teacher is to point you toward your own inner teacher. It was when I learned to look within that awake awareness showed me its own capacities, clarity, and love. It is important to have mentors and teachers who have traveled farther along the path to offer guidance. From psychotherapy studies, we know that transference, idealization, and projection are normal parts of our psychological relationship to a mentor. However, failing to recognize transference or overreliance on a teacher can keep you dependent. Those of us who know people who followed gurus into cults are aware of this potential trap.

Although teachers can share supportive energy, awake awareness cannot be transmitted from one person to another. Awake awareness is invisible and equally inherent within each of us. Whereas energy can travel from one person to another, awake awareness is already everywhere, so another person can only point it out to you. It needs to be discovered and realized by you.

A well-trained teacher can provide detailed instruction and cautions for avoiding traps, and he or she can help with an occasional checkup or tune-up. We can move from authority-based ways of finding truth to learning to look within and seeking methods of mutual exploration and support. Adyashanti says, "The keys to your happiness are no longer in anyone else's pocket from the past. They're in yours."[16] Although a teacher can give you a good map and point you in the right direction, only you can make the difference by prioritizing your own growth daily.

One example of a contemporary democratic model for physical, mental, emotional, and spiritual growth is a twelve-step program, such as Alcoholics Anonymous, in which leadership and speakers rotate. In twelve-step programs, there's a set of common principles, but each person is allowed to choose a higher power of their own understanding. People in recovery start as a sponsee and then become a sponsor as a way of mentoring one other.

There's no reason why awakening cannot be studied, learned, and taught like psychology, biology, or something seemingly ineffable like music. Many kinds of learning are conceptual, but awakening is more experiential and subtle. Like learning to balance on a bicycle, practicing these principles cannot be easily put into words, but it can certainly be learned. Historically, something has been called "esoteric" or "inscrutable" until its principles are revealed. For example, people originally thought that fire came from the gods, or that banging any two stones together would bring forth flames. Eventually they realized that two flint stones work best to produce fire. The science of flight and the ability to perform heart transplants were originally considered beyond possibility, but later a turning point occurred in which their basic principles were discovered.

One way to combine ancient spiritual practice and modern science is to consider everything I write as a hypothesis. I begin by stating a thesis, outlining experiments for you to try, and then encouraging you to discover what is true for yourself. You can share your own reports about what you find, read my reports, and hear the experiences of others. Here is a report from Dr. Jill Bolte Taylor, neuroanatomist and author of *My Stroke of Insight,* who describes what she experienced when a severe hemorrhage in the left hemisphere of her brain changed her consciousness:

I felt enormous and expansive, like a genie just liberated from her bottle. And my spirit soared free, like a great whale gliding through the sea of silent euphoria. Nirvana. I found Nirvana. I remember thinking there's no way I would ever be able to squeeze the enormousness of myself back inside this tiny little body.

But I realized "But I'm still alive! I'm still alive and I have found Nirvana. And if I have found Nirvana and I'm still alive, then everyone who is alive can find Nirvana." I picture a world filled with beautiful, peaceful, compassionate, loving people who knew that they could come to this space at any time. And that they could purposely choose to step to the right of their left hemispheres and find this peace. And then I realized what a tremendous gift this experience could be—what a stroke of insight this could be to how we live our lives. And it motivated me to recover. [17]

Dr. Bolte Taylor's initial shift happened unintentionally; she felt the boundless quality that Newberg's subjects described. Today, her hope and motivation for sharing her story are that people will experience a shift intentionally. The open-hearted awareness approach offers you tools to purposely choose to come into this awake, loving space at any time, but it works best if you are motivated to make awakening a priority in your life.

GLIMPSE 1 **Open-Eyed Meditation**

Modern brain research tells us that "vision is the product of a complex system of which the eyes are only one part. The processing of visual information—the receipt of visual stimuli through the eyes, its interpretation by various brain centers, and its translation into visual images—has been estimated to involve as much as 40 percent of the brain."[18]

When our eyes are darting around or scanning for a specific threat, then we're on alert. Sometimes our attempts to be calmer by having our eyes be more narrow and concentrated can keep our brain in a fixed, task-positive mode. Learning panoramic awareness will help us drop into a nondual, balanced flow state in which we are relaxed and confident.

There is a Tibetan Buddhist practice called sky gazing. You go to a place with a wide-open vista and become interested in looking at the open space. First you notice the open space in front of you, then within you, and then behind you.

The goal in this book is to help shift to another operating system, called open-hearted awareness, where all our senses and systems—including vision—are functioning in their natural state. In order for us to do this, we need to learn how to shift our awareness and live with our eyes open.

Here are some helpful hints for preparing to have your eyes open while shifting awareness. Throughout the remainder of the book, as you do different glimpses, these hints should come in handy. You don't necessarily need to experience all of them as I describe them. Use what works for you.

1. Relax your eyes and soften your gaze so that your eyesight is not dominant, and all your senses are experienced equally.

2. Instead of looking through a narrow tunnel of vision or in a pinpointed way at one object, see the forest as well as one tree. Put your pointer fingers together above your head and in front of you, then part them to either side, drawing a big circle in front of your body. Look equally at the periphery of that circular frame as you look at something in front of you. Open your gaze to include the entire circumference all at once so that you see in a broader, more open way.

3. Rather than looking at one object, create a diffused view like a soft-focus lens on a camera by looking to the wider scene of what's in front of you. You can try looking at the

top of a table that has objects on it. Instead of focusing on one object, see the tabletop and all objects on it equally.

4. Extend one hand in front of you with your palm facing you at the distance you would be looking at a friend's face. Look at your hand and the space around it. Now drop your hand and look at the open space. If your eyes habitually focus on the first object you see, repeat the previous steps until you get a feel for resting your eyes on objectless space.

5. Notice that your eyes do not operate like your hands. You do not go out to see something as your hands go out to pick something up. Your eyes work in a similar way to your ears. Just as your ears are receiving sound, light is reflecting off objects and coming to your eyes. Seeing is receiving.

6. Rest back as the light comes to your eyes then goes to open-hearted awareness within you, behind you, and all around you—all while all your senses are open. Feel like you are equally aware of all your senses rather than focusing on thinking or seeing.

7. Feel like you are receiving light as you soften your eyes while having a wide-open view of the periphery.

GLIMPSE 2 **Panoramic Awareness**

In this practice, you will move awareness around your body in a full circle, starting at the front of your body and moving to the sides and then behind you, so that you feel and perceive from a 360-degree panoramic awareness.

1. Sit comfortably with your eyes open and look directly in front of you. Allow your eyes to look into space rather than focusing on one particular thing.

2. Without raising your chin, bring your gaze slightly upward, as if you were on a beach, looking at the open sky.

3. Without moving your eyes or head, begin to slowly and gently expand your peripheral vision out to the sides.

4. As your peripheral vision widens, allow awareness to continue to open gently around the sides of your head.

5. Allow awareness to move from seeing to becoming aware of the space at the sides of your head through which sound is coming and going.

6. Continue to open awareness to the felt sense of space behind you where sound is moving.

7. Feel the sense of spacious awareness all around.

8. Notice how your view is open in a panoramic way.

9. Expand your awareness out until you reach the edge of the room. Then have awareness turn back to be aware from panoramic awareness to see thoughts.

10. Inquire: "Am I aware of the field of awareness or is the field aware of my thoughts, sensations, and feelings?"

11. Now, notice how awareness is mingling with space to discover spacious awareness.

12. Be aware that the panoramic field of awareness is spacious and pervasive within everything.

13. Feel the balance of awareness equally outside and within your body.

14. Remain undistracted, without drifting into thoughts or daydreams.

15. Breathe in and allow a smile to come to your face, and then feel spacious awareness and aliveness equally all around and within.

16. Notice how your ears are receiving sound without effort.

17. Notice, in the same way as sound, that light reflects off things and comes to your eyes.

18. Notice how the field of spacious awareness is alive, balanced, and continuous—and that it does not come and go.

19. Notice the dancing waves of thoughts, emotions, and energies within the ocean of awake awareness as you seamlessly welcome whatever is arising.

GLIMPSE 3 **Effortless Focus**

Unlike the everyday mind, spacious awareness is not made of changing thoughts. When we're looking from spacious awareness, we can focus effortlessly. This is a version of a Mahamudra practice called "King of Samadhi," which uses the image of a mother bird in the sky focused on its nest below. This glimpse practice is one I use in the Effortless Mindfulness Experiment that I discuss in chapter 12 (see pages 226–227). Observe how easy it is to count and maintain effortless focus from the witnessing self. Sustaining focus can become automatic after training your brain to remain in an awareness-based level of mind.

This practice builds on the previous one, so if you liked it, you can do that practice first and then move to step 4 below.

1. Have local awareness unhook from thought, go up to a corner of the room, and look back to become aware of thoughts, feelings, and sensations from spacious awareness.

2. Be aware of the vast, clear sky of spacious awareness.

3. Now see what it's like to be aware from spacious awareness.

4. Be aware from the sky of spacious awareness that is viewing from outside your body and the sensation of the breath moving within your body.

5. From the sky of spacious awareness, become interested in one point of contact within your body where your breath is moving, like your nostril or your chest.

6. From the sky of spacious awareness, begin to focus on the sensation and movement of your breath in this small area. Once you feel the breath has begun to move in, label it "One."

7. Then feel a natural pause at the top of the in-breath. Be aware of spacious awareness in the pause before the out-breath.

8. Then, feel the point of contact with your skin as your breath goes out, and label it "Two."

9. Feel the pause before the next in-breath and rest in the sky of spacious awareness.

10. Continue to focus effortlessly as you label each following breath, in and out, with a number up to thirty.

11. Now shift to look from spacious awareness at thoughts, sensations, and emotions arising and passing. Simply allow

them to pass by like birds or clouds. Notice any tendency to become drawn in by pleasant content or to contract against unpleasant feelings.

GLIMPSE 4 **Nondual Balance**

By experiencing balanced awareness of both outside and inside simultaneously, we can decrease the self-referencing mind-wandering associated with the default mode network. This type of daydreaming ceases when the two networks of the inner and the outward focus become synchronized. In this practice, we're shifting from a detached, witnessing self to embodied awake awareness. Try this glimpse practice a number of times until you get the feel of the equal balance of awareness outside and within as a continuous field. Once you get this for about three minutes, it seems to break the default mode habit; then most people experience a stable, nondistracted flow.

1. Unhook local awareness from thought and have it go to hearing from one ear.

2. Notice the effect of awareness focused on a small area and simply hearing.

3. Now, just as the local awareness can focus on a small area, experience local awareness opening to the space outside your body where sound is coming and going.

4. Instead of focusing on what is moving through the space, allow local awareness to become interested in objectless space.

5. Now, notice the shift from awareness of space to noticing that space is aware.

6. Allow awareness to be aware of itself as a contentless, formless, timeless, spacious field of awareness. Notice that awareness is knowing itself without using thought. Take as much time as you need to feel the shift into awareness aware by itself.

7. Now feel the discovery that the field of spacious awareness is already within your body as an ocean of awareness that is the same as the waves of aliveness and sensation.

8. Feel the continuous field that is aware both outside and within simultaneously.

9. Feel the seamless unity of awareness presence that has no outside or inside. Feel awareness embodied in a way in which you are able to easily be with pleasant and unpleasant feelings.

10. Without going up to thought or going off to a daydream, stay with the knowing from the field of spacious awareness that is naturally inclusive and undistracted.

The first section of this book presents research and practices designed to help you shift into the already-available level of mind that is experienced by seasoned meditators. The goal is to abide here. By doing these practices, you will eventually be able to: 1) be aware and knowing without going to thought, 2) feel the boundless, panoramic view that is free of ego-identification, 3) feel that spacious awareness is inherent within your body and is able to be free from clinging to pleasant feelings and rejecting unpleasant feelings, 4) live from open-hearted awareness with your eyes open, 5) feel the awake awareness that is balanced internally and externally so we can be in the now without constantly being distracted.

THE SHIFT
OF KNOWING
AND IDENTITY

6

THINKING AS THE SIXTH SENSE

In theory there is no difference between theory and practice.
In practice there is.

YOGI BERRA[1]

One of the most important developments in human evolution is the ability to think. However, an even more important development is the ability to grow beyond thinking. To do this, we need to discover the intelligence that's inherent in awareness itself. It is important to note that growing beyond thinking is not a regressive, dumb, or irrational state. Consider the innocence of a young child at an adult party, who asks the group of adults what they would do in this situation: "Imagine you are surrounded by hungry tigers with a cliff behind you. What would you do?" Each adult comes up with a different creative solution, but the boy just shakes his head. So they turn to him and ask, "What would you do?" The boy smiles and says, "I'd simply stop imagining."

When we are identified with our thinking, then that believing creates our perceiving. It is through our five senses that we receive information about the world. Hearing, seeing, touching, tasting, and smelling connect our bodies with our environment. In Buddhist understanding, thinking is considered the sixth sense. Each of the six senses (including thinking) processes a particular kind of information. For instance, our ears can hear sound, but they cannot perceive light. Thinking is a complex sense that performs several roles. One function is to mediate between the other five senses by categorizing: we hear a sound and then thinking goes to memory, finds a match, and labels it "dog barking."

We've spent a lot of time training our thinking mind, and this is important for functioning in the world. But the thinking mind is not meant to be the central source of knowing—let alone the foundation of our identity. Because cognition plays an organizing role, in Western culture we have elevated thought beyond the realm of the senses and overestimated the role of thinking. None of us would consider ourselves to *be* our hearing or even *what* we're hearing at any given moment. Yet we routinely take ourselves to be thoughts and emotions that come and go like sounds. When we place thinking at the center of our identity, we overvalue this mental process.

We can begin to wake up from identification with thinking by directly experiencing another way of knowing. If thinking is actually one of the senses, then *to whom or what does this sense appear?* We'll come to see that information from the senses appears to the always already-present and pervasive wisdom of awake awareness.

It's impossible to know awake awareness with our conceptual mind, our senses, or our attention! But once we discover awake awareness it can *use* thinking as needed. In making these important distinctions about ways of knowing, we return thinking to its natural role. Next, we can go beyond thinking to encounter the wisdom of nonconceptual knowing.

We Are Not Who We Think We Are

Conceptual thinking means creating an abstract image, symbol, or picture to represent our experience. Conceptual thinking is also called *reflective thinking,* because thinking looks to itself in order to know. When we look to thinking, we're reflecting; that means we're creating a conceptual image in our brain so we know what's happening. But here's the key: *Reflective thinking is always one second removed from direct experience.* If we get too lost in thoughts, we end up living in a virtual reality in our head. We then miss the direct experience—which does not need thought beyond its labeling function. Too often this kind of self-reflection alienates us from the direct experience of seeing and feeling.

We can end up living in a world of pictures, old stories, and imagination. We can also project our story onto other people and the world until we're unable to see things as they really are. Reliance on conceptual knowing can create a tremendous amount of suffering because it looks only to itself for answers. This perpetual loop of self-referential thinking is its own prison. We *think up* a sense of separation that's not really there. The thinker is always looking for one right answer, generating pressure to decide whether we are right or wrong, which leads to feeling like a good or bad person.

When thinking is elevated to a position above our senses, it can create a mistaken identity called ego-identification. In one Tibetan Buddhist map of consciousness, each of the six senses is a sense consciousness: seeing-consciousness, hearing-consciousness, etc. The seventh consciousness is called *afflictive consciousness* or *deluded awareness,* which is ego-identification. In this map, the eighth consciousness is a storehouse of past memories and actions. Afflictive consciousness creates a thinker out of thinking and ego function, and this thought-based sense of self forms the core of mistaken identity. Nothing more than a self-referential loop of thinking about thinking, our mistaken identity is actually a continuous conceptual proliferation that creates solid things out of images and a solid self out of thinking.

The most crucial mistake we make is turning to thought to know who we are. Unfortunately, philosopher René Descartes's famous statement "I think, therefore I am" is often misunderstood to mean "I am my thinking," or "I am a thinker." When we identify ourselves *as* our thoughts, we become anxious, isolated, and obsessively caught in our own self-images and stories. To grow beyond afflictive consciousness, we need to experience awake awareness, the feeling of "am" that is not thought based. Intellectually understanding this experience can be a helpful first step. But, because intellectual understanding is still the first kind of knowing, it is only a first step toward a much vaster, all-encompassing mode of knowing. When "the thinker" looks through our eyes, we wear the bifocals of dualism.

The thinker's way of knowing joins with a survival program that is meant to protect our physical body to create the afflictive consciousness of ego-identification.

Sigmund Freud described how children develop from *primary-process thinking* to *secondary-process thinking*. He defined primary-process thinking as the preverbal way a child perceives and knows the world. Freud considered secondary-process thinking the development of conceptual thinking and the highest level of mental development a human could achieve. Perhaps awake awareness, nonconceptual knowing, can be considered *tertiary-process knowing*.

Thinking is a great servant, but a lousy master. Thinking is not the center of who you are, and thinking is not the way to discover who you are. As soon as we shift into awareness-based knowing, conceptual thinking moves out of the driver's seat, yet it continues to be an important function of our operating system. When we're able to view thinking as a function of awareness-based knowing, we can even use our thinking more effectively when it's needed. When we stop identifying ourselves as the thinker, we gain the capacity to experience thought in the context of awake awareness, recognizing thought as movement and sensation without needing to regress to the old operating system.

In Figure 2, the illustration of Thought-Based Knowing shows experiences from the world coming to our five consciousnesses, then to our sixth consciousness (thinking), and then it goes in a loop of the seventh consciousness (afflictive). This loop of self-referencing thinking creates ego-identification and obscures awake awareness.

As the illustration of Awake Awareness-Based Knowing shows, when we turn awareness around to look through the loop of afflictive consciousness, we discover awake awareness, which includes all of our thoughts, feelings, sensations, ego functions, and unconscious storehouse. We have shifted.

Thinking As Inner Hearing

I've asked many people how they experience thinking. Most reply, "What do you mean? It's like . . . thinking. You know . . . just thinking."

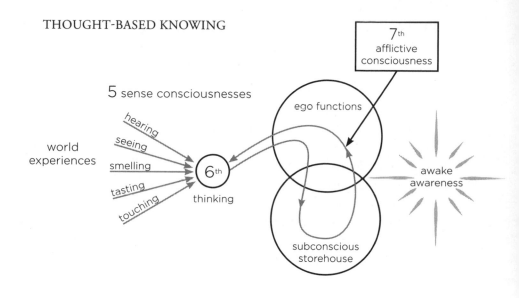

THOUGHT-BASED KNOWING

5 sense consciousnesses

7th afflictive consciousness

ego functions

world experiences

hearing

seeing

smelling

tasting

touching

6th

thinking

awake awareness

subconscious storehouse

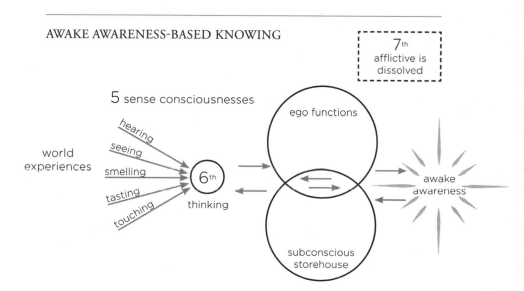

AWAKE AWARENESS-BASED KNOWING

5 sense consciousnesses

7th afflictive is dissolved

ego functions

world experiences

hearing

seeing

smelling

tasting

touching

6th

thinking

awake awareness

subconscious storehouse

FIGURE 2. The transition from thought-based knowing to awake awareness–based knowing.

They laugh or shrug their shoulders because they've never examined how they experience thoughts. Some people have a ticker-tape concept of thought; it's as if they're reading words scrolling across their minds. But thought is not written language like the CNN crawl. You're not reading it.

Thinking is a way of actively using all the sensory parts of the brain. It is inner sensing, inner seeing, and inner hearing. Thinking can be experienced as a vivid inner movie. The full sensory experience of thinking happens when we use our imagination. For instance, you can think about a beach, feel the sand under your feet, see the sky above your head, smell the salty ocean, feel the soft breeze on your skin, and even hear seagulls cry—all inside your head. As studies show, the same areas of the brain are activated in exactly the same way whether you're imagining a beach or physically sitting on the beach.

Some people are visual types, but for most of us, thinking is mainly experienced as inner hearing and inner talking. Yes, we all hear voices! Thinking is mostly hearing speech in your head without using your ears. It's also self-talk, speaking silently to yourself inside your head without using your mouth but with your brain hearing the words as if they're spoken into your ear.

Try this now: *Go ahead, take a moment now and see what the experience of thinking is like for you. You can silently say to yourself, "I am thinking this thought." And then listen to thought as inner hearing. Then wait, and you will hear the next thought spoken in your mind. What was that like, hearing the inner talk?*

Thinking as inner hearing includes all manner of inner monologue, commentary, and dialogue. Inner talking can take the form of a dialogue among subpersonalities who argue, debate, and plead with each other—all inside our heads. When we identify with one of these subpersonalities, we take the voice that is talking at that moment to be "me." The most common inner talker is a narrator who comments on what's going on, like a radio announcer at a baseball game: "Now I am going to take the garbage out. Okay, but first why don't I just see what's on TV? No, I watch too much TV. But there's a good show on Tuesdays."

The other main talker is the judging voice, the superego, the inner critic, or the doubter. This voice adds a second part of ourselves to create a continuous inner dialogue. We have an initial experience, and then the second voice judges it. The dialogue between these two parts generates a continuous tension; the push-pull of their dialogue never seems to stop. This is where the emotional qualities of fear, anger, despair, self-hatred, depression, and anxiety create an embodied feeling of "me" from what's just a bunch of opinions, points of view, and thoughts.

Most of us are so identified with thinking that we don't know there are options. We look *from* our thoughts—not *at* them. One reason it's hard to examine the thinking experience is that we constantly use thinking as what we're knowing with. When thought orients toward and believes the first thought, and then *that* thought refers to the next thought, a self-referencing loop forms. This conceptual loop gives rise to the illusion of a separate, thought-based identity. Becoming aware of the felt experience of thinking as inner hearing and inner talking is one step toward breaking free of the repetitive loop of senseless chatter. Stepping back from thinking and allowing our inner chatter to pass is an important skill to learn.

Automatic Thinking Moves to the Background

We tend to focus on *intentional thinking:* the analytic, problem-solving, calculating, decision-making, reasoning type of thinking. *Automatic thinking*—the continuous stream of consciousness and chattering thoughts—is another kind of thinking we all experience. Often we don't notice automatic thoughts because we're immersed in them, identified with them, arguing with them, or trying to ignore them. But automatic thoughts keep coming, whether or not we're paying attention to them. We can experience automatic thoughts as a kind of random commentary, like a tape playing on a continuous loop in our heads. We each have tens of thousands of thoughts per day, and the majority of them are the same thoughts every day.

We are in the habit of believing that if a thought arises, we need to check it out. After all, it could be an important life-saving message, such as: "Watch out for that car!" But few messages are that critical. Most are not even relevant. If we're always believing our thoughts, no wonder we're exhausted, anxious, and neurotic! Our relationship to automatic thinking is one of the most important things we'll learn to change—to our great relief. Much of the time we're identified with or lost in our own thoughts. But we can also step back to notice our thoughts as the contents of our consciousness. Mindfulness from everyday mind is done from another thought-based part of us, like a judge, commentator, or self-awareness. Awake awareness is the ability to be aware of thoughts and the contents of our consciousness from an awareness that is not a thought.

The field of cognitive behavioral therapy is largely based on the observation that identifying with automatic negative thoughts (ANTS) causes depression. But depressed people aren't the only ones who experience negative thoughts—everyone does. Or maybe everyone who identifies with their thoughts is a little bit depressed? A recent study of people on six continents showed that 94 percent of those surveyed experienced unwanted, intrusive, or impulsive thoughts. The most common type reported were doubts.[3]

The type of suffering that we are addressing in the open-hearted awareness approach is not caused by identifying with negative thoughts, but by identifying with *any* thoughts: positive or negative. You are not the voices in your head. The automatic thoughts that you hear are not you talking. You are not even the second voice that comments on the first thoughts. You start by listening to the thoughts, then you believe the thoughts, and then you believe the thoughts are you. It is important that you directly experience that you are primarily the awareness that hears all voices and thoughts. In order to experience awake awareness, it will be important for you to move beyond choosing good thoughts over bad thoughts on the level of identity. Of course, you'll still prefer positive thoughts to inform behavior. You will also be able to more easily accept negative thoughts.

Choosing not to listen to the content of automatic thinking and the narrator voice is an easy way out of ego-identification. When automatic thoughts move into the background, we no longer have to listen to each one or hypervigilantly monitor them all. It doesn't matter if automatic thoughts are negative or positive, because we don't have to listen to them. However, thought itself is not a problem or an enemy. We're not interested in stopping thoughts, but in returning thought to its natural function. Shifting our automatic thoughts to the background of our minds allows awake awareness to come to the foreground. When operating from awake awareness, we are better able to include and liberate our subpersonalities as well as inner shadow parts.

When you have shifted into awake awareness, it can be helpful to consider automatic thoughts as mental sensations. Most of us are in the habit of focusing on these mental sensations as they pass through our minds. However, if we can learn to not consciously engage with them, they can be relegated to the background, where awake awareness knows which few thoughts actually do need attention. Awake awareness precludes the necessity of going back to thoughts to orient ourselves on a constant basis.

What is it like when automatic thoughts are in the background? To find out, do a quick experiment now: *Bring your awareness to the sensations in your right foot. What do you notice when you focus your awareness in your right foot for a few moments? Do you feel a lot of sensations?*

Here's the thing: A minute ago, you didn't notice these sensations, although they were already happening. It's only when you focused on the sensations in your foot that they moved to the foreground of your awareness and began to seem so active and incessant.

You will see that you don't need to monitor your thoughts continuously any more than you need to constantly monitor the sensations in your foot. Paying attention to automatic thoughts is simply a habit we can change. When you shift into awareness-based knowing, automatic thinking moves into the background, and you experience true peace of mind. You'll learn to trust that the intelligence of awake awareness will tell you if there is a particular automatic thought that needs attention (which is not that often).

Addicted to Thinking

Neurobiologist Patricia Sharp, PhD, is an expert in addiction. She says, "Almost all of our repetitive thought patterns can be viewed as forms of addiction."[4] Pleasurable sensory or mental states are the rewards that condition us to seek the same experiences again. These pleasurable brain states are believed to be generated by dopamine and opioids released in the pleasure centers of the brain. However, as the activities associated with particular pleasures are repeated, the amount of dopamine released in the brain is reduced. We are left with a mental craving for pleasure, but decreased levels of neurotransmitter activity. Due to increased mental craving, we're driven to indulge more and more in activities that gave us pleasure in the past, hoping to experience that same pleasure, but disappointed because we keep receiving less and less dopamine.[5] The habit of continually looking to thoughts for satisfaction, even positive thoughts, creates a similar kind of addiction.

Sharp studied meditators and found that certain Buddhist meditations (similar to those you'll be learning in this book) stimulate the brain's pleasure centers. However, unlike dopamine surges, this pleasure does not diminish over time. Unlike addiction, this kind of awareness-based meditation does not lead to craving. When we shift to awake awareness, dopamine reduction doesn't occur. This means we can establish a natural bliss inside our bodies as a new baseline for living.

This background, low-level bliss is true to my experience, though I had never thought of it as a biochemical process before reading Sharp's study. This may be why the series of meditations you are learning is particularly helpful for people in recovery from substance addiction or physical pain. In fact, these meditations are helpful for everyone because we're all in need of recovery from thought-based addiction. This natural bliss is not a high, with fireworks and an orgasmic rush. Rather, it is as if your most intensely blissful bodily experience is spread out thinly throughout the sky. You can experience natural dopamine without becoming doped up! In this recovery program, instead of learning "Don't pick up the first drink," you learn: "Don't pick up the first *think.*"

Glimpses of Awake Awareness

The purpose of the following series of glimpses is to shift our primary experience of intelligence from thinking to awake awareness. We will break the habit of orienting ourselves by thinking. In the process, we'll go through a thought-free state. Eventually, we'll learn to use thoughts as tools when they're needed. Our goal is to be emotionally sensitive and vulnerable without becoming wounded or reactive.

Glimpsing awake awareness can help you establish a new baseline of peace in your life by introducing you to a silent presence of mind that's alert and joyful. Glimpses help you learn to trust the intelligence that knows which thoughts and emotions need attention as opposed to 99 percent of the stuff that doesn't. If all this sounds mysterious, it's only because you haven't experienced it yet. If it sounds too conceptual, remember that these words are designed to prepare you for a direct experience of nonconceptual, awake awareness.

GLIMPSE 1 **Inner Hearing**

In this glimpse, you're going to deliberately stop talking to yourself. Then you're going to stop being interested in what your automatic thoughts are saying. To accomplish this, you'll simply stop trying to understand the inner talk by no longer being interested in the meaning, words, or sentences you hear. In the process, your chattering thoughts will shift into being mental sensations, a background experience—like the buzz of conversation at a restaurant.

1. Start by noticing what it's like listening to yourself and speaking to yourself in your head. Talk to yourself internally by saying: "Thinking is inner talk and inner hearing." Then feel what it's like to experience thinking as inner talk and inner hearing.

2. Now give yourself these instructions: "I am going to stop talking to myself in a moment and move to only hearing what the thoughts are saying." See what this is like.

3. Next, give yourself the instruction: "I'm going to hear background chatter, but I'll become disinterested in

what the thoughts say. Instead, my interest will be in the
awake space."

4. Now choose not to talk to yourself for a while. Just listen
   to the background buzz as though it is a foreign language.
   Don't try to understand any inner language being spoken.
   Instead, be interested in alert, thought-free awareness.

5. Regard all thinking and inner self-talk as the movement
   of mental sensations. Focus on the sensations in your left
   hand and then on the mental sensations in your head.
   Then let all comments about experiences become mental
   sensations. Let awareness itself, which is already aware and
   intelligent, be your interest.

6. Notice the clarity and knowing that is here when you stop
   the habit of going to inner self-talk.

7. Once you discover this thought-free knowing without
   looking to thought, ask that your phone number slowly
   arise to awake awareness. Say it to yourself, hear it, and
   then go back to the awake, peaceful silence.

The key is to shift out of a thought-based operating system. So
it's not just about going beyond your story or a belief system.
Instead of asking yourself, "Who am I without my story or a
particular thought?" the shift is to go beyond orienting yourself
by any thought; "Who am I if I don't go to any thoughts to
know who I am?" Then from awake awareness we see that all
thoughts and emotions are not separate. These next glimpses
will give you some alternative ways of unhooking from thought
and shifting into one of your other senses so that awareness
becomes primary.

GLIMPSE 2 **Awareness Following the Breath Home**

Try hitching a ride on your breath to help local awareness unhook, drop, and know directly from within.

1. Begin by unhooking local awareness from thinking. Then have it move a short distance, from behind your eyes to where your breath contacts your nostrils. As inhalation occurs, let local awareness focus completely on this small area of sensation. As exhalation occurs, sense the breath touching the nostrils as it goes out. Do this for several breaths in a row.

2. With the next in-breath, allow local awareness to ride the air as it moves from your nostrils down your throat and into your chest.

3. Now allow local awareness to unhook from the breath and remain with the awake awareness and aliveness below your neck, even as the air goes back up and out again. Notice local awareness opening to the aliveness and spacious awareness both within and outside your body, while not returning to your head and thoughts.

4. Let the feeling of your chest rising and falling with each new breath be the place of contact for your awareness to stay interested in witnessing from within and opening out, letting go and being here and now. Notice the breath happening by itself as if you are being breathed.

5. Notice that the breath is happening by itself, just as awake awareness is also happening and knowing by itself.

GLIMPSE 3 **The Eighteen-Inch Drop from Head to Heart**

Take a few minutes now and glimpse open-hearted awareness for yourself.

1. Sit comfortably, eyes open or closed, and simply be aware of all your senses. Notice the activity of thinking in your head.

2. First, unhook local awareness from thoughts in your head. Next, let it move down through your neck and into your chest, and then know—directly—from within your upper body.

3. Become familiar with this kind of direct knowing, which is neither looking down from your head nor going back up to your thoughts.

4. Feel the awareness and aliveness together: rest without going to sleep, and stay aware without going to thought to know.

5. Feel that awareness can know both the awareness and aliveness from within your body.

6. Notice a feeling of an open-hearted awareness from within the space in the center of your chest.

7. Feel as if you have relocated from your head to this open-hearted awareness, which you are now aware from.

8. Notice that you can invite and welcome any thoughts and emotions into your heart space so that you can remain at home in open-hearted awareness and have information from the office of your head come to you by Wi-Fi.

9. Inquire within: "What does open-hearted awareness know?" Wait and feel what it's like to know, from this not-knowing that knows.

10. Be here, receive light with your eyes, and look out from the eyes of open-hearted awareness.

7

NONCONCEPTUAL AWARENESS

Nonconceptual wakefulness totally overcomes conceptual thinking.
If nonconceptual wakefulness were merely another thought, it could not
overcome thoughts. In the very moment of recognizing it, thoughts are cut
through and overcome. Is there anything more wonderful than that?

TULKU URGYEN RINPOCHE[1]

In recent years, scientists have begun to research and document nonthought-based intelligence. Countless people experience nonconceptual awareness every day while sitting still in nature or meditation. The amazing thing about the various types of nonconceptual awareness is that they can also be experienced with our eyes open, in the midst of our active daily life.

Three Types of Nonconceptual Intelligence

In his 1983 book *Frames of Mind: The Theory of Multiple Intelligences*, Harvard psychologist Howard Gardner expanded the definition of intelligence that had previously been based mainly on conceptual thinking, in particular as related to memory and IQ. Gardner added seven different modalities or lines of development in the following areas: musical, visual-spatial, verbal, mathematical, kinesthetic, interpersonal, intrapersonal, and naturalistic.[2] We all have different strengths and weaknesses in the various lines of development, and we develop each line at different rates. From experience, we know that an individual can be highly developed in one area, such as intellectually, and less developed in another, such as emotionally. Nonconceptual awake awareness is foundational intelligence to which each of these lines of development appears.

Recently, three types of nonconceptual intelligence have been recognized and studied: *flow, the hypo-egoic stage,* and *the adaptive unconscious.* Understanding these is a stepping-stone toward understanding the subtler, foundational type of nonconceptual intelligence based in awake awareness.

BEING IN A FLOW STATE

Flow is one of the most important modern areas of research in the field of psychology. Many of us know flow as "being in the zone"; it's the way I felt playing hockey in high school. In 1990, psychologist Mihaly Csikszentmihalyi, PhD, published his book *Flow: The Psychology of Optimal Experience,* based on years of research. Csikszentmihalyi and his team studied the ways people enter an optimal flow experience, which leads to deep enjoyment, creativity, and a total involvement in the "now." We can enter this flow state by bringing a type of awareness to our activity.

The seven qualities of flow Csikszentmihalyi's research identified are:

1. Knowing an activity is doable: that our skills are adequate to the task

2. Being completely involved in and focused upon what we're doing

3. A sense of ecstasy

4. Great inner clarity: knowing what needs to be done and how well we're doing

5. Sense of serenity: no worries about oneself; a feeling of going beyond the boundaries of ego

6. Timelessness: being thoroughly focused on the present so that hours seem to pass in minutes

7. Intrinsic motivation: whatever produces flow becomes its own reward[3]

Going beyond the boundaries of ego with a sense of clarity, ecstasy, and serenity is essential to the experience of nonconceptual awareness. However, the term "flow state" is often used to describe two very different experiences. The first type, which I call *absorbed flow,* occurs when you're so concentrated and immersed in a task that when you finally look up, you discover hours have passed in what seems like minutes. In this absorbed-flow state, your focus narrows and you have a kind of tunnel vision: you're unaware of what's going on around you. Examples of people in an absorbed flow include an artist deep in his own world while painting, a student writing a paper, and a carpenter hammering a nail.

The second type, which I call *panoramic flow,* happens when you're doing a task and are aware of every detail of your environment. Your focus is open, and you're panoramically aware of everything around you. You are in the "now," which means there is a timeless quality, yet you're simultaneously aware of events as they arise, moment by moment, in relative time. In contrast to absorbed flow, this experience feels as if time has slowed down. Consider the basketball player who sees the whole court, as well as each player's movements; she notices the time on the clock and the cheering crowd as she dribbles the ball across the court and throws a no-look pass to her teammate to win the game. In the movie *The Legend of Bagger Vance,* the main character, Junuh, gets into a flow playing golf, and Bagger says that he had learned "how to stop thinking without falling asleep."

BEYOND EGO

The famous quote from the *Tao Te Ching,* "When nothing is done, nothing is left undone," is sometimes misunderstood as "don't do anything."[4]

Mark R. Leary, a Duke University psychologist, has researched what he calls "hypo-egoic self-regulation," a state in which people accomplish their goals more easily by relinquishing conscious control. He noted that some of his subjects who'd been struggling to recover from addictions reported that their strong, willful egos—which they were using to try to stop their addictive habit—actually prevented them from recovering. Leary's study concluded: "The ultimate self-regulatory goal is to reduce deliberate self-control and to function hypo-egoically." Surrendering and letting go of ego-identification need not lead to regression or childish behavior but can instead open us to greater resources and a new foundation of identity. Leary argues that letting go of efforting can help people achieve difficult goals more easily.[5]

ADAPTIVE UNCONSCIOUS

Some psychologists call the adaptive unconscious the natural capacity of the human mind to know without referring to thought. In his 2005 book *Blink: The Power of Thinking Without Thinking,* Malcolm Gladwell likens the adaptive unconscious to a "kind of giant computer that quickly and quietly processes a lot of the data we need in order to keep functioning as human beings."[6] Gladwell gives the example of an art dealer who immediately and accurately knows that a particular sculpture is a forgery, although he can't explain how. The dealer's adaptive unconscious processes myriad details about the statue and compares them with details he's gleaned from years of experience in the art world. All of this processing is done so fast that the art dealer isn't consciously aware of it.

Everyone has had experiences with the adaptive unconscious, a kind of intuitive way of acting without overthinking. You probably know a great cook who doesn't measure or use recipes, but mixes ingredients and adds spices relying on this kind of adaptive unconscious—a mode of functioning like an airplane's automatic pilot.

This intuitive capacity could be called *adaptive awareness,* rather than adaptive unconscious, because going unconscious is not the only alternative to conscious thinking. You can be aware that you're doing something well without consciously thinking about what you're doing. When you're operating from nonconceptual awareness, you are not dumb, ignorant, zoned out, or blacked out. You're relaxed, alert, and able to draw on information as needed. Therefore the adaptive (so-called) unconscious is really a form of higher consciousness that uses nonconceptual awareness.

UPGRADING TO NONCONCEPTUAL AWARENESS

Nonconceptual doesn't mean irrational or the regression to a prerational stage like a baby—nor does it require stopping your thoughts. In fact, even a calm meditative state is not necessary. When one of my teachers, Tsoknyi Rinpoche, first came to the United States from Nepal, he noticed that many meditators here seemed to be practicing what he called "stupid meditation." He was referring to the practice that leads to the comfortably numb feeling I call the "sauna state." This kind of meditation suppresses chattering thoughts, but it reduces your alertness and ability to fully function. Although such meditation is relaxing, it's not based in the alert intelligence of awake awareness.

Moving from conceptual knowing to awake awareness is similar to learning to type. When you started, didn't you have to look at the keyboard? Then, with practice, you grew beyond thinking about where your fingers were going. Now when you type, you don't monitor your fingers or consciously remember the position of the keys. This new kind of knowing doesn't need to go to thought to check on your typing. In nonconceptual awareness, you don't need to keep looking at the screen of your mind, checking every pop-up or open file. Instead, thinking becomes useful as an instrument of awake awareness.

Our ability to swiftly process all the information coming to us through our senses is imperative for survival. However, it's now common knowledge that what appears to be multitasking is actually your attention alternating very quickly among several tasks, as opposed to doing these tasks simultaneously. This shows the limits of attention as a mental faculty. However, in a flow state, you are coordinating multiple aspects of one activity without being consciously attentive.

We use this ability whenever we drive a car in fast-moving traffic. Although you may not have noticed, you've likely already applied your ability to make high-speed decisions without consciously checking in with thought every moment.

"Intuition," "pure instinct," or "gut feeling" are some other terms for short moments of nonconceptual knowing. In our culture, we're not educated to trust the myriad types of intuitive, nonconceptual intelligence. Awake awareness is like continuous intuition.

We often associate the head with thoughts and the heart with emotions. When nonconceptual awareness becomes fully developed and embodied, we operate from open-hearted awareness, a subtler way of knowing that includes both thinking and feeling, head and heart, and being and doing—and goes beyond them. Open-hearted awareness has a quality of knowing that is completely different from dualistic thinking. One reason people often have difficulty transitioning to awake awareness is because it's an intelligence that uses paradox. Our everyday, conceptual minds can't really understand two seeming opposites as simultaneously true; our conceptual minds are designed to use the dualistic thinking needed to judge if the streetlight is green or red.

This way of knowing may initially feel paradoxical or slow compared to the fast-moving dualistic mind. In my classes, people answer the question: "What does open-hearted awareness know?" One person will say "emptiness," another will report "fullness," and a third will exclaim, "I agree with both of them: emptiness *and* fullness." Then the first two say at the same time, "Yes, that's it! Emptiness and fullness. That is what I meant." The linear logic of our trained, dualistic knowing could say, "That's illogical. It's either empty or full. It cannot be both!" But it *is* both, and the awakened heart perceives and embraces what looks like a paradox to the linear mind.

Open-hearted awareness doesn't consciously reference thoughts but instead rests deeply within an intelligence that is intuitively connected with all we know. When we take ourselves to be the ego-identification that is looking out of our eyes, the first thing we see is separation, difference, and judgment. Open-hearted awareness begins by sensing our oneness, unity, and connectedness, and then also acknowledges and appreciates our uniqueness. Open-hearted awareness can make distinctions without splitting itself into a subject and object.

For most of us, awake awareness is currently hidden in the background, but we can learn how it can become our primary mode of knowing and our new operating system. When we do, thought will return to its natural role, and we won't regress to the thought-based operating system that is our typical mode of knowing. You don't need to intellectually understand how awake awareness works any more than you need to understand how your body balances when you ride a bicycle. You need only to learn how to shift into awake awareness as the way you know. Then you live from it.

It's often easier to enter flow when we have mastered the basic skills of an activity to the point that they've become second nature. My hypothesis is that walking, talking, relating, and all the basics we learned from school and by growing up in our culture are already programmed into our brains. Once these functional abilities come naturally, we can shift out of conceptual thinking and self-consciousness and into awake awareness as our foundation. With practice, we'll be able to shift into flow and begin functioning from awake awareness. People in a flow state are not necessarily operating from awake awareness; however, people operating from awake awareness are in panoramic flow.

Embodied Knowing

The open-hearted awareness approach to coming back to our senses is a way of moving local awareness away from being overly involved with one sense (thinking) to awake awareness, which includes all of our senses. This results in a few important changes. First, awareness is freed of its identification with thinking, which creates a false sense of self, tremendous stress, and dissatisfaction. Second, we're able to experience the real sense of being in our bodies. Embodiment is not about stretching, strengthening, or bringing our attention to bodily sensations. Awake awareness embodied—also called presence—is actually feeling our bodies directly from within using awareness, rather than looking to mental images of our body or looking from our heads at our bodies using attention. When we feel our bodies from within, we discover that our bodies feel mostly like space, awareness, and changing aliveness—with some pressure where we're contacting the earth or a chair. When we feel embodied, our bodies feel light and alive, like a limber cat, but we also feel boundless on the level of identity and interconnected to everything on the level of awareness. Embodiment does not mean that awareness is *in* your body, but that you experience your body as appearing from and supported by awareness.

Embodied presence will change the way you know your body. As you shift to knowing the body directly from within, you're no longer filtering the body's experience through conceptual thoughts and images. When you know your body directly from within—without concept, image, or memory—it's not experienced as solid the way it appears to your eyes. You begin to feel a connection to all of life—a subtle sense of bliss and a support from awake awareness that relieves you of fear and shame. You feel your body as presence, as alive energy, as contracting and expanding sensations, as awareness, and as unity with all life.

Returning Emotions to Their Natural State

Emotional intelligence requires the capacity to feel our emotions, the ability to express them effectively, and the ability to distinguish between emotions related to the present and the past as well as those created by the cravings and fears of ego-identification. This level of awareness requires discernment between needs that are genuine and require satisfaction, in addition to awareness of desires based on ego-identification's cravings that cannot be satisfied.

We wake up from the mind by disidentifying with our thoughts, stories, and beliefs. By contrast, to have freedom from the grip of emotional identification, awake awareness has to wake in and embrace our emotions. Like thoughts and physical sensations, emotions are part of the subtle consciousness of the body. Emotions help us pick up information we need to survive, relate, and empathize. When the emotions aren't being confused and exaggerated by mistaken identity, they're returned to their natural condition and we are able to be sensitive and open-hearted. Emotions are like skin. Just as our skin is sensitive to physical contact, our emotions are sensitive to contact with other people. From open-hearted awareness, we do not transcend emotions but remain sensitive without shutting down or getting lost in the vicious cycle of thoughts and emotions that create ego-identification.

The brain can be imprinted by trauma involving strong emotions of loss, abuse, fear, violence, and tragedy. Emotional signals like fear and grief are meant to be strong, just like physical pain signals, so that we can avoid danger. Ego-identification, however, creates a vicious cycle of secondary suffering. Feelings of hurt and anger stemming from a single incident can turn into trauma or resentment that lasts for years. As a side note, there are two nonconceptual techniques that help heal trauma: EMDR (Eye-Movement Desensitization and Reintegration) and SE (Somatic Experiencing).

Awakening from emotional trauma cannot happen from an ego-identified point of view. Therefore, the psychological technique of intellectually understanding the history and causes of emotional issues does not by itself lead to their full resolution. Nor can we rely on merely observing our emotions from a mental or meditative distance, because this restricts us from experiencing life fully. Both mindfully witnessing and intellectually understanding the traumatic incidents that created our wounded feelings and subpersonalities is helpful, but we must keep going. We have to find a way to return to inhabiting our lives.

One of my longtime students lost her husband in the 9/11 attack on the World Trade Center, and she went through a process of shock, sadness, and rage about her loss. With the support of open-hearted awareness, she allowed every feeling to arise and be felt until she opened to what she called "the all-connected, all-loving, living grace." This experience brought up emotions she'd been keeping inside all her life. While supported by the ground of Being, she allowed the shell covering her heart to break. Subsequently, she grew to become a loving, accepting, and creative resource for all her friends and relatives who were going through loss.

Another example is a professor who'd lived in the tower of his head all his life, making the decision to—intentionally though reluctantly—shift into open-hearted awareness, only to discover what he described as "a wisdom and love that I had not imagined possible with all my studying." The professor couldn't help laughing when a quote from Shakespeare's *Hamlet* popped into his mind: "There are more things in heaven and earth, Horatio, than are dreamt of in your philosophy."[7]

The important distinction here is not just a positive experience, a change of attitude, or even healing for these people, but the discovery of a way of knowing and being that's not dependent on past experiences or future achievements. The experience of recognizing who you originally were is a deep, authentic sense of Being from which you feel a sense of wellness—free from fear, shame, and dissatisfaction.

When we begin to awaken, we discover that emotions like sadness, happiness, anger, and fear are simply signals that are part of our nervous system. They are important and vital parts of our full human experience now that they're untied from the stories of ego-identification. All basic emotions continue to rise to Being, but none becomes a vicious cycle of worry, anxiety, or resentment, or the basis of a continuum of dissatisfaction. We are already neurologically wired to feel the communication of our feelings without dwelling upon them. Neuroscientist Jill Bolte Taylor describes the biochemistry of emotion, saying, "My anger response is a programmed response that can be set off automatically. . . . Within ninety seconds from the initial trigger, the chemical component of my anger has completely dissipated from my blood and my automatic response is over. If, however, I remain angry after those ninety seconds have passed, then it's because I have chosen to let that circuit continue to run."[8]

When they drop their knowing from head to nonconceptual heart, many people describe a new feeling of "sweet sadness" or tender-hearted intimacy. Others describe going through a period of feeling like their hearts are breaking. When they look closely, however, they discover that their hearts are not breaking! Rather, the protective layers around their hearts are breaking apart to reveal a more tender heart underneath. For sure, there is real pain, but it is like the pain we feel when our hands are thawing after being outside in the freezing cold. With the support of open-hearted awareness, we can feel the grief of this transition and remain open-hearted.

There is also a deeper feeling of essential wellbeing, awe, wonder, unity, freedom, courage, and unconditional love that is an essential emotion, not based in thought. When we live from open-hearted awareness, there's an internal structure of essential qualities that are deeper and more primary feelings. These essential qualities are the foundation of a new emotional life that leads to more engagement and intimacy.

GLIMPSE 1 **Emotional Wisdom**

When you start this exercise, you'll be invited to bring your awareness within your body and find any emotion that is there now. You can do this exercise with an emotion, pleasant or unpleasant, but for the first time, please use an unpleasant emotion. If you don't have an unpleasant emotion available, choose your emotional "flavor of the week" or the unpleasant emotion that you deal with most often. If needed, you can go to a memory or a recent situation in your life to bring up an unpleasant emotion. You will learn that you can feel sad without being sad.

1. Find an emotion—fear, anger, jealousy, etc.—and begin by feeling it fully. (I'll use sadness as an example in the following steps; you can substitute whatever emotion you choose.)

2. Silently say to yourself, "I am sad." Fully experience what it is like to say and feel "I am sad." Stay with this experience until you feel it completely.

3. Now, instead of saying, "I *am* sad," take a breath and say, "I *feel* sadness." Notice the shift from "I *am*" to "I *feel.*"

Experience this shift and the new feeling of being. From here, feel your relationship to the feeling.

4. Now, shift again by saying, "I am *aware* of feeling sadness." Experience *awareness of* feeling sadness fully. Shift into an observing awareness. Notice the different emotional quality that comes from this.

5. Now, say, "Sadness is welcome." Starting from awareness, experience what welcoming the feeling is like. Feel the awareness embody and embrace the feeling. Notice the different emotional quality that comes from welcoming without reidentifying. Sense the support that welcoming brings.

6. Finally, say, "Awareness and sadness are not separate." Feel awake awareness around and within, permeating the emotion fully, but without identifying with the emotion or rejecting it. Feel awareness present with emotion fully from within. Feel the awareness, the energetic aliveness, the deep stillness of presence. Notice the feeling of looking out at others and the world from this embodied, connected, open-hearted awareness.

GLIMPSE 2 **"Om Sweet Home" in Your Heart**

Here's a glimpse practice that begins with making a sound, then feeling the vibration in the middle of your chest. This can be a helpful way to invite awareness to unhook from thinking and know the aliveness and awareness directly by using sound and vibration as support.

1. Place your hand on the middle of your chest. Feel your chest expanding under your hand as your breath comes in, and relaxing as your breath goes out. Sing, tone, or chant

the sound "Om," "Amen," "Home," or "Shalom"—or just "Hummmmm." Focus on the feeling of the vibration in the center of your chest. Continue to gently make this sound.

2. Now unhook local awareness from your thoughts and allow it to be drawn down to the vibration and awareness in the center of your chest. Feel as if your heart space is the new home of knowing from awake awareness.

3. Now, without using thought, become aware of the stillness, vibration, and awareness that is pervasive within; then open your awareness past your body's boundaries to mingle with the support of spacious awareness all around.

4. Allow the awareness of your heart space to know itself and then open to connect to all else as well.

5. Hang out and marinate in this continuous field of aware, loving presence.

6. Now relax into the silence that includes sound. Know from this open-hearted awareness without going back to your head to know.

GLIMPSE 3 **Embodied Presence**

In the "Experience Attention" glimpse in chapter 3, you moved local awareness to experience one of your hands directly from within. In this glimpse, you're going to move local awareness to experience the entire body at once, directly from within. If you've ever done a body-scan meditation, this is similar, but you're not scanning your body from your everyday mind using attention. This is an "ultimate-level" body scan that begins by unhooking local awareness from thought and knowing your whole body directly from within.

1. Unhook local awareness from thought.

2. Let local awareness drop down, feeling its way down through your face to your neck.

3. Be aware of not looking down from your head to your body. Notice what it's like when local awareness feels and knows awareness and sensations directly from within your body.

4. Now allow the local awareness to remain aware from within your upper body and continue to fill your entire body from head to toe.

5. Feel the local awareness scan from within your neck to include your shoulders, arms, and hands, and then further expanding to be aware within your chest, upper back, belly, and lower back.

6. Allow local awareness to continue moving downward to include and know your hips, waist, backside, and thighs from within.

7. As your awareness moves down the length of your body, notice the release from holding, and a deep relaxation. Be aware of the space, awareness, and aliveness within your knees, calves, shins, ankles, feet, toes, and soles of your feet.

8. Feel local awareness knowing and feeling your entire body from within, from the bottoms of your feet to the top of your head. Feel both a soft, boundless quality and a grounded embodiment.

9. Feel your breath happening by itself like waves in the ocean.

10. Enjoy the feeling of the natural, boundless freedom and awareness embodied.

11. Rest in the emptiness and fullness of embodied presence.

This is a good practice for helping you wake up out of your mind. You may also find this is a good practice to help you fall asleep at night.

8

A SIMPLE CASE
OF MISTAKEN IDENTITY

To study the Way is to study the self. To study the self is to forget the self.
To forget the self is to be enlightened by all things. To be enlightened by
all things is to remove the barriers between one's self and others.

DŌGEN[1]

Who am I? This is one of the most important questions people have asked throughout the ages. Learning how to inquire "Who am I?" can immediately clear up a great deal of suffering. To discover who we are, it's important to be clear about who we are not. In this chapter, we'll see how our current mistaken identity is constructed and held together in our minds, and we'll come to understand what gets in the way of discovering our true nature.

The problem of identity can be described in words, but the solution can only be known through direct experience. It can be confusing to discuss the topic of identity, especially when we get contradictory advice. The Greek oracle at Delphi said: "Know thyself." Jesus said that anyone who wanted to follow him had to "deny himself."[2] The Upanishads from India say that we need to move from a small self to a true Self. In Buddhism, one of the key foundations for awakening is realizing "no self." In modern psychology, some growth models promote building a strong ego, yet other models insist that ego is the problem and that we need to deny, kill, transcend, or get rid of our ego. The issue of identity is further confused by different definitions for concepts like *false self, true Self, selflessness, no self, ego strength,* and *egoless* from psychology and the wisdom traditions. Which "self" am I, and which "self" is the problem? What is ego? Is there a good ego and a bad ego? Which ego is the problem, and which is a normal part of being human? Because we are interested in both awakening and growing up, let's start by defining ego in a new way.

You Go, We Go, We All Ego

The word *ego* comes from the Latin personal pronoun "I." We are going to explore five aspects of ego: ego body, ego functions, ego personality, observing ego, and ego-identification. As we clarify our understanding of each aspect, we'll discover that we can simultaneously enjoy our human bodies, enhance our ego functions, appreciate our particular ego personalities, and learn how to grow beyond ego-identification.

Ego body is the acknowledgment that on the relative level each person is a separate individual because each has a distinct physical body.

Ego functions begin with the biological, innate, instinctual system that enables all human beings to survive and thrive. Ego functions are the ways living creatures organize and act upon information related to their particular physical bodies in order to respond effectively to their environments. Normal ego functions include perception, thinking, attention, memory, instincts, motor coordination, and socialization. Ego functions involve movement toward or away from things. The acts of craving ("I want") or resistance/pushing away ("I don't want") are normal feelings related to survival and are not the root of suffering. Natural desires and aversions constantly arise based on liking and disliking as a way of discernment that aids thriving and surviving. Ego defense mechanisms are also functions that help regulate our instincts and different parts of our personalities to avoid conflict and reduce anxiety. Ego functions also include will, or agency: the ability to choose and act on a physical level. What we choose is influenced by the location of our identity, but the ability to choose, react, respond, and initiate actions is an ego function. Healthy ego functions help us learn to adapt and socialize in communities as well as to thrive in our environment.

Ego personality is the combination of our particular genetics, personal experiences, and social conditioning. A product of both nature and nurture, ego personality includes our emotional life. Our likes and dislikes, our temperaments, and our style of relating to other people are all part of ego personality. Here, I'm including our autobiographical ego: our personal history and the stories we tell about ourselves. Our normal ego personality includes the roles we play in daily life, the masks we sometimes show the world (Jung called these *personas*), and the myriad internal aspects of ourselves, which we can understand as subpersonalities. Identification with any one persona (a professional role) or subpersonality (like the hurt child or inner critic) is a personality issue.

Your personality is as unique as your fingerprints. Ego personality can make life interesting and diverse; it can light us up from within. Most people go through a stage of maturity (or immaturity) where their personality is ego centered. At the level of ego personality, we can be ego centered, egotistic, prideful, self-obsessed, or even diagnosed with narcissistic personality disorder. But these personality traits are not what is meant by ego-identification.

Observing ego is the ability to step back and establish a witness within your mind of your internal thoughts, feelings, and sensations. Rick Hanson, PhD, and Rick Mendius, MD, founders of the Wellspring Institute for Neuroscience and Contemplative Wisdom, explain it this way: "The psychological term, 'the observing ego'—considered to be essential for healthy functioning—refers to this capacity (i.e., mindfulness) to detach from the stream of consciousness and observe it."[3] Observing ego uses mindfulness from self-awareness or subtle mind to be a nonjudgmental witness—similar to what Freud called "evenly hovering attention."

Ego-identification is the end result of a process, one that feels like who you are is a mini-me located in your head that looks out of your body's eyes. Ego-identification is not an entity but a mental process: a particular pattern of consciousness variously called ego-fixation, ego-grasping, or ego-clinging. This mental process only becomes ego-identification when it results in taking itself to be "I."

Ego-identification is not just an "I" thought, a resistance, a self-image, a personal story, or a belief that can be changed by an effort of will. Ego-identification is not "you" identifying with "your ego." Instead, self-awareness and ego functions cling inwardly to themselves, creating ego-identification, which then clings to outward things.

The process of ego-identification obscures our already-awake nature. The mental processes of thinking and ego functions can identify with each other and generate a closed loop: the feeling of "I." Ego-identification is a "selfing" process. However, we don't recognize this process because we're totally immersed in the experience, fused with our ego functions and looking at the world from a felt sense of "me" that has become ego-identification. Only when looking from awake awareness can ego-identification be observed as a mental pattern. Ego-identification is also ocurring on the unconscious level with our default mode network, where it creates unhappiness as a self-referencing mini-me.

Ego-identification creates a mistaken identity that believes it needs the same nourishment and protection as a physical entity. It co-opts our ego defense mechanisms even though there is nothing to defend. Ego-identification is not a physical creature; therefore this mental pattern needs no food, and there's no real threat to its existence. The delusion of a separate self struggling to survive leads to perpetual hunger, fear, dissatisfaction, and suffering. However, we can think of ego-identification as a transitional identity, a thought-based operating system out of which we can shift to awake awareness as our ground of Being.

THE RELATIONSHIP BETWEEN TYPES OF EGO

Ego body, ego function, ego personality, and observing ego are not in themselves obstacles to awakening—nor are they eliminated upon awakening. We can also see that our personality, body, ego functions, or the observing ego are not the center of our identity either, but only parts of us like our hands or our hearing. Full awakening includes our bodies, emotions, and personalities. From awake awareness you can see that "who you are" is not your appearance, job, age, race, income, or history. The dropping away of ego-identification does not leave you feeling vacant, spaced-out, disassociated, or depersonalized. With awake awareness as the ground of Being, there's a feeling of "I am," which is independent of "I am this" or "I am that."

Ego-identification is not a single character, but a me-system composed of our many different subpersonalities that rotate through the driver's seat of the self. We discover that these voices (or subpersonalities) are normal patterns of thought and feeling that most humans share. These patterns, or habits of mind, need to be liberated, not just stopped. When we can know and see from Being, our subpersonalities feel relieved that they no longer have to act as the driver. These parts can play or relax until they're called upon for their particular talents. With awake awareness as our ground of Being, these voices and opinions still arise, but they don't become the driver. Instead, all are welcomed and unburdened by the loving presence of open-hearted awareness.

Ego-identification is an organization and orientation built into our neural networks. It's so deeply wired into our brain that it appears as the main character of our default mode network when we're at rest. As a self-referential, looping pattern, ego-identification also projects images onto others and the world in an effort to feel safe. This habit is so ingrained that it starts first thing in the morning as soon as we transition from deep sleep: "Oh no, the deadline is today. Why do I always wait until the last minute? I'm such a failure." The judging function, needed to recognize unhealthy environments or "bad water," can get co-opted by ego-identification and turn against us. The mistaken identity causes shame, because we don't feel okay about being who we are. We confuse feeling unloved with being unlovable; we confuse making mistakes with being stupid or worthless. However, in spite of the strong, ingrained nature of ego-identification, we can still shift out of this level of mind. The big realization—when we go beyond ego-identification and discover awake awareness as our ground of Being—is that we've always been okay.

We all have basic needs. It's a mistake to try to reduce desire and aversion on all levels of ego as if they needed to be renounced, repressed, or transcended. We do need to seek and get food, money, sexual connection, social approval, joy, work, and safety. The issues of imbalance in these areas are about ego function, ego personality, and growing up. So we're not really awakening from ego-identification through renunciation, repression, denial, willful restraint, or stronger measures of abstinence or mortification. Nor do we awaken by transforming our emotions, personality, or thinking. Shifting into mindfulness and cultivating loving-kindness and acceptance can be a stepping-stone toward awakening, yet these measures don't help us cross the line into waking-up. When we get clarity about the different types of ego, awakening in the midst of worldly life is actually the most fully integrated way to go about it.

VIEW FROM NEUROSCIENCE

Neuroscience agrees that there's no separate self or subject located in any one area of the brain. An attendee of a 2002 New York Academy of Sciences conference, titled "The Self: From Soul to Brain," writes: "Most of us share a strong intuition that our own self is an irreducible whole, that there must be some place in our brains where our perceptions and thoughts all come together and where our future actions are decided. Yet this view is now known to be incorrect—different mental processes are mediated by different brain regions, and there is nothing to suggest the existence of any central controller."[4]

The brain is a symphony, but no conductor can be found. Neuroimaging research has begun to identify key brain regions involved in self-referential processing, like the default mode network. Studies with meditators have revealed that the self-referential process can be dominant, turned off, or experienced as a mental process instead of being identified with as "my self." Neuroscientist Sam Harris agrees that "this is where meditative insight actually makes contact with science: because we know that the self is not what it seems to be. There is no place in the brain for a soul or an ego to be hiding.

And it is possible to examine this illusory self closely enough to have the feeling that we call 'I' disappear. As it happens, this comes as quite a relief."[5]

Your current ego-identification is not an independent entity, but a pattern of consciousness that's less than optimal for living. The interesting thing about this seemingly solid, mistaken sense of self is that it is a biological neural network operating both when we're conscious and when we're daydreaming. It runs on autopilot in every person's brain, regardless of their history, conditioning, and culture. Neither the conscious operations of the mistaken identity called ego-identification nor the unconscious default mode network are set in stone. It seems to be a stage of development that we can grow out of. We can positively transform our consciousness and train our brains to discover a whole new way of seeing and being.

VIEW FROM PSYCHOLOGY

In psychoanalysis, *ego* is defined as: "The part of the mind that mediates between the conscious and the unconscious and is responsible for reality testing and a sense of personal identity."[6] The problem here is that *ego* means both ego function and ego-identification. There is no acknowledgment that the ego function is only a part of our identity and not the same as identity.

Separating ego function from ego-identification will begin to solve this case of mistaken identity. It is important that we don't mistakenly deconstruct ego functions. It's also important not to end up in the mindful witness of observing ego or to stop our awakening process at deconstructing ego-identification without also transitioning to awake awareness. Transitioning to awake awareness as an essential part of waking-up will help us avoid the pitfalls of depersonalization, dissociation, and becoming overwhelmed with unconscious material. Once we have recognized our new identity in the ground of Being, ego-identification can semiretire, giving up its second job of trying to fill the shoes of identity. We can let the ego relax, with full retirement benefits, returning to its natural role as ego function.

BOUNDLESS GROUND

Most contemplative traditions agree that the root of suffering is the belief there's a separate self within us. Realization that there is no separate existing self, *anatta,* is used in the early Buddhist texts as a strategy to view the self as a series of conditioned processes instead of an entity. When the Buddha was asked whether or not there was a self, he wouldn't give a simple answer. He didn't say the self was a complete illusion, but he considered the self the same as other relative phenomena: nonsubstantial and constructed on a moment-to-moment basis from the contents of consciousness.

When you go beyond ego-identification, who are you? You are still human, but with unconditioned awake awareness as the foundation, it is hard to say whether you are a true self or no-self. Once you have a direct experience beyond ego-identification, questions of self and no-self are no longer of philosophical interest. Our bodies, our personalities, and our ego functions are helpful tools within an ever-changing, interconnected field of awareness and consciousness. Let's see if we can get a sense of how the process of ego-identification occurs, how it maintains itself, and how it can relax and allow ego functions and ego personality to return to their natural roles.

A Wake-Up Story

Once upon a time, only the simplest forms of life existed on Planet Earth, among them single-celled microorganisms. What distinguished these particular organisms from other forms of life was their semipermeable membrane, a kind of "skin" that formed a boundary, separating life inside from the life outside. Each of these microorganisms, whose primary purpose was survival, treated everything inside its boundary as "self" and everything outside as "other." Evolutionary biologists tell us that a single-celled creature in its earliest, most primitive form could respond only at the part of its boundary that contacted another object. If one part of the creature bumped into an obstacle, that part would stop, while the sides oozed around the obstacle and tried to keep going forward.[7]

As time went on, an important evolutionary change occurred: the organism developed a simple representational system that enabled it to relay information from its boundary's surface to an inner part of itself. When any stimulus was perceived at the boundary surface, the information traveled through the organism and got recorded in a kind of processing center, which gave the organism the capacity to store representations of past situations in order to respond more effectively to the environment, thereby increasing its chances for survival. For example, when the temperature rose, the organism retrieved the negative experience of feeling too hot, registered dislike, and then moved away. When the organism was hungry, it craved food and then retrieved information about what was nourishing, and moved closer to the nourishing source.[8]

FROM EGO FUNCTION TO EGO-IDENTIFICATION

Like those single-celled creatures, each of us is a bounded lifeform with an information-processing system. As our human ancestors acquired language and the present-day brain developed, an evolution in consciousness occurred that gave us many advantages. Modern science estimates that a human body is made up of 100 trillion individual cells. The web of nerves going from the body's boundary (the skin) to the brain and back again is forty-five miles long. However, evolution also created an ongoing self-loop, out of a representational storage center, which has outlived its usefulness. The self-awareness that resulted from this human development co-opts our boundary survival program and is the key to understanding the bind of mistaken identity we face today.

Ego functions are the natural system by which humans organize information. Like a simple computer program, some of the ego functions say things that include: "I need to survive," "Monitor the boundary," "Protect the body from danger," "Acquire nutrients," "Procreate," and "Bond with my group." This intense part of our consciousness includes basic human needs and instincts.

The processing center mistakenly identifies with the pattern and creates the feeling of a separate entity out of its own thoughts.

The type of thinking that co-opts the boundary-survival program is what psychologists call *self-awareness*. This is the process of splitting our thinking into two parts by creating an observing self within our mind. The term *self* refers to our ability to become a consciously observing subject. Researchers have demonstrated that we are not born with the capacity for self-awareness; it begins to emerge at around one year of age. The capacity for self-awareness becomes much more developed around eighteen months, the age when children can recognize themselves in mirrors. Children then begin to use the pronouns "I," "me," and "mine" to refer to themselves. However, it's not the naming of oneself as a separate person that causes ego-identification.

Self-awareness leads to ego-identification when we split our thinking into two parts, creating a separate subject. Your everyday mind is aware of your body and environment; self-awareness is the observer of the thoughts from your everyday mind. Instead of reacting to a situation from our current ego personality, self-awareness gives us the ability to step back and think about what we'll say or do. When we're self-conscious, or overly self-aware, we feel anxious because we feel viewed as a separate object that others can judge, criticize, or potentially attack. Self-awareness creates a separate sense of self that can observe the "me" made of the contents of consciousness as an object—as in: "I'm so mad at myself." It's as though the "I" (the viewer) and the "me" (the physical person) are two different entities. Self-awareness is one of the highest human developments, yet in some ways this gift also limits our growth and development.

The self-referential process locates itself within our brain and then starts to loop around itself, creating the sense of having its own boundary. The same programs for the body's skin boundaries and its perceived conceptual boundary seduce us into feeling that the intangible ego-identification in our head is as solid and separate as our body. It's almost as if the processing center, trying to do its job, carried its job one step too far by applying the boundary rules to itself. The information-processing center is like a security guard who monitors everything that comes in. Self-awareness has made itself the arbiter and last reference for identity. This situation self-perpetuates until our story can move to the next chapter by having our identity upgraded to awake awareness.

Like the representational center of the single-celled organism, self-awareness doesn't know our body's boundary directly; it only knows indirectly through representations like thoughts, images, or concepts. Ego-identification personifies self-awareness as if it were a physical entity, a physical "me," living in our brain, needing to be protected. In some cases, even your physical body can be considered "not me," but a part of the environment to be dealt with. For instance, in the science fiction film *2001: A Space Odyssey,* the spaceship's computer, Hal, begins as a monitoring system but ultimately takes over as the decision maker. However, ego-identification is not an evil master but a transitional identity that developed and is now innocently protecting itself because it doesn't know any better. We can see how ego-identification is part of human evolution—a developmental stage we can grow out of—rather than a false self.

In the following story, Eckhart Tolle, author of *The Power of Now,* describes the way his ego-identification collapsed and revealed "pure consciousness."

> I woke up in the middle of the night. The fear, anxiety, and heaviness of depression were becoming so intense, it was almost unbearable. . . . Everything was totally alien and almost hostile. . . . And the thought came into my head, "I can't live with myself any longer." That thought kept repeating itself again and again.
>
> And then suddenly there was a "standing back" from the thought and looking at that thought, at the structure of that thought, "If I cannot live with myself, who is that self that I cannot live with? Who am I? Am I one—or two?" And I saw that I was "two." There was an "I" and here was a self. And the self was deeply unhappy, the miserable self. And the burden of that I could not live with. At that moment, a disidentification happened. "I" consciousness withdrew from its identification

with the self, the mind-made fictitious entity, the
unhappy "little me" and its story. And the fictitious
entity collapsed completely in that moment, just as if
a plug had been pulled out of an inflatable toy. What
remained was a single sense of presence or "Beingness"
which is pure consciousness prior to identification with
form—the eternal I AM. I didn't know all of that at the
time, of course. It just happened, and for a long time
there was no understanding of what had happened.[9]

For Eckhart Tolle, the dissolution of ego-identification happened
quickly and dramatically. We too can see how the process of self-
awareness divided his consciousness into two parts, one of which was
an unhappy "little me." Tolle's story is an example of sudden, unin-
tentional awakening. For me and for many others, the same process
happened more gradually, through a series of shifts.

While the idea of sudden awakening may hold a strong appeal,
we need to remember that Eckhart says that it took him ten years
to integrate his awakening. I know many people who've had similar
experiences of awakening but were never able to integrate them. This
kind of identity transition does not fit into our conventional cultural
understanding of human growth, and so these individuals who experienced sudden awakenings had no context in which to place them.
Their experiences were too foreign for them to categorize and make
sense of. Many did not have the resources (books and people) that
described the process of going through this kind of consciousness shift.
Most of these people didn't know how to familiarize themselves with
and stabilize in their new sense of Being.

The Co-Opting of the Boundary Program

On the physical level, if we forget to eat, we will die, so our body
registers our need for intake of food as hunger pains. Hunger creates unpleasant feelings of dissatisfaction that motivate us to crave
food, seek it, possess it, and consume it. As such, desire, seeking, and

dissatisfaction are natural on the everyday level. When our bellies are full, our bodies produce sensations of pleasure and satisfaction.

Our suffering begins when ego-identification mistakes itself to be a real physical entity and then looks outside for "nourishment." Because ego-identification is a mental construction and not a living creature, it doesn't need food. Nor does it need to be fearful or protective, because it is only a pattern of thought and cannot be hurt. However, when ego-identification believes it is the physical creature "I" that has a boundary, it uses the biological survival programs of our ego functions and constantly feels unfulfilled cravings and worries about imaginary potential dangers.

The boundary-survival program is designed to serve the physical body. As soon as self-awareness creates ego-identification as a location, it syncs up with the biological boundary program to crave, seek, possess, and consume. These drives are natural and useful at the physical level, but they create suffering at the level of identity. Nothing can relieve the mistaken identity's desires, resulting in a perpetual feeling of lack, fear, and dissatisfaction. The attempt to solve this feeling of dissatisfaction through seeking from ego-identification reinforces the problem. Ego-identification is driven to be constantly seeking, which makes us feel like something is always missing, that who we are and whatever is happening is never quite enough or right. This is the root of suffering that can be relieved by awakening.

When ego-identification co-opts the body's survival strategies to defend its illusory identity, it builds a fortress around itself for protection and then feels isolated. Ego-identification perpetually tries to solve problems that are not real, and then—not succeeding—it feels more anxious and develops more strategies. A set of defensive attitudes and patterns of behavior multiplies to preserve its perceived existence. When self-awareness identifies with our boundary-survival program, we contract our natural boundless nature and feel as if all our life energy is being squeezed into a narrow point of view. Identification with this narrow point of view severely limits us and obscures our connection to the larger and subtler dimensions of life. Our brain, driven by the mini-me, is constantly on alert for potential danger, often ending up overwhelmed, anxious, or depressed.

False Fears

The mini-me responds to exaggerated or imaginary situations that frighten it with physical survival strategies, including fight, flight, freeze, or please. When we fight imaginary enemies, we end up feeling frustrated, confused, or anxious. When we run away from them, we end up in denial, dissociation, or fantasy. If we freeze, we get depressed or shut down. If we please, we often end up feeling minimized, oppressed, or victimized. The more we try to think our way out of situations that frighten the ego-identification, the more neurotic and confused we become. Because we don't know what to do with our mistaken perceptions of danger, we frequently act out our feelings instead of expressing or examining them. We may react aggressively as if we are being attacked. Or we may repress our feelings, resulting in painful, energy-sapping shame, hopelessness, or self-hatred.

When the mistaken identity feels threatened, it's as though a car alarm has gone off accidently and the mind immediately scans for suspects—even though no crime has been committed. Ego-identification begins to strategize, creating multiple delusional scenarios that are confused with memories of actual physical and emotional threats that occurred in the past. The mistaken identity's conclusion—I am in danger—sends fear signals cascading through our innocent bodies, releasing a flood of chemicals such as adrenaline and cortisol that increase the very real feelings of immediate physical danger. Since fear is a biological experience, fear cements the mistaken identity's belief that someone real is being threatened. The strong emotions accompanying fear can be acted out through attack, blame, or addiction; or they can be suppressed, often leading to anxiety or depression.

From the perspective of mistaken identity, making a slight error or engaging in a disagreement can be interpreted as causing a potential risk of death, and thus a threat to its sense of "me." Our mistaken identity feels that it has to maintain control and avoid criticism; it must be right or the ego-identification feels it could become "dead wrong." One student told me that she'd just been promoted at work, but the very next day when her boss frowned, she watched the ego-identification's story play out on the screen of her mind. She went from joy to an immediate fear of being fired, of losing her home and her partner for being such a failure, of becoming homeless on the streets, and of ultimately falling sick and dying alone. However, she was able to realize no real threat of being fired existed. In addition, she saw that ego-identification had co-opted her physical-survival program. Next, she was able to step back to awake awareness, and from there she watched how she had contracted into ego-identification. She was able to soothe her scared personality and body while feeling spacious and connected.

We can learn to shift levels of mind and see what is true. Feelings aren't facts. It is a fact that she was feeling fear, but it was *not* a fact that there was a threat to her physical safety.

At root, our chronic pain and suffering comes from a simple case of mistaken identity. Ego-identification is happening by itself; it is not something we intentionally create. We often don't know that it's happening or that there's an alternative—and from our current level of mind, we can't see how it's created. This lack of knowing is often called "ignorance" or "confusion." Most of us do the best we can with what we know from our current level of ego-identification. It's often only after shifting out of ego-identification, and looking back, that we recognize ego-identification for what it is. By directly experiencing life from the awareness-based operating system, we can begin to free ourselves from the suffering caused by our mistaken identity.

The Problem of Attachment and Addiction

Ego-identification can piggyback on existing biological or psychological cravings such as an addiction to cigarettes, alcohol, or food; or it can create its own addiction out of anything. In its attempts to find satisfaction, the mini-me gloms onto different potential solutions. But these attempts can never succeed in restoring balance; instead they result in a perpetual feeling of lack, dissatisfaction, and craving that feels as painful as physical hunger. There is nothing wrong with desire, which is a strong biological impulse wired within us. Desire is not the problem. The problem occurs when awareness attaches to a limited type of consciousness, creating the feeling of "I," which then desires and seeks relief from the loneliness and separation that the small self has just created. When we find some relief, pleasure, or satisfaction, then we addictively return to this until there is another option.

There are three kinds of cravings: physical, psychological, and those caused by ego-identification. Suffering and addiction can happen on any of these levels, and each has its own methods and treatments. Sometimes working on one level is enough, but often all three levels are needed for treatment. For instance, in treating substance abuse, the twelve-step program uses all three levels. Abstinence from the substance is the physical level. On the psychological level, group support, behavioral changes, and personal honesty are added. The third level of treatment involves moving beyond reliance on ego-identification by finding a power greater than the self. When we realize that our will, our everyday mind, and our ego are unable to overcome addiction—and that they actually stand in our way—then we can choose to find, rely on, and identify with a vast support of awake awareness that can be called by any name.

Distinguishing ego-identification from ego body, ego functions, and ego personality is the key to waking up and growing up. When we don't see this creation of ego-identification as an unnecessary mistaken identity, we may try to get rid of the suffering it causes by trying to change or control our body, personality, or ego functions. When you've stepped out of ego-identification, you immediately leave behind the seeking, craving, and aversion it created. From the ground of Being, on the level of identity, you feel fulfilled, interconnected, and complete. Thus, there is nothing to be pushed away. Nothing is needed. You feel fundamentally well and whole.

GLIMPSE 1 **The Now**

A set of famous Mahamudra instructions is called the Six Points of Tilopa, also known as the Six Ways of Resting the Mind in Its Natural Condition.

Don't recall	Let go of the past
Don't anticipate	Let go of what may come in the future
Don't think	Let go of what is happening in the present

Don't examine	Don't particularize or analyze
Don't control	Don't try to make anything happen
Rest	Relax naturally, right now

Figure 3 is a pointer to help you discover and remain in the Now. The Now is the timeless time that includes the three times of past, present, and future. The Now is not the present moment, but is aware of present moments arising and passing. We can learn not to collapse into identifying with one particular time or state of mind. From awake awareness, familiarize yourself with the view from the Now.

1. Allow yourself to find a comfortable place to sit and settle in. Take a few comfortably full breaths and let a smile come to your face. Become aware of your breath as it comes and goes. Relax and be here Now without needing to change anything.

2. As you notice your next in-breath, let local awareness unhook from thought and ride the breath down below your neck.

3. Feel the intelligence of awareness that knows your senses directly from within your body. Rest in your heart space that is open and knowing without going up to thought.

4. Begin to be aware of each passing moment, each passing thought that comes and goes, appearing and disappearing.

5. Look and feel from timeless spacious awareness. Open to the Now that includes past, present, and future and doesn't get stuck in any present moment.

6. Inquire: When am I? Stuck in the past? Chasing the future? Trying to hold on to the present moment? Or in the Now that includes everything? Rest here, deeper than sleep and wide awake, and simply:

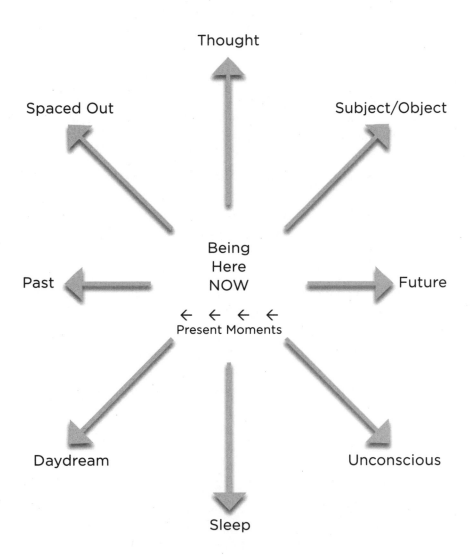

FIGURE 3. Learning to be here and now with the past, present, future, and passing present moments.

7. Don't go up to refer to thought.

8. Don't go down to sleep.

9. Don't go back to refer to the past.

10. Don't go even one moment forward to anticipate the future.

11. Don't cling to the passing present moments.

12. Don't look out to the world to create a subject/object relationship.

13. Don't fall into daydreaming.

14. Feel the magnetic pull forward to the future, the pull back to the past, and the pull to hold onto the present while remaining in the Now.

15. Rest your awareness equally inside and outside. Open to the Now and notice the timeless, continuous field of open-hearted awareness in which all of these present moments of experience are appearing and disappearing.

16. Let be and relax in the all-at-onceness of the Now.

GLIMPSE 2 **Infinite No-Self**

In this practice, we're shifting away from the witnessing self and any tendency to contract into a single point of view. The feeling of being a self is the feeling of being an observer with a particular location. No-self is the realization that we are viewing from everywhere, nowhere, and here. We can let go of the tendency to construct a subject-versus-object view and to hold onto positive qualities that arise, such as bliss, clarity, and nonthought. We will no longer be looking from a particular location of the ego, the meditator, or skylike spacious awareness. When you shift away from self-location, then you can let everything be as it is. Paradoxically, you will feel ordinary in an open-hearted way.

In this practice, you'll check for any remnant of the location of an ego or self-viewpoint so awake awareness can show us clearly that it's the natural ground of being. If you like, do one of the previous glimpse exercises as the first part of this practice until you feel as if you're an ocean of awareness with waves of experience appearing. Then, let local awareness search for any remaining sense of self.

1. Unhook local awareness and have it search your entire body-mind system from head to toe to see if a self as an object or subject can be found. Allow the awareness to scan quickly and thoroughly until nothing is found.

2. Upon not finding a self located in any one place or looking from any one place, notice how awake awareness and aliveness are free and unconfined—and seamlessly permeating.

3. Notice that the field of open and empty awareness is aware of itself, by itself, as itself. The awake field is infinitely aware from everywhere, interconnected to everything. The ocean of awareness knows all waves from inside the wave.

4. Feel that there is no boundary, no center, yet continue to observe with no observer.

5. Notice the arising of the aliveness in your human body out of formless awareness moment to moment.

6. Notice the quality of the Now, where everything is here all at once.

7. Let everything be as it is, ordinary and free.

9

THE ANATOMY OF AWARENESS

That everything is included within your mind is the essence of mind . . .
Even though waves arise, the essence of your mind is pure;
it is just like clear water with a few waves. Actually water always
has waves. Waves are the practice of the water. To speak of waves apart
from water or water apart from waves is a delusion. Water and waves
are one. Big mind and small mind are one. When you understand
your mind in this way, you have some security in your feeling."

SHUNRYU SUZUKI[1]

What we experience is based on our way of perceiving. If we use our eyes, we see one thing, but if we use a microscope or a telescope, we see other realms of reality that have been there all along. I have enjoyed witnessing thousands of people discovering their natural capacity to see in a new way for the first time. People have described it as putting on a pair of glasses, or moving from black-and-white to color TV.

Most people tend to focus on appearances and objects that exist. "Existence" comes from the Latin root word *existere,* meaning to "stand forth" or "appear." Our common understanding of existence is "that which is real," but the word actually refers to appearance: what can be seen or felt. Awake awareness is real even though it's invisible and empty. There is existence and the awareness of existence, but it is also possible for us to be aware of awareness. There are other dimensions of consciousness that we can experience when we discover awareness-based knowing.

One reason we don't usually see our basic awareness is that we're always looking out *from* it. We can only look from awake awareness when it has recognized itself. Awake awareness is like a lamp that illuminates both itself and objects in the room. Usually we turn our focus outward, becoming fascinated with objects and the interpretations our thoughts offer. Discovering awake awareness means learning how to look back to the source of light and then how to look from the clarity of awareness.

Awake awareness is natural to all human beings. It is not exclusive to any religion, creed, or culture. We've all had glimpses of awake awareness. At those times we've felt like we're resting in our true nature—open, loving, connected, free of worry, and yet able to respond to things as they are with curiosity and courage. These experiences of feeling free and alive are our most cherished times.

Awake Awareness, Consciousness, and Thinking

Awake awareness as spacious awareness is formless and contentless, yet knowing. It is the foundation of all types of thinking and knowing. Spacious awareness is what makes consciousness aware. Spacious awareness is independent of circumstances and conditions, thoughts and emotions. Consciousness is the appearances, the formations, the patterns—like a ray of sunshine, a flower, or an ocean wave. Awake awareness is inherent within all types of consciousness. Like a wave, consciousness moves, but it never separates from the ocean of awake awareness, which is inherent within all consciousness. Consciousness is the spontaneous expression and creative activity of awake awareness. Awake awareness is always the ground of being—permeating and connective—like the quantum field from which individual particles or waves appear.

There are many types of consciousness (patterns of experience) such as emotional consciousness and hearing consciousness. Thinking is a form of consciousness. When we say we're doing something consciously, we're using thinking consciousness, which uses thought to look to other thoughts to confirm that we know what we know. Awake awareness is nonconceptual awareness. Whether or not there are thoughts on the screen of our mind, awake awareness is the background intelligence we can learn to recognize and trust.

Awake awareness is inherent within thinking consciousness, but when awareness becomes identified with thinking, it creates an "I" consciousness. The witnessing awareness gets lost in the world of thoughts. This type of consciousness is called ego-identification because we consider this identified state to be normal, to be "me." The purpose of separating awareness from thinking consciousness is to liberate us from the illusory sense of self that is at the root of our suffering. Patanjali, author of the Yoga Sutras, said: "As soon as one can distinguish between consciousness and awareness, the ongoing construction of the self ceases."[2]

By using glimpse practices, we can discover directly that awake awareness is the primary dimension of consciousness, and thought is secondary. Spacious awareness is like empty space. Not inert space, but knowing space. It is the innate, formless intelligence that exists prior to thought, yet it also exists within thought; it is able to know thought and can use thought when needed.

The Hindu tradition identifies four natural states of consciousness. We know the first three very well: ego-consciousness, our everyday waking state; sleep; and dreaming or daydreaming. The fourth natural state, *turiya* in Sanskrit, is spacious awareness that is inherent within all four states. It also recognizes a fifth "stateless state," *turiyatita,* which is when spacious awareness is realized as the ground of our Being.

When awake awareness is experienced as the source of consciousness, there's a lack of craving and fear, along with a sense of peace, wellbeing, and clarity. When awareness remains as the primary dimension from which we experience life, other dimensions of consciousness can move freely and return to their natural functions.

When you are abiding in awake awareness, you can experience different essential qualities when formless awareness first contacts different aspects of your consciousness. When awake awareness connects to hearing, you may experience silence. When it contacts thinking, you may feel peace of mind or have an insight. When spacious awareness is embodied, you may experience it as inner-body presence or bliss. When it contacts your emotions, you may feel joy, wellbeing, or a compassionate connection. If it contacts your language center, you might experience a "still, small voice." When awake awareness experiences your physical senses you may feel it within as stillness. From the visual sense, the experience can be boundless space, emptiness, or clarity. Every experience of awake awareness in touch with consciousness is somewhat different.

Distinguishing conceptual thinking from awake awareness has three steps: first, we glimpse awake awareness; second, awake awareness becomes primary and knows itself; and third, we know *from* awake awareness within our physical, emotional, and thinking consciousness. As you explore the practices in this book, you'll find that you can experience spacious awareness just as naturally as you experience the other, very familiar states. The important thing is to recognize that spacious awareness is the source of knowing and to begin to see that it's not dependent on thinking.

What Is Spacious Awareness?

Awake awareness is like a diamond with different facets that show up at different times. Spacious awareness is the boundless, timeless, contentless, invisible, and yet knowing expression of awake awareness. Spacious awareness is also inherent within physical forms and energetic patterns. It is important for spacious awareness to know itself as the primary dimension, both as the nature of mind and the ground of Being. Then spacious awareness can include all dimensions of consciousness without becoming identified or lost. The journey of awakening does not end with spacious awareness but continues to reveal presence as awareness embodied without going back to ego-identification.

The natural qualities that we search for externally—peace, joy, connectedness—arise from within on their own when spacious awareness is primary. Spacious awareness, though empty like space, is knowing. Getting used to the feel of this new, nonconceptual knowing without checking back with thought is one of the most important transitions for abiding and living from open-hearted awareness. We can begin to understand the feeling of spacious awareness that reveals itself in two ways: through emptiness and knowing. Then we discover embodied awake awareness and its compassionate expression as open-hearted awareness. Spacious awareness is absolute pure potential, the potential to know, manifest, create, or to be anything or nothing.

SPACIOUS AWARENESS IS EMPTY

Emptiness, which is so essential in Eastern meditation traditions, is often misunderstood in the West as meaning the "absence of anything," like an empty cup or a vacuum. The word *empty* in this context does not mean "blank" or "vacant." The Sanskrit definition, *sunyata,* comes from the root word *svi,* meaning "ripe with possibilities"—like an empty womb. A traditional definition for emptiness is "the invisible life force within a seed that makes it capable of growing into a tree." Invisible, but alive and real. This invisible life force is not only empty and alive, but also awake and aware.

Emptiness also emphasizes that there are ultimately no independent, separate things; not because everything is unreal or an illusion, but because everything is essentially interconnected and interdependent. The apple on your table does not exist independently from the soil, the sun, the rain, the air, the farmer who picked it, the trucker who brought it to market, the grocer, or the checkout person at the store. None of these things or people is separate from the apple—or from each other. There is no independent, separate apple.

Another important emphasis from Buddhism is the emptiness of self: anatta. One aspect of anatta is similar to neuroscience's insights: there's no entity or part of the brain that is the location of a self. Through mindfulness meditation, we see how the experience of "I" is a continuously changing process of consciousness. Having stepped out of ego-identification, spacious awareness is aware but selfless. We also begin to see the emptiness of possessions and accomplishments that we believed would satisfy this illusory self. From spacious awareness, we experience relief from suffering created by the feeling that we should get something or get rid of something.

Spacious awareness is invisible. It's not solid, nor is it a thing, separate from anything else. Although awake awareness is not a substance and is empty of all relative existence, it is not empty of itself. It is not empty of true nature. While absent of content and form, it's full of life. Spacious awareness is not energy. It is formless, pure consciousness that precedes the arising of patterns such as thoughts. For this reason, it's variously called *pristine awareness, naked awareness,* or *contentless awareness.* Spacious awareness is vast and infinite, unlimited by boundaries; when we realize the emptiness of a separate self, we feel *boundless awareness.*

Spacious awareness has been described as *unconditioned awareness* because it's not reliant on conditions. Unconditioned awareness doesn't change when circumstances or conditions change. It knows without the use of conditioned memory.

Others refer to spacious awareness as *unmanifest awareness.* The Latin root word *mani* means "hand," so *un*manifest means that spacious awareness can't be held in our hands. Importantly, it cannot be experienced by our five senses or thinking.

SPACIOUS AWARENESS IS KNOWING

Spacious awareness has been called *natural wakefulness* because it's not information-based intelligence that's created or developed, but is discovered to be already naturally awake and aware. It is also called *clear light awareness;* however, it's not energy or physical space, nor is it literally light. Here, "light" is used as in the term *enlightenment.* Think of a light bulb in an unused attic room. The moment the light turns on, everything is seen—no matter how long the room has been in darkness. Light represents the clarity of the new, nonconceptual knowing that sees things as they are.

Nonconceptual awareness is another term that might be helpful for getting a feel for this expression of awake awareness. Nonconceptual doesn't mean we're experiencing a babylike prerational stage. Spacious awareness is more of a postconceptual, advanced level of intelligence that's sometimes called *wisdom mind,* which includes and permeates conceptual knowing. Wisdom mind is the subtlest, most primordial dimension of mind and the source of intelligence, also known as the *nature of mind* or *mind essence.*

Thinking or believing cannot experience spacious awareness, which has been called thought-free wakefulness because it doesn't use thought to know. However, when spacious awareness is the primary way of knowing, thoughts and experiences continue to arise and are included within spacious awareness. While spacious awareness is free of thought and concepts, it is nevertheless inherent within all human activity, and able to use thought.

When local awareness—the second expression of awake awareness—goes to spacious awareness, then spacious awareness is aware of itself, without subject or object. Thus, it's been called the "unseen seer." Spacious awareness cannot be known as an object; it can only know itself.

As pure perception, spacious awareness can see everything directly, as it actually is, without projection. Pure perception sees through delusion to perceive the awake, empty nature within everyone and everything. As poet William Blake wrote, "If the doors of perception were cleansed, every thing would appear to man as it is, Infinite."[3]

When we're operating from thought-based knowing, we look to thought to know; we think about thinking, ruminating, obsessing, and orienting by thought. When we shift into spacious awareness as the ground of Being, then thinking goes into the background and we don't see pop-ups and multiple programs running on our mind-screens. Then, our conceptual minds are quiet but, just as we can use our hands at any moment, we can use thought whenever needed. Awake awareness in its fullness is empty, knowing, loving, and embodied.

What Is Nonduality?

The art and beauty of practicing dharma becomes more and more subtle and profound as we learn the dance of the relative and absolute truths . . .
When we first start practicing, we are typically at the conventional or relative level, which when practiced well can eventually lead to a realization of the absolute. However, the final stage, which we are speaking about here, is the realization of the inseparability of the two.

TSOKNYI RINPOCHE[4]

Shifting into freedom is not a matter of transcending the human condition; it's an expression of nonduality, of formless awake-awareness living that expresses itself as different forms of human consciousness. The goal of awakening is to realize our full potential as human beings. Understanding the experience of nonduality is essential for living from open-hearted awareness. There are a number of definitions of nonduality. My understanding of nonduality is that it encompasses two simultaneous levels of reality: the relative and the absolute. Relative reality is how things appear to us in everyday life, the experience of different patterns of energy and forms that are observable with our senses.

Absolute reality is empty spacious awareness. Spacious awareness as the absolute level of reality is the underlying ground of relative reality. From absolute reality there are no separate or isolated things. On the relative level, a tree is a distinct object. Don't try to drive through it with a car! On the absolute level, however, a tree is not a separate entity. The tree is made of cells, chemicals, atoms, and quarks that are mostly empty space.

Some people define nonduality as exclusively absolute reality and consider relative reality to be an illusion. Some use the word "nonduality" to mean emptiness only, and others mean "pure" awake awareness only. These two definitions emphasize going beyond perceiving from our dualistic mind. However, if you don't consider including dualistic thinking, then you've created a new duality. My understanding of nonduality is closer to what's described in the Heart Sutra: "form is emptiness and emptiness is form."

When you shift into timeless, contentless, spacious awareness, you're experiencing what could be called "not duality," because you're not operating from the dualistic mind. However, that is not nonduality because it does not include relative reality. Some people use "nonduality" to mean "oneness," but there are many words in Sanskrit for "oneness." The word *advaita* means "not two" and refers to the paradox that the two levels of reality are not separate. That the two levels of reality are inseparable doesn't mean they're reduced to one; instead they're paradoxically experienced as two, one, many, empty, and simultaneously all.

In Buddhism, nonduality begins with distinguishing that there are two truths before seeing that they are simultaneous. Those with the view of relative truth only fall into the traps of materialism, intellectualism, and ego-centeredness. Those with the view of absolute truth only fall into the traps of nihilism, escapism, and world-denying ethical relativism.

Nonduality simultaneously includes both oneness and the many, both empty awareness and all appearances. Rather than being the opposite of duality, nonduality includes duality. In fact, it includes everything. Nonduality recognizes the inability to conceptually describe reality. It tries to avoid the extremes of nihilism (says everything is really empty), materialism (says that relative reality is the foundation of reality), and externalism (says an essence or oneness is unchanging).

Our everyday thinking mind, our senses, and our ego-identification cannot perceive absolute reality; they can only view the world from relative reality. We cannot live in the world from absolute reality only. Awakening does not change reality. Awakening shifts our view so we can perceive from absolute reality, which is already inherent within relative reality. This is why when you are based in awake awareness, you can drive a car without crashing into that tree I spoke of earlier.

Nondual Wisdom

A high IQ, being at the top of your college class, or winning at Trivial Pursuit has nothing to do with nondual wisdom. Wisdom begins when awake awareness is the primary operating system that organizes information, memory, relationship, communication, and your sense of identity. In Tibetan Buddhism there are two types of ignorance that create suffering. Shifting into the awareness-based operating system clears up the first type, called "conceptual ignorance," which is when conceptual thinking creates an illusory sense of self. The second type, co-emergent ignorance, is when appearances and forms are not recognized to be spontaneous self-displays of awake awareness, and they are taken to be either illusion or real, separate things.

Nondual wisdom begins with embodied awareness that includes the necessary discriminating functions of the mind, but it leaves behind the internal critic with its fear, sense of separation, and controlling aggression. Self-judging and self-consciousness are absent. Instead, our normal judging functions are transformed into the discriminating wisdom of open-hearted awareness. As we shift into nondual embodied awareness, we feel less judgmental and more compassionate. Then we develop a more mature conscience, along with a humble sense of integrity and compassion.

The wisdom and knowing from awake awareness may initially feel very slow compared to the fast-moving thinking of the everyday mind. Awake awareness doesn't consciously reference thoughts; instead it rests within a wisdom that's intuitively connected with all that we know. When the everyday mind looks out through our eyes, the first things we notice are separation, differences, and judgment. In comparison, embodied awake awareness first recognizes that which is the same in all of us, and then sees and appreciates our individuality. From this way of knowing, everything in the world feels interconnected, like dancing opposites or a unified field.

The following glimpse practice will allow you to experience the expressions of awake awareness as four fields of your ground of Being.

GLIMPSE 1 The Four Fields of the Ground of Being

Physicist Stephen Hawking, PhD, says that in order to create a universe, "You need just three ingredients: matter, energy, and space."[5] These are three of the fields that we are going to experience. However, we are adding a fourth field, awareness, which allows us to be aware of all four fields. The first field of the ground of being is objectless, thought-free, boundless space in which things are happening and appearances arise.

The second field of the ground of Being is energy, the aliveness happening within the boundary of the body. This second field can be called the subtle body and mind. The body at its most physical or coarse level is often thought of as what it looks like: skin, bones, and muscles. But the subtle body is what our bodies feel like from within as aliveness in many patterns of consciousness. In order to feel this second field, we won't focus on any particular thoughts, emotions, or stories, but directly feel aliveness, energy, and sensations. This second field is where ego-identification could form, but in this subtle-body level of experience, patterns of thought won't form into an ego-identity.

The third field of the ground of Being is matter, what we see in front of us in the physical world. It includes interaction with people, nature, situations, and activities. The fourth field is awake nondual awareness that is within all the other three fields and perceives a unity without a self-referencing viewpoint.

You can begin this glimpse with any of the three main ways of unhooking awareness: unhooking and dropping into the body, panoramic awareness, or shifting from hearing to spacious awareness. Select the way to begin that works best for you (physical, visual, or auditory). Or just begin with the first step below if that works for you.

1. Have local awareness unhook from thought and intentionally shift to the space behind your back.

2. Allow local awareness to surrender and mingle with the formless and contentless space, until spacious awareness is discovered to be already aware by itself.

3. Take your time until awareness has fully detached from your thoughts and sensations.

4. Be aware of discovering and shifting into the already-awake field of spacious awareness. Wait here until awareness is aware of itself.

5. Now, as you intentionally surrender back, feel the field of spacious awareness that is already looking forward and mixing with the aliveness and energy in your body.

6. Observe what it's like when awareness is the primary way of knowing your body from within. Feel the waves of aliveness dancing within the ocean of awareness.

7. Marinate in this embodied awareness.

8. Now notice that awareness is already unified with all your senses, thoughts, and feelings from head to toe without any effort needed.

9. Now notice awareness going out from the middle of your chest to connect with everyone and everything in front of your body.

10. You may feel a connection to everything, or as if everything is alive or lit up from within.

11. You may see everything as simultaneously connected, empty, and particular, or just simply Being itself as it is, without any thoughts projected onto it.

12. Now, feel spacious awareness equally behind, within, in front, and all around your body.

13. You may now feel the three fields of matter, energy, and space as one continuous self-sustaining field of aware presence.

14. Begin to feel spacious awareness moving from in front into your body and then back to the support of spacious awareness behind your back.

15. Notice that any information coming in through the senses naturally continues back and through the subtle-body field to be received by spacious awareness.

16. Notice what it is like when your identity is not centered in the field of ego-identification. Ask: "Where is 'I'?" Scan the middle field to see if a separate sense of self as an object or subject can be found. Upon not finding any point of view, notice the seamless field of aware presence, both formless awareness mixed with aliveness within and objects in the world in front that are not separate on the essential level but simultaneously are unique appearances of energy and physical form.

17. Surf the ocean of awareness. Your breath is a wave moving from inside to outside, and outside to inside. Local awareness is the surfboard. Ride your breath back to spacious awareness, then forward through the inner-body field to connect to what's in front of you; then ride back again through the inner-body field to the spacious awareness behind you without creating an identity in the middle field of your body-mind.

18. Now feel all four fields at once. Feel aware, infinite, finite, nowhere, everywhere, here, and now.

19. As you move from the support of spacious awareness behind you, feel the embodiment of love. Go out with open-hearted awareness to connect to all beings.

10

OPEN-HEARTED AWARENESS

When I look inside and see that I am nothing, that is wisdom.
When I look outside and see that I am everything, that is love.
And between these two, my life turns.

SRI NISARGADATTA MAHARAJ[1]

On a crisp autumn day in New York City, I headed downtown for a meeting. Arriving at the entrance of my neighborhood subway station on 116th Street and Broadway, I heard the train pull in below. I reached for my MetroCard, passed through the turnstile, and hurried downstairs, reaching the platform just in time to see the subway doors slide shut and the train pull away.

I stood there, looking at my watch, feeling frustrated because I'd probably be late for my meeting. The subway station was completely empty. As I walked toward the back of the platform, I felt disappointment arise as a physical contraction in my stomach. Then I noticed I'd begun to worry, and those thoughts were sending me up into my head, where I was starting to think up future worst-case scenarios. Then it occurred to me: *"Oh, I'm caught in my thoughts, but there is another way to be."* I realized my current situation was an opportunity to shift into embodied awake awareness.

As I shifted out of ego-identification and into embodied awake awareness, I began to feel safe, grounded, open, and joyously alive. My emotions and thoughts about missing the train and being late were naturally included in the luscious unified feeling and clarity of seeing from awake awareness. It was clear to me that awake awareness was not something I'd created, but an existing dimension of reality that was always already here. With a small shift, awake awareness had become spontaneously and immediately available to me, changing my feeling of myself and the whole situation for the better.

Waiting in a subway station, an activity I'd thought of as boring, had transformed into a mini-retreat, the most precious opportunity of the day. After a few minutes, I was so relaxed and open that I mused: *"This is great. What could be better than this?"* So I didn't expect what happened next.

The train arrived, the doors opened, and I stepped inside. Looking to my right for a seat, I felt stunned when my eyes met those of the few people who looked up. It seemed as if a veil between us had been lifted; our masks had dropped away. I felt vulnerable, yet safe, and connected to everyone and everything. It was as if I truly understood—for the first time—the saying "our eyes are the windows to our souls." It was as though the other subway riders and I were seeing each other heart to heart. This new kind of knowing is what I now call open-hearted awareness. There seemed to be no separation between the other subway riders and me. I had a profound sense of both the awakeness and imperfection in all of us. Taken aback, I gasped in awe at this new way of seeing and being. Then I started to laugh because, in some ways, this mode of seeing from open-hearted awareness felt so simple and ordinary—and it was such a relief!

A New Way of Being, Knowing, and Relating

The philosopher Jiddu Krishnamurti said, "There is no intelligence without compassion."[2] Open-hearted awareness is that compassionate intelligence so greatly needed in our world today. However, open-hearted awareness is not a far-off ideal. It's a natural capacity within each of us, and we're all capable of discovering and familiarizing ourselves with open-hearted awareness until it becomes the new normal in our lives. Open-hearted awareness is the meeting of mind and heart, wisdom and love, contemplation and action. It's a shift from head to heart, from conceptual thinking to a new way of knowing from nonconceptual heart-mind. It's a different way of seeing and relating to the world and other people. When we operate from open-hearted awareness, we have the ability to see how we are all the same and act with courage.

We shift out of thought-based knowing into awake awareness. As Anam Thubten says, "An open heart can only be experienced when we go beyond the realm of the intellectual mind."[3] Our first experience of awake awareness may be as spacious awareness, which is free of thought, but also a detached witness of emotions and sensations. Then we may feel we shift into an embodied presence, which knows from within rather than from outside our experience. Open-hearted awareness is awake awareness that is embodied and also feels connected to everyone and everything. It's not possible to experience open-hearted awareness from an ego-identified sense of self. We can't just *do* open-hearted awareness from where we start. It's not an attitude, an emotional feeling, or positive thinking. It's a natural capacity within each of us that requires that we shift levels of mind.

Open-Hearted Awareness throughout History

Recognized and valued since ancient times, the reality of open-hearted awareness has many names, among them: "heart wisdom," "sacred heart," and "heart-mind." The early Catholic theologian St. Augustine used the term *oculus cordis,* "eye of the heart," and recommended finding it by "returning within yourself." As the writer G. K. Chesterton said, "There is a road from the eye to the heart that does not go through the intellect."[4] In modern times, Brother Wayne Teasdale called this way of knowing "the mystic heart," and spiritual teacher Adyashanti calls it the "spiritual heart."

In the Bön Dzogchen tradition, open-hearted awareness is known as the "sphere of knowing." In the Sufi tradition, it is the "heart of hearts." Tibetan Buddhist teacher Tsoknyi Rinpoche calls it "essence love." A number of spiritual traditions have called this way of knowing "the diamond heart," emphasizing its preciousness, clarity, and indestructible nature. In Tibetan Buddhism, the word that corresponds to open-hearted awareness is *bodhicitta*. In Sanskrit, *bodhi* means "awake," and *citta* can be translated literally as "consciousness," so it is describing when our consciousness is awake. But interestingly, the translation of bodhicitta is not "awake consciousness" but "heart-mind," "awakened heart," or "the wisdom that leads to compassionate activity."

There is "relative" bodhicitta, which is having positive intentions such as doing loving-kindness meditation to benefit all living creatures. Then there is "ultimate" bodhicitta: open-hearted awareness that is living from your natural awakened heart. Those who live from open-heartedness are sometimes called bodhisattvas, because they dedicate their lives to increased awakening, love, and wellbeing in all they meet.

Open-hearted awareness is not physical heart, nor is it our heart chakra or our emotional heart. It is more like an open door of love and wisdom in the middle of your chest that goes out to connect to others and to receive support from our loving ground of Being. This new mode of awareness requires a shift into a different type of consciousness that, fortunately, is always already available—once we know where and how to look. Open-hearted awareness is a modern term for a reality that has been recognized by the world's ancient wisdom traditions.

Embodying Heart-Mind

When we shift our consciousness, we discover that our biology is capable of adapting to the new way of seeing and being. At a 2014 talk at the Education of the Heart symposium in the Netherlands, Daniel J. Siegel, MD, described the potential of the mind as "fully embodied and relational."[5] He spoke about how the mind is not enclosed in a skull, but is distributed across the nervous system within the body, and through relationships links us with other people and the environment. He described our neural networks as weblike configurations around the heart and stomach, explaining that they engage—along with the brain—in what neuroscience calls "parallel distributed processing." Among the things that parallel distributed processing does is making human intelligence more efficient than computers in some significant ways.

Siegel reported that recent neuroscience research suggests knowing from a full body-mind network actually moves from cells in the heart and gut and travels up through the spine into the brain. These neural structures use "mirror" neurons to perceive other people's subtle communications, whether or not we're conscious of it. These neurons literally mirror the behavior of others, causing emotional resonance in the observer and providing a sense of the other's felt experience. When you see someone smile, for example, your mirror neurons for smiling fire, causing a sensation in your own brain that is the feeling of smiling.

Although the brain is in the head, recent scientific studies demonstrate that "the mind" is fully embodied and relational, requiring a new, more holistic definition—similar to the description of open-hearted awareness given here. One man recently told me that when he shifted into open-hearted awareness, he felt as though his head dropped down into his heart, and his heart dropped down into his belly. A woman told me that her heart had opened, and she could feel a connection to others "heart to heart." Another person reported: "My awareness, which has always seemed located behind my eyes, is now equally distributed throughout my body, as if every cell in my body is lit up." This description is reminiscent of the image of the Bodhisattva of Great Compassion, who is depicted as having eyes on every part of her body.

Emotional Intelligence

Most of us remember times when we've gone beyond our normal, self-centered fear to help someone else in need. When we think about it later, we might say to ourselves, "I can't believe I did that, but I'm glad I did." In these moments when we transcend personal fear, we are spontaneously operating from open-hearted awareness—even though we may not recognize it as such. From open-hearted awareness, we can see when others are acting out of fear or self-preservation, and we can respond to them with empathy and compassion instead of defensiveness. Open-hearted awareness has natural qualities like strength, safety, and courage that arise when we learn how to shift into it.

There seem to be two ways humans suffer when we haven't yet learned to live from open-hearted awareness. Being overly mental is one way: trying to avoid feelings by being "rational," "objective," and focused on worldly achievements. The suffering here arises from detachment, dissociation, and living trapped in our heads. Being overly emotional is the second way we suffer: by taking everything "personally" and by feeling overwhelmed, anxious, fearful, and/or depressed. This happens when we're sensitive and vulnerable but lacking the support of awake awareness, as our ego-identified system is too small to handle full emotional life.

Having a closed heart is as painful as going through our day with an overwhelmed emotional heart. Like Scrooge in Charles Dickens's *A Christmas Carol,* we can live most of our lives with a closed heart and even be successful in the world without knowing there is an alternative. However, the opportunity for transformation and a shift into open-hearted awareness is available to each one of us—no matter where we're located in the journey of our lives.

When we don't shift into open-hearted awareness, our hearts can be painfully closed, or they can be too open so that we're frequently overwhelmed. Then we end up looking to our thoughts to create a sense of self. The result is a small, mental sense of self that makes us fearful and unworthy. Sadly, a thought-based identity cuts us off from our greatest resources for connection, loving-kindness, and wellbeing. While identified solely with a mental self, we may not be able to hear the call of open-hearted awareness. No wonder we become confused about our own heart's desire and end up looking for love in all the wrong places.

Some people are caught in their emotional heart: feeling everything, worrying, and feeling wounded and unsupported most of the time. Shifting into open-hearted awareness has transformed many people who say they "pick up every feeling and are too sensitive to others' emotions." These people don't have to shut down. They can continue to feel others' emotions, but instead of holding them in their bodies, they can let emotions continue back through the open heart's door to the support of the field of awake awareness within and behind them.

Open-hearted awareness builds on emotional intelligence, which is the ability to recognize, distinguish, and articulate our emotions. It's also the capacity for understanding and appreciating the emotions of others and the way they communicate with us. Open-hearted awareness does not have to defend against emotions. From open-hearted awareness, we're able to "be with" emotions that formerly would have been overwhelming. From open-hearted awareness, we need not consider ourselves underdeveloped or weak if we go through what St. Teresa of Ávila called the "gift of tears."

Even when we've awakened from ego-identification, we still need to unlearn and relearn about love. What we call love, or what we think is love, is often mixed with a lot of early personal conditioning, old belief systems, and emotional attachments. When the heart doesn't go *out* to look for love, but looks instead back to its source—the ground of Being—we can discover unconditional love as who we have always been. Then this new experience of love can become the foundation from which relationships are formed. A whole different emotional way of being and seeing gives rise to a new, vastly more compassionate and connected way of relating.

Open-hearted awareness, which is operating from our heart-mind, begins to include necessary judging functions of the mind, but leaves behind the fear, separation, and controlling anger that made us "judgmental." Our normal judging functions are transformed by open-hearted awareness into discernment and discriminating wisdom. The judge, the critic, and the superego are not essential or rigidly fixed parts of the human psyche. As soon as we shift into open-hearted awareness, an immediate feeling of being nonjudgmental and more compassionate arises. We develop a more mature conscience, a sense of integrity, and an acceptance of what is, while having the capacity and motivation to change what needs to be changed.

Even when we are not as identified with thoughts or stories, some deeper moods and long-held emotions continue to arise. But in the context of open-hearted awareness, this is the natural phase of detoxing our repressed emotions and returning the energy they held back to our natural life force. Discovering open-hearted awareness is the beginning of a whole new way of being with emotions that can only be done from this state, which can become a stable stage in our development.

Open-hearted awareness begins with the discovery of the support of awake awareness. Then we feel not only love for others, but also tenderness and compassion for ourselves. We can feel both vulnerable and courageous because our foundation is awake awareness. Our emotional heart will no longer need to create a shell of protection around itself. When we experience a great loss or hurt that feels like "brokenheartedness," we now realize that our heart is not broken. It's actually the heart's protective shell of defenses breaking open to allow us to feel all emotions fully. Open-hearted awareness gives us the capacity to experience a full emotional life without shutting down or being overwhelmed. We can feel both vulnerable and courageous, while knowing that—essentially—all is well. When we first shift into the phase of embodied presence, there is often a period of deep rest and just being with the inner silence, stillness, and wellbeing that's not based in thought or action. When we shift into open-hearted awareness, there is a generous acceptance of others and ourselves that makes us not passive, but curious and creative instead.

In the shift from embodied presence, we move from unconditioned awake awareness to the unconditional love of open-hearted awareness. One person offered this description: "I feel like I'm moving from awareness aware of awareness to love loving love." The quality of the formless awareness meeting physical form can feel like a fabric of love, a dance of opposites, or a field of unity. The key here is that heart-knowing allows us to experience our identity not only as a limited, separate, physical person, but also as someone inextricably connected with a community, the fabric of love, and something greater than our individual self.

Awakened Heart-Wisdom

When people first discover open-hearted awareness, they often report feeling relief, as though they've let go of a burden. When you first make contact with open-hearted awareness, you may feel its physical and energetic forms of unconditional love, bliss, or stillness. People report that when they know from open-hearted awareness rather than from their heads, they feel safe, connected, curious, and tenderhearted. This is a profoundly beautiful experience for many, who spontaneously describe it in poetic phrases such as "having a heart as big as the world," "feeling a sweet sadness," "knowing all is well," or "feeling a tender trust."

When people who have shifted into open-hearted awareness are asked, "What do you know from open-hearted awareness?" they often reply:

> Love—a sense of unity, oneness, compassion, and relationship.
>
> Safety—everything is okay, all is well.
>
> There is no fear, shame, or worry at all.
>
> Nothing is missing. And nothing needs to be pushed away.
>
> Who I am cannot be threatened.
>
> I thought I was lost, but it turns out open-hearted awareness has been here all along.

When you shift into open-hearted awareness, you may realize that its tenderness and vulnerable strength are connected to the vastness of Being. Many people also report becoming more involved in activities like social justice, service to the needy, animal rescue, and other spontaneous acts of charity. The day after 9/11, I found myself drawn to Lower Manhattan, and over the next few years I continued working with families who'd lost loved ones. I met many people nationwide who felt called to be present during the 9/11 tragedy, and when I talked with them it was clear that many seemed to be acting from open-hearted awareness.

When we operate from open-hearted awareness, we no longer listen to the internal narrator and the random chatter of our automatic thoughts. These voices become little more than background noise, like children playing in the backyard. Awake awareness has moved into the foreground of the mind, where it's quiet. We're no longer exhausted by efforts to organize our thoughts. We feel embodied, refreshed, and alert, with the potential for knowing what needs to be known, when we need to know it. We're no longer looking to thought to know. As we experience and perceive through open-hearted awareness, we allow more of the world in, and more amazingly, we also stop projecting our thoughts and emotions onto others.

From open-hearted awareness the world seems lit up from within, and what once seemed "other" is actually interconnected. Open-hearted awareness can shift you into a new way of seeing. Your eyes connect not only to the brain but through your heart-mind to the ground of Being. Your ego-based identity is no longer looking out of your eyes. Instead, looking from open-hearted awareness is like seeing directly through the eyes of your awakened heart, without the thoughts, beliefs, and projections of the mind interpreting your experience. There are no fears or worries about what the other person might be thinking; there is trust that you will know how to respond—with a natural, intuitive heart-mindfulness.

Trust and patience are needed during the transition from ordinary consciousness to open-hearted awareness. When we begin to shift, our thinking and ego functions are not yet fully online. Therefore we may feel that the transition is too slow, but it's vital not to give up. There is the stage of waiting for the response, without looking to the mind—even if you feel no response will come. The ego-mind says, "Hurry up!" or, "See, I said you'd become a lazy couch-potato without me as the leader." But the new wiring will lead to another way of speaking from open-hearted awareness. One person offered this description: "Speaking becomes like breathing. It's easy and natural and just flows without needing to plan what you're going to say."

Amazingly, we don't have to try to create this experience of open-hearted awareness. We just need to learn how to shift out of the ego-identified mind into heart-mind; over time we grow more and more familiar with being this way. Living from open-hearted awareness makes you feel like you've come home again, like you're whole again, and like you'll never be alone again.

GLIMPSE 1 **Open-Hearted Connecting**

The Buddhist Tonglen practice is interesting because it's the opposite of some contemporary practices like breathing in positive energy and love and breathing out negative energy and suffering. Tonglen practice is a relative-level practice of giving and receiving, in which you are instructed to breathe into your heart

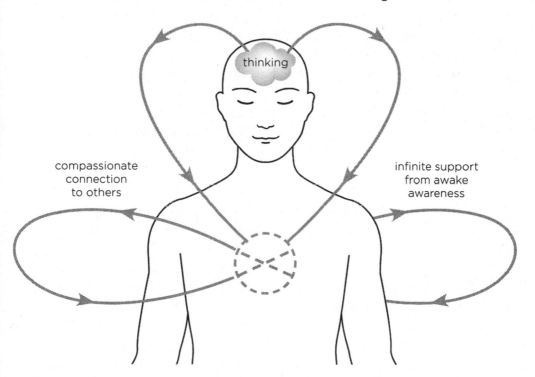

FIGURE 4. Relocating to open-hearted awareness.

the suffering of others, with the wish to take away their ignorance and pain. Then you breathe out of your heart, sending good feelings, compassion, and happiness to particular individuals or groups of people.

This next practice is a version of an ultimate-level Tonglen practice. It is the same as the relative-level Tonglen practice, except that when you breathe into your heart, you don't stop at taking the suffering into your body. Instead, you allow it to continue through your heart space to the support of awake awareness behind your back. Then you feel the support of awake awareness coming into your body. Next, you feel the loving awareness go out to the person in front of you and connect to the awake awareness within and behind them. As you breathe in, you feel their ignorance and suffering coming back to and through your body—and then back to the support of awake awareness. The key experience could be summarized this way: *awake awareness has your back.* We can learn to receive and give from here. Figure 4 is a visual representation of this practice.

In this practice, take a few minutes to glimpse open-hearted awareness for yourself.

1. Sit comfortably, eyes open or closed, and simply be aware of all your senses. Notice the activity of thinking in your head.

2. First, unhook local awareness from thoughts in your head. Next, let it move down through your neck and into your chest, and know—directly—from within your upper body.

3. Become familiar with this kind of direct knowing from within; it neither looks down from your head nor looks back up to your thoughts.

4. Feel the awareness and aliveness together: rest without going to sleep and stay aware without going to thought to know.

5. Feel that awareness can know both the awareness and aliveness from within your body.

6. Notice a feeling of an open-heart space from within the center of your chest.

7. Feel as if you have relocated from your head to this open-heart space, from which you are now knowing and aware.

8. Notice that you can invite and welcome any thoughts down, so that you can remain at home in your heart and still have information from the office of your head come to you via Wi-Fi.

9. Be here, receive light with your eyes, and look out from the eyes of open-hearted awareness.

10. Feel how local awareness can move behind and through your heart space to become aware of spacious awareness behind your body.

11. Surrender local awareness until local awareness merges with spacious awareness so that it's aware of itself.

12. Wait until you are knowing from within the timeless, contentless, thought-free awareness.

13. Notice that as you surrender awareness, the field of spacious awareness behind your heart already includes your whole body.

14. Feel how awareness knows itself as pure awareness behind your body, and as the aliveness within your body from your toes to your head. Feel the joy and lightness of this inner-body presence.

15. Now notice how local awareness is also moving and looking out at the world through your heart space.

16. Be aware from this field of spacious awareness— behind, within, and in front. It's simultaneously spacious and pervasive: a continuous field of awareness, stillness, and aliveness.

17. Notice that you don't have to alternate being aware outside and then inside. Awareness is both outside and inside at the same time.

18. Without going to thought, ask, "What does open-hearted awareness know?"

19. Simply let go and let be. Rest in this new knowing and flowing; see from being.

Notice the loving awareness happening effortlessly.

THE NEW NORMAL

11

THE NEXT STAGE
OF HUMAN DEVELOPMENT

We are not human beings having a spiritual experience.
We are spiritual beings having a human experience.

PIERRE TEILHARD DE CHARDIN[1]

Over the past thirty years as a practicing psychotherapist and meditation teacher, I've had the privilege of listening to thousands of people share their inner journeys with me. I've seen the full range of people's development unfold before my eyes. Folks from diverse nationalities, socioeconomic groups, races, genders, and ages have given me the opportunity to work with them. My clients have included graduate students, individuals in psychiatric halfway houses, college professors, corporate CEOs, homeless people, firemen, doctors, recovering alcoholics, full-time parents, artists, actors, ministers, plumbers, yoga teachers, and a tugboat captain.

Over the six years I worked at a community mental health clinic in Brooklyn, I discovered that clients with challenging brain chemistry, or those who lacked early sufficient nurturing, could still have a direct experience of awake awareness as their ground of Being. This experience of recognizing who they are at the root—a kind of basic goodness or original innocence—proved deeper and more impactful on my clients than the equally important work of helping them grow up in areas in which they were stunted. They realized their true nature had never been damaged, and they were able to see that the traumatic events of the past were no longer occurring in the here and now. One client reported: "Now that I know the normal me, I don't care if people think I'm not normal." Another announced: "I feel so great these days. Trying to be 'a somebody' was exhausting. It was driving me crazy." Many of the people I worked with immediately recovered their sense of humor and lightness of being. They still had some disabilities, but once an individual has glimpsed and connected with the ground of Being, she or he can better deal with the many unresolved emotional issues that accumulated all throughout life.

Many private-practice clients who came to me for awareness-based psychotherapy were sometimes outwardly successful in their careers, family lives, and communities. Most were baffled about the cause of their pain. Though they all had the same underlying reason for their suffering, each one presented different symptoms: depression, anxiety, addiction, despair, alienation, fear, worthlessness, self-loathing, or resentment. They all had grown up in most areas of their lives. Some had done years of psychotherapy, meditation, or other forms of self-improvement, but most had reached a place of unbearable dissatisfaction. Even with all their success and ego strength, they would report: "I can't figure it out," "I can't bear it," "I can't go on like this," "Nothing that worked before is working now," "I'm overwhelmed and can't handle so much pain," or, "Is this all there is?" These clients felt as if they'd hit some sort of wall: an emotional bottom or, more likely, a ceiling of growth. Most people discover by midlife, if not sooner, that even the most successful, well-maintained ego-identity will end up feeling dissatisfied because it's not capable of living a fully intimate human life.

Many of my clients had already tried to fix their problems by altering external situations and behaviors or by changing internal thoughts and attitudes. Having given up on escape, they tried to make the best of their situations by decorating the walls of the ruts in which they were stuck. This particular population had reached the limit of their current operating system: their ego-based identity. To grow up further, they needed to begin the process of awakening beyond ego-identification.

If we don't wake up out of ego-identification and grow up psychologically, we may find ourselves caught in a midlife or quarter-life crisis. Current research shows that people in their twenties are reaching higher levels of stress and depression than in any previous generation.[2] Unless we grow up into a new identity, we may regress back to adolescentlike behaviors, settle for a false persona, shut down into depression, or feel continually overwhelmed with anxiety. We may act out or try to medicate ourselves with an addiction. We can intentionally begin shifting out of ego-identification and learn to rely on the ground of Being *before* a crisis occurs. Then if a life crisis happens—one that might otherwise have led to a dark night of the soul—it can be experienced as beneficial growing pains, emotional detoxification, and rewiring to live from open-hearted awareness.

I began to notice that many of my clients and students were beginning to awaken beyond conventional developmental models. I've seen people move into another stage of awakening right before my eyes. For some, the shift happens unintentionally and spontaneously, often born out of crisis. These people may experience a breakdown before they can shift and break through. A few make this shift simply by opening to the light of awake awareness, but many have already been going through their dark night of the soul when I meet them. Some people simply surrender, stop searching and struggling, and allow themselves to open. Others kick and scream, leaving fingernail marks as they try to hold on. Some people need to feel the fire at their backsides—the sting of heat and the fear of getting burned—before they're willing to let go of old ego defenses and shift into a new sense of being. Yet more and more people I currently work with intentionally take a leap into the unknown, allowing themselves to rest there, letting go of whatever they were holding onto, while continuing to show up and grow up in their lives.

The question that emerges today is: Can the average individual access the potential for a new stage of adult human development that previously seemed limited to only a few wise women and men? Can we choose to do this *before* a breakdown or without joining a monastery? As we combine modern psychology, neuroscience, and ancient wisdom, we can start mapping the particular changes needed to initiate and support the next stage of growth. To expand the potential of our full human development, we need to explore and study this new stage of life together.

The Beginnings of the Model of Human Development

When my nephew Justin was five years old, we went fishing together for the first time. That summer, he was so excited about fishing with his uncle that he talked about it every day for weeks before I arrived. When we finally stood side by side at the pond with a single fishing pole, Justin wouldn't—and developmentally *couldn't*—share the pole with me.

"One more fish, and I'll share it." His five-year-old voice was full of determination. "Ten more minutes of my turn, and then you can try." But my nephew couldn't let go. The following year, when Justin was six, he was delighted to share. What a difference a year can make! We all know, from our experience and from observing others, how radically we change as we grow throughout our early lives.

In the early 1900s, anthropologists and developmental psychologists began to realize that children worldwide, regardless of their culture or environment, tend to reach developmental milestones in the same order. Using careful, scientific observation, these social scientists were able to delineate common stages and transitions as people grow up.

Stages and levels of human development have been observed in many areas. Psychologist Jean Piaget famously worked with cognitive development; physician Margaret Mahler researched early-childhood development. Psychoanalyst Erik Erikson mapped the stages of life from infancy through adulthood. Lawrence Kohlberg explored stages of moral development, while Carol Gilligan researched ethical development in the context of the female gender. More recently, Ken Wilber extended the concept of developmental studies into areas such as spirituality, meditation, and consciousness.

When we refer to normal human development, we're discussing the mammal called *Homo sapiens,* and like all other animals, we humans have a natural development that's typical within our species. Both "nature" (our biological, genetic makeup) and "nurture" (our relationship with caregivers, environment, and social learning) contribute to normal human development. A unique thing about human development is a type of consciousness that allows us to observe the internal contents of our minds and the external patterns in the world. However, this self-reflective ability of human consciousness, called "self-awareness," may have become overdeveloped and creates a limited sense of self, which is what we need to awaken from.

Early psychological descriptions of the full human development have ended in the stage of ego-identification based on conceptual thinking. Western psychologists tell us that infants do not come into the world with a sense of self. We develop a sense of self at the same time we develop conceptual or representational thinking: from age eighteen months to two years. At this age, we develop self-representations, which are mental images of one's self, and object-representations, which are internalized images of other people. Conceptual thinking and self-awareness are important developments that move us toward independence, allow us to function, and help us relate with others. Self-awareness is also the way we create a distinct self-image that's important for ego function. This normal way of distinguishing "me" (as in "my body") from surroundings is important for surviving and thriving. We've all watched two year olds exercise this new development: *My* toy," "*My* mommy," and, "I do by *myself!*"

Extending the Model of Human Growth

Discovering a new foundation for identity is necessary to grow up. In fact, the later stages of emotional and psychological work that lead to essential wellbeing cannot be done until after awakening begins. To achieve this next stage, we must extend the developmental models and create new ways of growing into these next stages. Just as parents support a child's progress through each level, we also need to support each other's awakening and growth.

Although awakening is different for everyone, there seems to be an unfolding process with common principles and stages. Many spiritual traditions acknowledge that there are stages of development after the initial shift of awakening. For example, even in traditions like Zen, which emphasizes sudden initial awakening (*kensho* or *satori*), there's an acknowledgement of the need for maturation. Zen teacher Tozan identifies five stages of development after the initial recognition. The Dzogchen tradition refers to four progressive stages of recognition, realization, stabilization, and expression. Christian mysticism discusses the movement through purgation, illumination, and union. The Mahamudra tradition describes four stages: one-pointedness, same taste, nondiscrimination, and nonmeditation. Contemporary teacher of awakening, Adyashanti, describes stages of "head awakening, heart awakening, gut awakening, and root awakening." Although each of these is described in different cultural languages, they all agree that there are stages of unfolding after initial awakening.

In order to continue developing past a certain point of adulthood, we need to shift our identity into the awareness to which all lines of development appear. We can bring together psychological knowledge and ancient wisdom about awakening to reach a new stage of development. Most people reading this book are already at a level that's mature enough to begin the awakening training discussed here.

This new model of human development is built on the previous one. Although no model can be static because people do not grow in the same cookie-cutter way, there are general principles that can be very helpful to recognize. I propose a consciousness model that describes three traditional stages of psychological growth—*dependence, independence,* and *socialization*—and three parallel stages of awakening—*transcendence, embodiment,* and *interconnectedness.* I'll refer to transcendence as "waking-up," embodiment as "waking-in," and interconnectedness as "waking-out."

EGO-DEVELOPMENT STAGES	AWAKENING STAGES
Dependence	Waking-up (transcendence)
Independence	Waking-in (embodiment)
Socialization	Waking-out (interconnectedness)

When we come into the world as infants, we're unable to take care of ourselves and are *dependent* upon adults for survival. In the first stage of life, we form strong bonds with our caregivers. As we grow older and are able to fend for ourselves, we develop *independence*. As we get older still, it's important that our ego functions continue to develop, that we continually internalize new levels of information, and that we continue to grow emotionally so that we're ultimately able to live independently. *Socialization* requires children to begin sharing and cooperating with others. By young adulthood, we've learned to interact with others at work and take on roles in our communities. In order to develop empathy and compassion, we learn to see another person's point of view and to feel what it would be like to be in their shoes.

It is possible to recognize and describe these stages in contemporary, accessible language. Awakening begins with waking-up by transcending ego-identification to abide in awake awareness, continues with waking-in to our body and emotions, and then moves to waking-out to relationships and functioning in the world. Waking-up knows from awake awareness. Waking-in knows from awake awareness embodied. Waking-out knows from open-hearted awareness.

WAKING-UP

There are two parts to this stage: the first is waking-up *out of* ego-identification, and the second is waking-up *into* awake awareness as our new operating system. When we're looking from awake awareness, we're immediately free of the suffering of greed and fear. We have shifted our identity from ego-identification to witnessing self and knowing from nonconceptual awareness.

In waking-up, what we're transcending is not our ego functions, not our bodies, not our personalities, but our ongoing process of ego-identification. One of the main reasons we don't naturally develop into the first stage of awakening is that our ego strengths and defenses, which were so vital for early development, are now keeping us from developing further. Like kindergarteners who have a hard time letting go of their parents' hands on the first day of school, it can be difficult for us to let go of our familiar ego-identification. Developing healthy ego function is important for getting through school, learning a job skill, building a career, and raising a family. But because we've created a limited ego-identification out of conceptual thinking and ego functions, we've created a defense against our next stage of growth! In fact, it seems the smarter we get, the more complex our defenses against letting go of an old identity become. We will discover that we do go through rewiring of ego functions like memory and language when we shift into awake awareness as the ground of our Being.

Waking-up is an important but dramatic change in life. As we go through the initial phase of letting go, it might seem like we're going backward or falling into a void—and it can feel dangerous and frightening. One student reported that transitioning through not-knowing "feels like I'm letting go of all I know, letting go of solid ground—and moving into a gap of not-knowing." If we stop with the first part of waking-up out of ego-identification, fear of the unknown can paralyze us. Our strong ego defenses tell us to "avoid the void." We need to continue to the second part: waking-up into awake awareness.

Although it may seem strange or esoteric to the average person on the street, waking-up is actually natural and can become the new natural. For both a baby and a person in an early stage of awakening—a "baby being"—a sense of safety and trust are essential. For the baby, safety is found in physical contact and healthy bonding with caregivers, which is known as *attachment*. A solid sense of the physical body contacting other bodies, of being held and comforted, leads to a healthy, secure psychological foundation.

Instead of finding identity in attachment to another person, a baby being's identity is founded first through nonattachment: the letting go of holding onto the physical world, his or her own body, other people, and mental self-images. Then the baby being finds security and trust in nonphysical awake awareness and changing aliveness. Here's a table that illustrates the commonality and differences between the first stage of growing up and the first stage of awakening.

FIRST STAGE OF CHILD DEVELOPMENT	FIRST STAGE OF AWAKENING
Issue: security and trust	**Issue:** security and trust
Mode: physical bonding	**Mode:** awake awareness as ground
Behavior: holding	**Behavior:** letting go
Task: attachment	**Task:** nonattachment

WAKING-IN

We begin to wake in as we experience that formless awake awareness is not separate from energy and forms. Waking-in brings the formless awake awareness together with our human body. Our identity moves from witnessing self to Being. The early stages of a child's development unfold by themselves, but later stages need training, support, and reinforcement in order to reach these potential higher stages. For instance, the stage called *school-age development* does not occur by itself. Children at this age have the natural capacity to read and write, but they won't develop to the next stage unless they actually train those skills. Waking-in works in a similar way. We have the capacity to wake in and live from an embodied, awareness-based knowing and identity. As we grow up and awaken, we need to be actively involved and learn how to intentionally participate in the unfolding process.

Upon initially waking-up, we are free of much of the internal suffering of egoic craving, aversion, worry, and depression. However, we can get spaced out, remaining detached from the ability to live a fully embodied human life. Until you can continue to wake in and wake out, you can remain ethically relative and emotionally detached.

Waking-in is where waking-up meets growing up. In order to continue to wake in, we learn how to remain grounded in awareness inherent within physical form. When awake awareness becomes embodied, we discover natural qualities of courage, compassion, and acceptance that help us grow relationally, ethically, and emotionally. Awake awareness is our common ground of Being. When we wake in, we discover our individual human being as an innocent and wise "Being." From here, the core stories and the old feelings of shame—"I'm not good enough," "Something's wrong with me," "I'm unlovable"—are no longer convincing.

On the ultimate level, unfolding happens by itself. The learning required to embody Being is not done by the conceptual thinking mind, but by the new knowing. Awake awareness unfolds by itself, and local awareness is active and has curiosity, intentionality, and creativity.

WAKING-OUT

Waking-in naturally leads to a realization of our unity with all people and all creation so that we feel a spontaneous, compassionate motivation and begin to wake out. The big shift is in the experience of our identity. When we shift, we're no longer limited to feeling like only a separate, individual, physical person. Instead, we're also interconnected with all life, the same way a wave is inseparable from the ocean. From open-hearted awareness, we feel love and sensitivity toward others and ourselves, yet we're not overwhelmed by our vulnerability because we also feel a fearless support. When we begin to wake out, we discover heart mindfulness, which is the ability to connect to others and rewire so we can live from a flow state—as we learn to do from Being.

The Relationship between Waking-Up and Growing Up

It's important to develop psychologically *and* to progress through levels of consciousness. Ken Wilber says, "Stages are how we grow up; states are how we wake up."[3] Wilber calls the way we progress through levels of consciousness "state-stages," and the way of moving through our developmental stages "structure-stages." We know the enormous difference when we grow from one stage to another, the way my nephew did when he matured enough to share his fishing rod. We also can see the dramatic difference between the everyday-mind state and seeing from awake awareness.

You can be more developed in psychological structure-stages or consciousness-based state-stages, and many people focus on either meditation or psychology, as if one will somehow include the other naturally. We cannot see our structures of psychological development by focusing on internal meditation states. Your meditation experience will be interpreted through the lens of the structure of your current level of development. However, without meditation and awareness training, you will not naturally develop subtle levels of consciousness simply by growing up.

During the state-stage development, using inquiry and meditation, we're not just having restful meditative states; we're also changing the structure of our brains and shifting our identity. Through recent studies using the fMRI, we know now that meditation changes our brain not only in the short term, but also long term. Using meditation to change the way the brain processes emotions, information, and identity is one of the most important discoveries of modern times. When we use meditation to shift our identity, we can continue to grow up in new ways.

Identity moves from ego to self to Being. This awake-identity process is only available when growing up and waking-up meet. The awake-identity stage of development allows us to detox our repressed emotional storehouses and rewire our brains so that we can respond to life rather than merely reacting.

Two things have become clear to me from years of observing people as they go through the process of growing up and awakening. First, no ego-identity—no matter how strong—can live a fully intimate, happy human life. If we don't wake up, we'll experience perpetual dissatisfaction. Second, in this day and age, it's actually more difficult and dangerous to try "holding it together" and "doing the best we can" from the level of ego-identification than it is to begin the journey of awakening. We just need to know it's possible to awaken, and we need a sense of how to proceed. Our choice today is to break down, shut down, act out—or break through and wake up.

Awake awareness itself never develops or grows up. At its essence, awake awareness is always the same. It's inherent within all changing dimensions of our experience, just the way space exists within atoms. Awake awareness is similar to physical space in that it is within us, invisible and pervasive, but different from physical space because it is a knowing space. When this unconditioned awake awareness becomes primary and includes our human conditioning, then there is the potential for a new, higher stage of human development. Meditation training, study, and preliminary spiritual practices are part of the spiritual and meditation lines of development. But you can glimpse awake awareness at any time, regardless of your developmental level. You can awaken with no prior meditation training or spiritual practice. Awake awareness does not go through any developmental process. Whether it is recognized or unrecognized, awareness is always already awake. Ultimately, no ego-identified person can awaken; the one who starts the journey does not arrive. Ego-identification, as who we take ourselves to be, is what we awaken from. Awakening is when awake awareness becomes the primary dimension of our consciousness, the ground of our Being.

You can wake up, but still not grow up. Making progress in meditation skills or mystical states alone will not lead to full human development. In fact, you can initially awaken from your ego-identification and remain in a detached, nonjudgmental witness location. From this location of a spacious awareness, we are free of much of the internal suffering of egoic craving, aversion, worry, and depression. However, until we continue to wake in and wake out, we may remain ethically neutral, emotionally detached, and spaced out.

We have examples of spiritual teachers from all countries who had initial awakenings. Some of these teachers act in immature ways: abusing people, power, money, sex, drugs, and alcohol, while claiming they've transcended basic ethical behavior. In *Toward a Psychology of Awakening,* John Welwood points out this potential trap: "There is a tendency to use spiritual practice to try to rise above our emotional and personal issues—all those messy, unresolved matters that weigh us down. I call this tendency to avoid or prematurely transcend basic human needs, feelings, and developmental tasks spiritual bypassing."[4]

You can grow up, but only to a certain level, without waking-up. Our thought-based ego-identification is an operating system that, like a computer's operating system, has a limited capacity.

There is a limit to our human development unless we wake up out of our ego-identified sense of self and begin to live in awake awareness. Even if we're progressing well in our psychological growth, we eventually hit a wall because the small sense of self has limited capacity. An ego-based sense of self can only get us so far. If we want to continue developing, we're going to have to shift out of ego-identification—which in turn requires waking-up. Living an awakened life also requires waking-in, waking-out, and growing up.

You do not have to wait until you're fully mature, have your life "together," or reach old age before you begin to wake up. In fact, many of the opportunities for initial awakening come during periods of transition, crisis, loss, and chaos in people's external and internal lives. This is a time when the ego-identification collapses because it can't maintain control or handle life's intensity. You can begin awakening now, before you get your life completely together or before it falls apart.

WHERE GROWING UP AND AWAKENING MEET

While the stages of early adulthood are culturally supported with rituals and celebrations—graduations, weddings, first jobs, children's births, housewarming parties, promotions, and so on—the subtler awakening stages of life remain culturally unacknowledged. The meeting place of awakening and growing up is the shift of our identity, or sense of who we are. Only by shifting from ego-identification to ground of Being do we have the capacity to handle a fully emotional, intimate life and function with compassion. Open-hearted awareness allows us to feel life fully, without becoming overwhelmed and anxious, depressed or addicted. Only from open-hearted awareness can we bear what seems unbearable.

Now that we live in a time of global access to information and dialogue between cultures and spiritual traditions, my hope is that our understanding of the way awakening and growing up combine and unfold will support people proceeding to these next stages of human development.

GLIMPSE 1 **The Memory Door**

One of the helpful pointers often used by meditation teachers is to tell a student not to attempt to recreate a positive meditation experience or chase after a good state. Instead, the instruction is to simply let everything arise naturally without hope, fear, or expectation. This is good advice. However, here is a way to use memory to open a door to what is here now.

A first-time student came up to me during a break at a daylong introduction to open-hearted awareness. She said, "I'm very frustrated. I don't get the spaciousness or the peace or the wellbeing that everyone else seems to be experiencing." I asked her, "Can you think of a time when you *did* feel peace, spaciousness, and wellbeing?"

She looked perplexed, but then said, "Oh yeah. A couple of weeks ago, when I went hiking with my friends and we walked to the top of a hill and looked at the view."

"Great," I said. "Let's use that past experience to help you realize that the same capacity is here now." I did the following exercise with her, which took just a few minutes.

Please adapt this exercise to a particular remembered experience of your own. Try it now after you read this example:

1. Close your eyes. Now remember when you were hiking. In your mind, see and feel every detail of that day. Hear the sounds, smell the smells, and feel the air on your skin. Notice the enjoyment of being with your friends. Feel yourself hiking that last stretch as you get toward the top of the hill.

2. Now, visualize and feel yourself as you have reached your goal and are looking out over the wide-open vista. Feel that openness, your connection to nature, your sense of peace and wellbeing. Having reached your goal, feel what it's like when there's no more seeking and nothing to do. See that wide-open sky with no object to think about, and fully feel this deep sense of wellbeing.

3. Now begin to slowly but completely let go of the visualization, the past, and all associated memories. Remain connected to the joy and freedom of being that is here now. Slowly open your eyes. Realize that the wellbeing that was experienced then is also here now, and it does not require you to go to any particular place in the past or the future once it's discovered to be within.

GLIMPSE 2 **Cave of the Heart**

This practice is similar to the yogic meditation practice called *nirvikalpa samadhi*, a practice of absorption without any self-referencing, and what Tibetans call the practice of "the mind of black near attainment." It's also similar to *yoga nidra* ("yogic sleep"), a practice of deep rest. You may be familiar with the yoga nidra practice called *shavasana,* commonly done at the end of yoga class, which has great benefits for resting the entire nervous system on a very deep level. It is like an even higher-powered "power nap."

This practice is one in which you can experience no-self in a way that's more restful than sleep, yet you remain wide awake without content or a self. Most glimpse practices have revealed a pristine, infinite day-sky view. In the Cave of the Heart practice, the experience of no-self is like the infinite night sky: an experience of black-velvet awareness.

Ramana Maharshi, the great modern sage, often recommended two practices. One was self-inquiry that directly looks into "Who am I?" The second practice, which is less well known, is what Ramana called "resting in the cave of the heart on the right side of the chest." He never described in much detail how to do this practice, but I played around with it to see what it felt like. In using local awareness to go within the cave of the heart, it seemed to open up a profound dimension of awareness. Here's a version that makes sense to me and that seems to work for many others. Many of my students say this is one of their favorite practices.

On the left side of your chest is your biological heart. People feel that their emotional heart is at the top of their chests near their throats. The heart chakra—or energy center—has been described as being in the lower middle part of the chest. On the right side of the chest is the cave of the heart—the safe space of the heart. It's where the physical heart would be if it were on the right side of your chest—but instead there is a space.

In this exercise, you unhook local awareness from thought and drop it down to the safe, restful place that is the cave of the heart. It's a way of resting deeper than sleep, though you are wide awake. When your body rests deeply, the normal tendency is for our minds to fall asleep. Here, when you allow your body and brain to rest deeply, see if there's also an awareness that remains wide awake—a kind of black-velvet clarity, like the night sky.

Some people report that a short period of resting in the cave of the heart makes them feel like they've had the equivalent of the best full-night's sleep of their lives. Enjoy.

1. Sit comfortably or lie on your back. Close your eyes, and take a full breath or two so that you feel alert, alive, and awake.

2. Now allow local awareness to unhook from thought. Let it slowly drift down like a leaf below your neck and find a safe, restful place inside your upper body on the ride side of your chest. This safe space may feel like it has a little light, or pinpoints of light—or it may be completely dark, like black velvet.

3. Allow your awareness to rest in this black-velvet silence without falling asleep. Feel each cell drinking in this rest and renewal. Let awake awareness surrender into the cave of the heart and rest as this deep, dazzling darkness, deeper than sleep, yet wide awake. Remain here for ten to fifteen minutes, or until you naturally arise or open your eyes.

12

EFFORTLESS MINDFULNESS

The meditator said, "I experience a state which is not created through
meditation yet which lasts for a while, by itself." "Right on!" Jamgön
Kongtrül said. "Now spend the rest of your life training in that!"

TULKU URGYEN RINPOCHE[1]

Mindfulness has become very popular in our culture today.
Applications of mindfulness have been found effective in
many different contexts: psychotherapy, spirituality, pain
reduction, addiction treatment, and improved mental focus. *Effortless
mindfulness,* a next stage in mindfulness training, is very helpful for
people who have difficulty concentrating at work or school because it
teaches a way to focus from spacious awareness.

One of my student's teenage son, who was diagnosed with Attention
Deficit Hyperactivity Disorder (ADHD) and struggling in class, came
to me specifically to learn effortless mindfulness. When we met, he was
having difficulty on tests and completing longer written assignments.
Frustrated, he had angry outbursts at school and home. He told me
that, paradoxically, he became more distracted the more he tried to
concentrate. To this, I said, "It looks like trying hard to pay attention
is costly to you." He joked, "Yeah, I was paying so much attention that
I felt like I was going to go broke."

I asked him what activities he enjoyed, and he told me he loved
playing the trumpet in his school band. He also mentioned this
was the only time he felt he could stay focused. I taught him to use

effortless mindfulness, and he took to it right away. He reported, "I know this way of focusing! It's what I do when I play music."

I explained how to intentionally access effortless mindfulness whenever and wherever he needed it, and he was able to master the skills involved in six weeks. He learned to step back into spacious awareness, which gave him the ability to focus from a panoramic view. He was able to observe his emotions of frustration and anger when they first arose, and then to realize he had a choice not to act them out. By the end of the next semester, effortless mindfulness was second nature for him, and he was doing better than ever in school and actually enjoyed learning.

After helping many more people learn this new way of focusing, I now believe that the phenomenon we call "attention deficit" should be renamed "attention overload" because we are trying to overuse a type of attention that has limits. It's good that we have another option: effortless mindfulness.

Mindfulness is important no matter where you are in the process of awakening because ultimately mindfulness is the connection to what is happening in the relative world. Mindfulness is the ability to remain connected and related from any level of mind. However, what you can be mindful of depends on what level of mind you're mindful from.

Deliberate Mindfulness and Effortless Mindfulness

In his book *Rainbow Painting*, Tulku Urgyen Rinpoche says that in Dzogchen there are six kinds of mindfulness, and then he talks about the two main categories: "There are two types of mindfulness: deliberate and effortless."[2] You can use deliberate mindfulness as an initial practice leading to effortless mindfulness, or you can begin meditation training with effortless mindfulness. When you start with effortless mindfulness, you still get all the benefits of deliberate mindfulness.

Deliberate mindfulness is the basic form of mindfulness most of us have encountered. The Theravada Buddhist word for mindfulness (in the Pali language) is *sati*, often translated as "remembering." But it does not mean remembering in the sense of recalling past events.

When used in the context of deliberate mindfulness, sati means remembering to return to the object of your focus when your attention wanders. Deliberate mindfulness requires us to continuously return—re-remembering and re-attending.

Lack of willpower is not the reason we lose focus. The reason we cannot stay focused is that the everyday mind we're looking from is always moving and changing. In deliberate mindfulness, we must continuously reapply ourselves to our task by actively re-creating not only the focus but "the focuser" over and over within the everyday mind.

The two most common practices of deliberate mindfulness are one-pointed attention and nonjudgmental witnessing of thoughts, feelings, and sensations. Traditionally, deliberate mindfulness refers to both: *shamatha* ("calm abiding") and *vipassana* ("insight"). Researchers have extensively studied both these types of deliberate mindfulness in recent years, and they refer to shamatha as "focused attention" (FA) and vipassana as "open monitoring" (OM).

Some traditions of deliberate mindfulness focus on stilling the chattering mind with disciplined concentration; others encourage a more patient approach based on gently returning every time the mind wanders. The first method of concentration uses practices like breath counting (from Zen) or the Nine Stages of Attentional Development (from Tibetan Buddhism) to sustain concentration until the ability is learned. The second method of deliberate mindfulness begins with the task of trying to sustain attention. Then, when the mind inevitably wanders, you become aware of being distracted and then bring back your attention again and again. This approach emphasizes nonjudgmental awareness over concentration.

Effortless mindfulness—the second type of mindfulness—is also called *innate mindfulness*. Effortless mindfulness doesn't mean that we don't have to make an initial effort. You aren't being asked to "do nothing" or to "try to be effortless." (Trying to be effortless can be quite an effort!) The adjective "effortless" refers to the discovery that awake awareness is spontaneously aware without our help or effort. Effortless awareness is a description of the way we naturally experience life when operating from awake awareness.

One way to begin effortless mindfulness is to have local awareness look back toward the mindful meditator. When the meditator is looked for, none can be found. Instead, spacious awareness is discovered to be effortlessly aware. Living from awake awareness, we are supported by that which is already aware. With this support, we are able to effortlessly focus from spacious awareness. There is no need to willfully concentrate from effortless mindfulness. Spacious awareness is the foundation of the awake-aware mind—which, unlike the everyday mind, is not made of moving thoughts—this is why you can focus and attend to things effortlessly. When awake awareness moves from the background to the foreground, our way of knowing is no longer located in or bounded by the contents of our consciousness.

We can be mindful from any of the five levels of mind I mentioned before: everyday mind, subtle mind, awake-aware mind, simultaneous mind, or heart-mind. Deliberate mindfulness is practiced from the first two levels of mind: everyday mind and subtle mind. Effortless mindfulness occurs from the next three levels of mind. Most importantly, we can't practice effortless mindfulness from everyday mind or subtle mind.

One famous modernizer of mindfulness meditation, Jon Kabat-Zinn, defines deliberate mindfulness like this: "Mindfulness means paying attention in a particular way: on purpose, in the present moment, and nonjudgmentally."[3] This definition can apply to deliberate mindfulness from both the everyday mind and subtle mind. Everyday mind has to intentionally try to be nonjudgmental because it is located in dualistic thought, which is always comparing and judging. However, one sign that you are mindful from the subtle mind is that you're naturally nonjudgmental. Deliberate mindfulness without an object, sometimes called "objectless shamatha," or choiceless awareness, is still viewing from the subtle-mind point of view.

Consider the difference between effortless breathing and deliberate breathing. Imagine having to remember every time you needed to take a breath. Noticing effortless mindfulness is like noticing that our breathing happens by itself. When looking from awake awareness, we need no effort to be effortlessly mindful. From effortless mindfulness, we have the ability to use local awareness for intentional focus while awake awareness remains wide open. Effortless mindfulness empowers us with the natural capability to be with our thoughts and emotions, without constant monitoring. We find effortless mindfulness by shifting to spacious awareness and then focusing from there.

There are two additional types of effortless mindfulness. When we shift to awake awareness embodied, we can utilize *nondual mindfulness.* The next type of effortless mindfulness is called *heart mindfulness,* which is being aware, not from transcendent spacious awareness or from embodied presence, but from open-hearted awareness.

In the gradual path many meditative approaches offer, effortless mindfulness is considered an advanced practice, but it can be just as easy for beginners to learn as deliberate mindfulness. Effortless mindfulness is somewhat like riding a bicycle on a gradual, downward-sloping road: once we learn to balance, we can coast without deliberately pedaling.

The Dzogchen tradition says, "Sustain primordially free awareness with innate mindfulness."[4] This saying is both a description of what happens on the level of awake awareness and an instruction for operating from awake-aware mind. Here, the first difference from deliberate mindfulness is that awake awareness is both the subject and the object. The second difference is that you're aware from within your body and mind rather than observing from outside. It is like saying: "Sustain your love for the person with whom you're totally in love." There is a quality of devotion, willingness, interest, focus, and also surrender. The sustaining is not done from any effort made by your current ego-identification or by the ego's will. Yet sustaining is an important instruction for stabilization, abiding, and expression that also avoids taking a too-passive attitude. Effortless mindfulness makes the transition from initial realization to the ability to live from primordial, free awareness. From open-hearted awareness, heart mindfulness is the connection from the infinite to the finite, and from each human being to other people and to the world.

In the Mahamudra tradition, the deliberate mindfulness way of focusing is called the "event perspective" because we're looking at events or the contents of our mind. Effortless mindfulness uses a method of focusing called the "mind perspective" because we change the direction of our focus to look back at the nature of our own mind. Effortless mindfulness often begins with the practice of awareness of awareness. This turning around of awareness is called an "orientation instruction." The effortless mindfulness practice of looking from spacious awareness is called "king of samadhi" and is described as a soaring eagle looking back at its nest.

Though used in Tibetan Buddhism, effortless mindfulness can be found in other meditation traditions as well. In his book *Mindfulness: A Practical Guide to Awakening,* Joseph Goldstein, cofounder of the Insight Meditation Society, writes that although most of the focus in Theravada Buddhism is on deliberate mindfulness, effortless mindfulness is nevertheless acknowledged as "unprompted mindfulness." Goldstein writes that unprompted mindfulness "arises spontaneously through the force of its own momentum. No particular effort is required. It's just happening by itself. In this state of effortless awareness, we can further discern the presence or absence of a reference point of observation, a sense of someone observing or being mindful."[5]

With effortless mindfulness, we have shifted to viewing from spacious awareness. We are in a different level of mind that is stable, calm, and able to remain naturally undistracted. Spacious awareness has the ability to effortlessly observe the arising of thoughts, feelings, emotions, and even subpersonalities—without needing to identify with them; to judge them; or to deny, oppose, or project them onto others. Like space itself, spacious awareness can be neither increased nor diminished by any forms arising within its field; there is only a natural acceptance of everything. Effortless mindfulness is like a mirror that reflects without judgment.

Deliberate mindfulness can be reached either by pulling back from the contents of the mind or by resting until the contents of the mind are separate from the mindful meditator. Effortless mindfulness is not a matter of progressively stepping back farther and farther, like an infinite regression to a bigger and bigger witness. It begins with turning awareness around to look through the observing ego. When we do so, the location of the observer opens or dissolves. The goal is to discover the absence of ego-identification and realize spacious awake awareness as our new foundation.

Two Approaches to Calm and Insight

Although the ultimate goal of awakening is the same, deliberate mindfulness and effortless mindfulness each approach calm abiding and insight differently. In effortless mindfulness, instead of trying to calm the contents of the mind, we step out of the everyday mind and into an already calm, alert, awake-aware mind. Deliberate mindfulness approaches calm abiding by using one-pointed concentration and loving-kindness meditation. One-pointed concentration means focusing on an object such as your breath, noticing nonjudgmentally when your attention wanders, and continually coming back to focus on the object. Loving-kindness meditation uses simple, positive phrases to generate feelings of emotional, physical, and mental wellbeing. Loving-kindness meditation creates calm abiding and reduces fear, hatred, and anger by affirming and feeling love toward yourself, loved ones, acquaintances, and even difficult people in your life.

One-pointed concentration represses the everyday mind and the default mode network. While it gives you a rest, it also represses some creativity, emotions, and higher functioning. The calm abiding of effortless mindfulness *balances* the default mode network rather than repressing it. Therefore self-referential mind wandering does not take us away, and we still have our creative abilities available. When using deliberate mindfulness, we look at our thoughts as if they were possessions or pieces on a chessboard that we can move around. Mingyur Rinpoche describes the effortless mindfulness approach:

> We access the mind of calm abiding through recognition. What do we recognize? Awareness: the ever-present knowing quality of mind, from which we are never separated for an instant. Even though normally we do not recognize awareness, we can no more live without

it than we can live without breathing. For this reason, I often use the terms shamatha and awareness meditation interchangeably. Discovering our own awareness allows us to access the natural steadiness and clarity of the mind, which exist independent of conditions and circumstances, and independent of our emotions and moods.[6]

In heart mindfulness we learn how to shift into the loving consciousness—ultimate bodhicitta—that always permeates the field with pervasive, compassionate wisdom. Rather than beginning with calm abiding, we start with the direct recognition of awake awareness and the profound discovery that awake-aware mind is already present, naturally calm, insightful, and loving.

When we're using effortless mindfulness and heart mindfulness, we start to relate to our thoughts and feelings more intimately. We can listen to the voices and needs of subpersonalities, with whom we used to be identified, but we no longer believe these parts are the center of who we are. Now we easily recognize these parts as mere ego functions—roles we could play—but not who we are. When we discover open-hearted awareness, we don't have to go back to ego-identification because nonconceptual awareness has shifted us out of our previous thought-based operating system. As we become free of ego-identification, we are no longer at the mercy of our moods, our fears for the future, or our regrets about the past.

The Effortless Mindfulness Experiment

Over the years, I have tested the effectiveness of effortless mindfulness in meditation workshops in many different settings. The thirty-four different groups of people I tested have ranged in size from 12 to 150 participants. Their levels of experience varied from beginner to long-time meditator.

For the experiment, the groups tried to maintain continuous focus while using two distinct styles of meditation: deliberate mindfulness and effortless mindfulness. I gave participants the following instruction: "Focus on the sensation of your breath, either at your nostrils or your belly, and to try to maintain continuous focus." As a means of measuring whether they were maintaining continuous focus, I asked participants to label their in-breaths with a number, counting from one to fifty. During the out-breath, I asked them not to use a number, but to "remain aware of the felt sense of the out-breath." I also instructed: "Try to continuously maintain focus on your breath without losing your count or letting your mind wander. If your mind wanders or you lose count, notice that. You can begin to count again from one or pick up where you left off."

In a recent group of eighty-five men and women, I started by asking people to use deliberate mindfulness first. Only two students out of eighty-five reported being able to maintain continuous focus without losing count. Then, after I spent fifteen minutes teaching the same group effortless mindfulness, eighty participants reported they were able to count to fifty without losing track.

I often conduct this experiment at the beginning of workshops without telling participants the purpose, so as not to influence their outcomes. I have alternated between giving the effortless and deliberate mindfulness exercises first. I've also had people act as a control group, asking them only to try counting fifty breaths without any other instructions. The results are always similar: in every group, an average of five percent of people counted to fifty breaths without any instructions, and about ten percent were successful using deliberate mindfulness. In contrast, eighty-five percent of meditators in my groups were able to count to fifty without losing track of their breaths when using effortless mindfulness.

The Advantages of Starting with Effortless Mindfulness

In deliberate mindfulness, we deconstruct ego-identification without providing an alternative foundation. When we step out of ego-identification, related ego defenses are also deconstructed, and a flood of unconscious material and repressed emotions may arise. The intensity of this flood can be difficult to bear when you don't have your old identity or a new foundation—a condition that's sometimes called the "gap of egolessness." Brown University neuroscience researcher Willoughby Britton, who has studied some of the potentially negative side effects of mindfulness meditation, says, "A lot of psychological material is going to come up and be processed. Old resentments, wounds, that kind of thing."[7]

Alternatively, I have found it a great advantage to start with the direct recognition of awake awareness so that we can avoid becoming trapped in the gap of egolessness. One important reason for beginning with effortless mindfulness is that you're immediately introduced to awake awareness, an infinite resource capable of coping with all difficult emotions. Beyond that, awake awareness is a much more powerful and compelling foundation for functioning in the world than ego-identification. Dealing with the gap of egolessness is difficult enough, but it's compounded when our ego defense mechanisms keep pulling us back to ego-identification. Many people get scared back to ego-identification. From awake-awareness, we can feel the fears, hear the doubts—and welcome them.

To practice deliberate mindfulness insight, you usually need a special place—a meditation hall, retreat center, or quiet room—to observe your internal experience. Conversely, effortless mindfulness insight can be done with your eyes open, in the middle of your day. It's crucial to realize that the type of attention used in deliberate mindfulness cannot be used to transition into effortless mindfulness.

Deliberate mindfulness approaches insight by using the four foundations of mindfulness found in the Satipatthana Sutta: the practice of observing four different types of internal objects. These four are body sensations, feelings of pleasantness and unpleasantness, consciousness, and mind objects. Practicing the four foundations of deliberate mindfulness deconstructs the mini-me by observing the parts of consciousness that create a sense of separation. Deliberate mindfulness leads to insight into who we are *not*. In contrast, effortless mindfulness insight allows us to realize the foundation of who we *are* by leading us to directly recognize awake awareness.

Five Foundations of Effortless Mindfulness

As a way of organizing effortless mindfulness practice in a style similar to deliberate mindfulness, I am offering the five foundations of effortless mindfulness: awareness of awareness is mindful of awareness; awareness is aware of itself as nature of mind; awareness from spacious awareness is aware from awake-aware mind; awake awareness embodied is aware from the simultaneous mind; and open-hearted awareness uses heart mindfulness to create and relate.

1. **Awareness of awareness is mindfulness of awareness.** The mindful attention that was used in deliberate mindfulness to focus on your breath and thoughts cannot be used to find awake awareness. Therefore, we need to find a way to rest in the nature of mind or to use local awareness to become aware of spacious awareness. In deliberate mindfulness meditation, we're located in subtle mind, looking at the contents of our consciousness. However, this first foundation of effortless mindfulness is a You-turn, moving away from looking out through our eyes at the contents of our mind and body. Awareness of awareness is not an endless progression of pulling back of awareness, but a turning around of awareness to look through the meditator to discover that awake awareness is already aware as both subject and object.

2. **Awareness is aware of itself as the nature of mind.** When local awareness becomes aware of spacious awareness, it begins to recognize itself. When local awareness and spacious awareness unite, they realize they have always been united. The experience is like air escaping from a balloon and mixing with the rest of the air in the room. Similarly, subject and object merge; there is no longer a subject knowing an object—from this perspective, there is just awareness. Awareness knows itself by being itself. We discover that awareness is already awake without our help.

Awareness of awareness takes us beyond ego-identification and knows, without referring to thoughts or our senses. In this second foundation of effortless mindfulness, we go beyond spacious awareness as the object of meditation. One way to check this is to inquire: "Am I aware of spacious awareness, or is spacious awareness aware of itself?" Please don't skip past the experience of awareness resting as itself, and go prematurely to the next foundation of witnessing awareness. If you can abide as awareness of itself—contentless, timeless, boundless, knowing—for even three to five seconds, that experience can shift you into the ground of Being.

3. **Awareness from spacious awareness is aware from awake-aware mind.** This is the experience of turning back toward your body and mind and witnessing from an open-sky, panoramic view. A radical shift of perspective, this principle can move you out of ego-identification and into spacious awareness as the witnessing self. Who we are, from the nature of mind, is not a single point in a field. We can remain effortlessly focused from awake-aware mind because its foundation is spacious awareness rather than changing thoughts and perceptions. We learn to trust that knowing is happening from spacious awareness, then we no longer need to return to thinking for a second opinion. As the witnessing self is established in spacious awareness, it's able to use effortless mindfulness to focus and function in the world. Local awareness, the vehicle that helped us discover spacious awareness, now becomes a tool the witnessing self uses as needed to focus on particular tasks.

4. **Awake awareness embodied is aware from simultaneous mind.** It is an alive, embodied awareness similar to being in a "flow state" or "being in the zone." We began by only experiencing ourselves as separate, solid selves who

then realized we were formless awareness. Now formless awareness is realizing that it's also inherent in form. Awake awareness takes a second You-turn and steps back within to include the mind's contents and the energies of the body, but with a new perspective this time. We are now observing whatever arises not only from outside, but also from within our body. We are not a detached witness, but we feel our thoughts, emotions, and sensations from within—without needing to re-create an ego-manager. From effortless mindfulness, we can openly monitor internal levels of consciousness that are not available to deliberate mindfulness. Effortless mindfulness can clearly see the process of self-awareness, subpersonalities, long-held assumptions, shadow parts, self-representations, and self-images. Awake awareness embodied is often called "unity consciousness" or the stage of "one taste" in the Mahamudra tradition. The shift of location is from the witnessing sky to the ocean of awareness in which waves of experience arise, crest, and return, without ever separating from the sea. Simultaneous mind experiences all levels of reality from nondual awareness: emptiness and fullness, absolute awareness and the relative world, infinite and finite—as well as being nowhere, everywhere, and here. From this fourth foundation of effortless mindfulness, we can be aware, from spacious awareness, of our reality within and outside simultaneously. This brings the default mode network into balance, and we can learn to remain connected and effortlessly undistracted. People who learn this foundation of nondual mindfulness are astounded that they can immediately shift into embodied awake awareness while doing everyday activities in a stress-free flow—with their eyes open.

5. **Open-hearted awareness uses heart mindfulness to create and relate.** We now discover heart-mind and the

nonconceptual awareness that's the important source of our new way of knowing. From open-hearted awareness, we welcome all thoughts and emotions, and we recognize the same awake awareness in others. We move from witnessing self to no-self to seeing from Being, where you feel nothing is missing, and "you"—as open-hearted awareness—cannot be harmed. We are aware of our emotions, patterns of ego-identification, and our subpersonalities arising within us, yet we don't become identified with any of them. This ability to remain connected to everything gives us more space and wisdom, more capacity to choose how to respond when emotions, opinions, and thoughts continually arise. From the support of open-hearted awareness, we can begin to detox repressed emotions and rewire our brain for the better. Feeling part of the field of life, we can focus with local awareness. Compassionate activity becomes the natural expression.

GLIMPSE **Effortless Mindfulness**

The effortless mindfulness practice that I used in the experiment (discussed earlier in this chapter) can be done using the two practices of Effortless Focus or Panoramic Awareness in chapter 3. These two practices are being done from the third foundation, which is awareness from spacious awareness.

To practice all five foundations of effortless mindfulness, try any of these full practices from earlier chapters: Unhook, Drop, Open, See, Include, Know, Let Be in chapter 4; the Four Fields of the Ground of Being in chapter 9; or the Open-Hearted Connection in chapter 10.

One of the most important, unique, and sometimes tricky parts of the five foundations of effortless mindfulness is the two You-Turns. The first You-Turn, called recognition, is turning from looking outward using our ego-identified mind to have local awareness look back to awake awareness. Many people who attend my groups or see me in individual sessions are able to have this initial glimpse. However, awake awareness is not just a temporary experience happening to you but can be realized as the foundation of who we are.

The second You-Turn, called realization, is shifting into and abiding as awake awareness, which then looks and feels back to include our body from within and looks out to experience the connection with others. I have found that just taking even a minute or two to completely let go and feel awareness aware of itself before looking back from spacious awareness is the foundation of this shift into freedom.

13

LIVING FROM BEING

This being human is a guest house. Every morning a new arrival.
A joy, a depression, a meanness, some momentary awareness
comes as an unexpected visitor. Welcome and entertain them all!
JELALUDDIN RUMI[1]

Have you ever used a rope to swing from the shoreline out over a lake? Letting go of a rope swing can be frightening because we relinquish control of our grip on known safety in order to fly through the air and then drop into the water. Despite our trepidation, we jump and swing out over the lake, knowing how exhilarating the experience will be. Splashing into the lake, we realize the water doesn't have the same qualities as the land we just left. Although our plunge into water brings joy and refreshment, at first there is also slight disorientation. Then, once we surface, we experience support and buoyancy provided by water.

This is very much how it feels to transition from ego-identification into Being. When we first discover Being, it's a great relief. We can finally rest. There is nothing we need to do in order to be. We don't need to think because Being is not dependent on thought. Being doesn't need anything to change; it doesn't have to get healed in order to be okay. Although we all have the natural capacity to abide as Being, most people find it disorienting at first. Because of this disorientation, ego-identification may attempt to reassert itself. It's as if we're being pulled back into ego-identification, back to the seemingly safe shoreline. Usually, we have to grab the rope and plunge into the water again and again before we can remain as Being, and eventually live from Being.

Don't be surprised by the inner resistance you may encounter when you begin training to remain as Being. As we transition away from ego-identification to identification with Being, we're switching from one operating system to another. The old programs related to the current operating system of ego-identification are designed for its survival. Ego-identification co-opts these survival programs so that we hear the voices of fear—like children telling us there are monsters under their beds. If we believe those voices, we could go into fight-or-flight mode—as if awakening were a threat. When you feel fear, you need to check to see whether it's coming from the ego-identification system. With practice, you'll be able to distinguish these voices. You'll end up seeing them as kids with a backseat steering wheel pretending they're actually driving the car! They just need reassurance that they're safe so they can relax and enjoy the ride.

When we shift out of ego-identification, we feel free from perpetual dissatisfaction and separation. The absence of the mini-me leads to relief, relaxation, peace of mind, and freedom from striving. However, we cannot live our lives from absence. The initial stage of non-ego and not-knowing is not the destination of the water but the transition of letting go of the rope. We must discover the presence of the ground of Being and learn how to operate from there. A group of essential qualities arises as support from the ground of Being: joy, boundlessness, embodied presence, connection, open-hearted love, and creativity. The most important of these is the new knowing that doesn't return to the everyday mind for a second opinion. This new "not-knowing that knows" has to be developed for us to stabilize our functional awakening. When we become familiar with the new awareness-based operating system, we can begin to live from Being.

When we're seeing from open-hearted awareness, we find that thoughts, feelings, and sensations (both pleasant and unpleasant) still arise in embodied awareness, but there's no separate self to attach to them or feel threatened by them. Therefore we can experience a level of basic goodness, equanimity, compassion, and unconditional love that's not limited to the physical pain-pleasure system. Both our body and mind experience the freedom and bliss of presence. Then we need to stay with the process of rewiring the body-mind and learning how to create and relate from Being.

It's very rare to live from Being after a single, initial glimpse. We can have recognition and even realization, but stabilization and expression take some unfolding because ego-identification and the default mode network have strongly established survival habits. It's important to rest in aware presence and allow awakening to unfold by itself, but simply abiding doesn't always lead to the capacity to live from open-hearted awareness. If we become too active in the unfolding process, the dangers are intellectualization or creating a spiritual ego. If we're too passive, then the danger is remaining in meditation states of bliss, clarity, or stillness. We can learn to unite awake awareness with our human conditioning by actively and intentionally doing from Being. Shifting into awake awareness and then performing small actions from Being, like typing an email, is a way of building trust and new neural networks to support the unfolding of awakening.

The ego-identification's misperceived need for safety continues to reconstitute old defenses that obscure awake awareness. If we are ego identified, we are contracted and our perceptions arise from this level of mind. When we shift out of ego-identification, we can recognize our own thoughts, feelings, and subpersonalities as changing contents of consciousness. If we get on board with the unfolding of awakening and become familiar with living from open-hearted awareness, our old, defensive conditioning will gradually become less dominant. The qualities of Being and the new knowing from open-hearted awareness will guide us, but we need to actively nurture the next stage of growth or else we may slide back.

A period of integration occurs as formless, awake awareness becomes embodied as presence and then connects to others through open-hearted awareness. You can allow yourself to be held and supported by the loving arms of awake awareness. From there, you'll discover new motivation so you reach out to support others in need.

During the transitional period, you'll see defense mechanisms arise that were created to help your ego personality thrive and survive during your formative years. These defenses need to be welcomed, liberated, and reconfigured. Even when you're caught in the grip of old patterns such as fear, guilt, shame, and anger, you can learn to step back more easily into the awake awareness and then realize it is inherent within everything. Believe it or not, we can all feel a pervasive wellbeing—a basic goodness—that's not grounded in the ongoing ups and downs of daily life. As awakening unfolds, you'll naturally alternate between ego-identification, witnessing self-awareness, and living from Being. We can learn to make small shifts during this unfolding process that engender big changes.

Psychology Before and After Initial Awakening

A certain amount of emotional maturity and psychological insight is needed to prepare for embodying awareness. However, even the best psychological work from ego-identification can only take us so far. If our goal is to abide, create, and relate from Being, we need a different approach after awakening has begun. One reason it's so difficult to deal with repressed emotions, shadow parts, and traumatic memories is that these energies are stronger than the mental pattern of ego-identification. For our emotional knots to dissolve, open-hearted awareness has to embrace traumatic feelings and liberate the corresponding subpersonalities that are trapped in the prison of our past memories. Our neural networks continually fire off memories of trauma until those traumatic patterns have been both welcomed and unburdened. Only when we've shifted into Being do we have the capacity to detox, liberate, transform, and love all repressed emotions, karmic patterns, and shadow parts of ourselves.

Vestiges of earlier developmental stages survive in the brain, and strong emotional experiences create preverbal knots of emotion in a child's brain and sensitive nervous system. These neuronal imprints create not only emotional patterns, but also patterns of identity. Sub-personalities are brain habits formed around ways of coping with difficult emotional situations at an age when we had fewer resources and less cognitive capability. Although their aim is to maintain stability so that we can survive a trauma, they can unintentionally end up preserving childhood wounds.

From the beginning of Western psychology, there's been an acknowledgment that various parts of ourselves can cause suffering when they dominate our identity. Sigmund Freud divided the psyche into three parts; *id, ego,* and *superego.* Carl Jung also developed a psychological theory with multiple parts, including personas, shadows, and archetypes; Jung considered the Self an archetype. Roberto Assagioli, another great thinker, mapped multiple interacting subpersonalities in a theory he called psychosynthesis. Fritz Perls, who developed Gestalt therapy, asked clients to envision and talk with different self-aspects, most famously Top Dog, Underdog, internalized Parent, and inner Child. Richard Schwartz developed Internal Family Systems therapy (IFS), which acknowledges different inner parts as exiles, protectors, firefighters, and managers. One unique thing about IFS is the goal of working with subpersonalities to establish a non-ego-identified Self, similar to what I refer to as Being. Schwartz says the Self is talked about in esoteric traditions of religions as a "manifestation of the absolute ground of Being," and he goes on to say that it "often doesn't take years of meditative practice to access because it exists in all of us, just below the surface of our extreme parts. Once they [subpersonalities] agree to separate from us, we suddenly have access to who we really are."[2]

When we experience a difficult life situation in the present, our nervous system may reactivate a part that feels victimized or a part that tries to protect us. The power of a neuronal habit (or subpersonality) is so compelling that when we are in its grip, we *regress* to the brain pattern forged at that age. We actually feel as though we are once again the defenseless child. Subpersonalities and hidden shadow parts can emerge when triggered and hijack us if we don't bring them out into the light, where we can welcome and unburden them. Because these childhood hurts are hidden so deep within, many people believe that bad feelings are at their core. When they shift out of ego-identification, they begin to realize these bad feelings are just patterns of energy and belief systems that need to be liberated. As you wake in and learn how to live from Being, you can start including and liberating some of these exiled shadow parts.

Until you are seeing from Being and expressing from open-hearted awareness, you will be rotating through different subpersonalities—or more accurately, they will be rotating through you. Before waking-up, subpersonalities take turns in the driver's seat of our identity. One subpersonality drives us too hard; another feels tentative, young, and confused. One part wants to be taken care of; another is fiercely independent. These subpersonalities are often in conflict with each other, and they battle for control. After initial awakening, subpersonalities and thinking patterns continue to arise and try to occupy the driver's seat of identity. When a subpersonality sits in the seat of identity, it feels like it's truly "me." So the important new skill is heart mindfulness, to become aware of these arising patterns from open-hearted awareness, without becoming identified. Many people who have come to see me have said, "I have seen through the small self. It seems backwards to relate to these patterns of thought as if they were personalities." This makes sense intellectually—and I have also tried to approach them this way. But this is the way they have formed and appear, so if we don't meet them as they are, the subpersonalities can sneak up and cause havoc in our lives.

Working with various inner parts helps overcome the illusion of a single, solid, separate self. Overcoming this illusion is necessary for awakening and growing up. For instance, in couples' therapy, one partner is able to say: "One part of me is really angry that you don't want to go to my sister's house this weekend, and another part is able to hear why you don't want to go. Can I tell you about the angry part first?" This allows the individuals to maintain their loving connection—and not feel attacked—even when the partner is expressing strong emotions. Noticing inner parts allows us to take a step back out of ego-identification into an observing self, and then we can lean forward again to open-hearted awareness, which embraces all our many aspects. After initial awakening, the ability to include all parts is one of the most important developments toward stabilization.

From open-hearted awareness, we have the capability to perceive these subpersonalities as parts of us instead of our primary identity.

I have found that it's possible to start from working with subpersonalities and reach the ground of Being. But more often I begin by introducing people directly to the ground of being and then encourage them to welcome, relate to, and unburden their subpersonalities. These parts may feel needy, fearful, and hostile, but no part is inherently bad. All parts are trying their best, from their limited perspective, to be safe and find love. When we actually meet the shadow parts we've fearfully avoided, we realize they're only scared, hurt, or angry subpersonalities expressing their upset about not being seen or heard. Ego-identification lacks the capacity to give these parts the love they need. But even shadow parts that seem most injured or hateful can be unburdened when embraced by unconditional love from being. What started as a wounded inner child—frozen in time, continuously fearful in a traumatic movie scene—can eventually evolve into a contributing, playful part in an energetic human life. During the awakening process, subpersonalities continuously arise as pretenders to the throne of identity; Being can welcome and integrate them all with open-hearted awareness.

Simply abiding in Being may permit painful emotions, beliefs, and strong subpersonalities to begin arising spontaneously to liberate themselves. Three images often used for spontaneous liberation are: 1) when an old emotion arises, you begin to feel like you're seeing the face of an old friend; 2) uncomfortable emotions can also spontaneously unburden themselves in the way a coiled snake simply unfurls; 3) emotions arise, but there's no one to react to them—as though thieves were breaking into an empty house.

Your new sense of Being is exactly what your wounded inner parts have been looking for all along. When these subpersonalities feel seen and loved, they can finally be unburdened, and their destructive and painful habits lose fuel and motivation. When subpersonalities are repressed, denied, or attacked, they interpret the intense energies of the physical body as a threat to their existence, co-opting the "flight," "fight," "freeze," and "please" instinctive responses. These defensive strategies end up creating more painful mental and emotional layers on top of the original pain signal. From Being, we can practice heart mindfulness and cultivate the ability to detect the influence of strong thoughts, emotions, and subpersonalities before—or soon after—identifying with them.

One of the most important ways to support living from Being is by recognizing the difference between subpersonalities and personas. Personas (masks or functional roles) can be natural and helpful in daily life. However, they're not the source of our identity. We have various personas that come front and center at appropriate times. Consider the worker, the friend, the family member, and the significant-other personas. These roles help us get along in the world, but we can learn to wear them like clothes we change to suit the occasion, without becoming identified. When we're comfortable with our emotions, personality, and personas, we don't have to worry that awakening will limit us to one role or a single expression of identity. In fact, the reverse is true; as we grow more comfortable and less at the mercy of our emotions, we gain greater personal range and flexibility.

Some of our core stories are intricately embedded within us. When we access these stories, emotional soreness results. Further, when anything difficult or unpleasant happens, a dualistic split of me-versus-them arises. Typical core negative beliefs are: "Something's wrong with me or them," "I'm bad or they're bad," "I'm worthless or they're worthless," "I'm unlovable or they're unlovable," "I'm stupid or they're stupid," and infinite other variations on shame, blame, guilt, and hatred. When we take on ego-identified positions with their accompanying feelings and beliefs (such as "I'm worthless"), we merge with them. We mistakenly experience these beliefs and emotions as who we are, instead of feelings we have. It can seem as if there's no way out, allowing us to wallow in negativity. Or we can develop methods for splitting off from negative thoughts and defending ourselves against the feelings they bring up.

In contrast, from Being, we are insightful and show compassion for our subpersonalities without becoming seduced by their arguments. The issue is not the intensity of these energies, but who or what these energies are rising to. We don't need to flee from strong emotions once we find the vast, embodied sense of Being that comes with open-hearted awareness. The key to handling the disorientation, detox, and growing pains of awakening is to develop familiarity and trust in the ground of being and the process of unfolding. When subpersonalities arise to open-hearted awareness, previously disowned childhood feelings and experiences can be accepted, liberated, and integrated. The wisdom of open-hearted awareness understands how ignorance and confusion caused the hurtful actions that coalesced subpersonalities in the first place. When we are living from Being, those previously split-off, unfulfilled basic human needs such as "I want to be seen" or "I want to be valued" can be addressed and satisfied. We come to realize: "I am valuable and unique . . . just like everyone else." With this profound shift in perspective, the remaining emotional energy from a core wound or knot is returned to the individual as life force and creativity.

A student once told me about a small incident at work that made her feel ignored: she was not invited to lunch with some colleagues. When she saw them laughing as they walked out the door, a strong emotion began to overwhelm her. Because she'd been practicing small glimpses many times, she was able to return to Being quickly. She immediately unhooked and returned to open-hearted awareness, even as the feeling of "being ignored" became stronger. Then she heard the feeling speak with the voice of an inner child: "I'm unlovable. Nobody sees me. Why should I even try?" Staying with this feeling, she discerned the response from her loving presence of Being. A compassionate voice emerged to address the hurt inner child: "Okay, sweetheart, I'm here. Tell me more."

At first, this invitation made the wounded inner child even more indignant: "Everybody ignores me! Nobody listens to me!" But from Being, she was able to respond with empathy: "Yes, I'm here. I hear what you're saying about how nobody listens to you." She felt her wounded inner child begin another protest and then stop, realizing it had finally been met with compassionate listening from Being. She was able to be with deep, uncomfortable sadness fully—for the first time. Something deep inside her softened and began to shift. At this point, she felt that her real identity was the loving presence of Being, grounded in the unconditional love that even embraced the "unlovable" parts of herself. She later explained that she felt as though she "was love itself"; only her old habits of identifying with past pain had previously prevented her from realizing this. The weight of an ancient pattern began to lift. In subsequent months and years, the thought patterns "I'm unlovable" and "Nobody listens to me" continued to arise periodically, but they no longer had the power to possess her. Upon arising, these thoughts were recognized and liberated, sometimes quickly and sometimes slowly, but with increasing ease.

Detoxification

Open-hearted awareness allows us to begin to wake out into creative expression and relationships with others. Open-hearted awareness means not only the ability to rest as Being but also to create and live an awakened life. It's the new way of knowing from Being. Shifting into open-hearted awareness releases subpersonalities from the burden of acting as our primary identity. Patterns of thought untangle; the emotions and story that kept cycles of suffering in place eventually loosen and unravel. Open-hearted awareness is the beginning of a process of emotional reintegration. Shifting into living from Being opens us to a level of emotional sensitivity that wasn't available before.

Once we learn to begin by shifting, what has traditionally been called a "dark night of the soul" becomes a period of detox. As awake awareness becomes embodied, there can be a period of necessary mourning, or what I call "good grief" in honor of the *Peanuts* character Charlie Brown. We've all had losses: the death of a loved one, divorced parents, the end of a life dream, a romantic breakup. A common occurrence when people reach the stage of open-hearted awareness is the discovery of heart mindfulness and the capacity to allow previously frozen, unresolved grief to thaw, process, and dissolve.

Many people talk about experiencing a new feeling of "sweet sadness" or tenderhearted intimacy when entering this stage. Others describe feeling like their hearts are breaking for no reason. However, upon inquiry, we discover that our hearts are not breaking! Rather, the defenses around our hearts are breaking open. The emotions that were too big for ego-identification to handle can now be fully experienced.

With the support of open-hearted awareness, we can feel great grief, while remaining both vulnerable and courageous.

We may initially experience Being as resting in silence or stillness, but in order to remain primary, Being must get to know itself. That means avoiding getting stuck in stillness or spaced-out in the detached, mindful witness. Instead of staying in a transcendent state, we can learn how to allow formless awareness to mix with our bodily form and provide support for our detox.

We can detox on all the levels: physical, mental, energetic, emotional, and spiritual. To stay with the detox process, it's important to distinguish between two types of pain: There are pain signals that point to real danger and need an immediate response—for example, the bolt of fear when you step into the street and see an oncoming car. Then there are growing pains. With growing pains, we may experience a pain signal, but there's no real threat—it's like the sore muscles you get after a workout. This kind of pain signals that improvement is occurring because you're intentionally breaking down your muscles as one step in the larger process of making them stronger.

The pain of detox or the melting of repressed emotions signals that we're taking a step toward becoming stronger. When we come in from freezing outdoor temperatures and feel the pain of our hands thawing out, we don't try to relieve it by putting our hands back into the cold. Recognizing that we're thawing out allows us not to shut down during the detox process. Instead we can learn how to be with the positive, yet painful, process of our body coming back into full life. Learning to be with painful emotions during "detox" changes your relationship to your whole emotional life.

In terms of identity, we grow from ego to witnessing Self to Being. When we're ego-identified, we're in chaos and denial, and we're struggling with or overwhelmed by disturbing emotions and situations. When we step back to the witnessing Self, we have the space to observe, but we're detached from the fullness of life. When we discover presence, we can be embodied while witnessing from within. At a certain point, we will see that Being is welcoming all our feelings, knowing they're not a real threat. Being is like a wise grandmother who can stay with a screaming two-year-old child, allowing him to move through his tantrum without overreacting.

As our primal energies release, we may feel as though something inside is literally being shaken free, as if we are knocking the dirt off our boots or wringing out a rag. We may feel as though the heat of our released energy is slowly baking us, purifying us to our essence. During this period of detox, we may feel unusually strong emotions: not just anger, but rage and even murderous rage; not just fear, but terror. Sometimes a personal situation or traumatic memory goes with the strong feeling and sometimes not. In somatic experiencing, the healing trauma work developed by Peter Levine, it is recommended that you titrate, or regulate, the amount of energy you release, and that you resource yourself with something supportive. We can resource ourselves within the source of awake awareness and utilize intentional choice to regulate the detox process, although it can sometimes take on a life of its own. When we realize—as Being—that there's a feeling of terror but no real threat, we can face what previously seemed unbearable without needing to resist or identify. Within open-hearted awareness, it's important to find and nurture the qualities of courage, guided by our heart's desire to be free.

Several years ago, I was undergoing a detox phase. While sitting in a café with a cup of tea, listening to pleasant background music, and speaking with an old friend I hadn't seen in a while, my body was suddenly flooded with primal terror. I felt the need to flee. I didn't notice anything happening in the restaurant that could trigger this response, so I searched my mind to see if there was a memory or recent emotional situation that was particularly frightening. Then I realized that the experience of terror was part of my ongoing detox. My whole life I had been defending against intense feelings such as rage, terror, and loneliness. This detox was thawing out my deeply repressed emotions. You know how we say, "I'll deal with that later"? Well, later was now. This realization changed everything for me. I decided to take a "Dog Zen" approach to my terror. Just stay, sta-a-a-yyy, I thought. Don't control, don't resist, don't identify.

My friend must have seen the sweat dripping down my face, because he asked, "Are you okay?"

"Yes," I answered. "It's something I'm feeling. It's nothing personal."
When I heard myself say, "It's nothing personal," I laughed. This
terror wasn't a personal response to anything my friend said; in fact,
the strong emotion wasn't even a personal threat to me. My friend
went back to telling his story, and I continued to breathe as the terror
moved through me.

I call this type of detox "shake-and-bake." The pain I felt was a
normal growing pain. The energy that first shook me like a rag next
opened me to a vitality I'd never felt before. A kind of fearlessness and
courage followed and became more available to me. It's pretty typical
that some subpersonalities think they're going to lose control and "die"
when this kind of intense feeling occurs. When subpersonalities fear
their own death and we're identified with them, we also feel as though
we're going to physically perish or remain in a "hell" of unchanging
pain. By contrast, when we live from Being, subpersonalities and life
energies, even strong ones, are not a threat.

A student undergoing her own shake-and-bake detox reported that
while talking to her boss at work, she felt a strong impulse rise from her
belly. The impulse traveled up her spine, into her jaw and shoulders,
and even into her eyes before triggering a fight response. She identified
this fierce feeling as a need to be right, even though her boss wasn't
implying that she was wrong. She recognized familiar, childhood feelings of being dismissed, unseen, hurt, and mocked. She then noticed
a subpersonality who was defending against these feelings—the very
feelings that had also driven her to succeed in life. In a moment, she
was able to shift into Being. From Being, she spoke to this childhood
part: "You don't have to be in charge anymore, sweetheart." Her whole
body softened. After that she was able to articulate her opinion to her
boss in a simple, clear, and heartfelt way.

Rewiring to Remain as Being

The identity that begins the journey is not who we know ourselves to
be upon awakening. But, because we initially can't conceive of how
we'd live without our ego as the manager, living from Being seems like

an impossible project. It is not. You do need to recognize the rebound effect that can bounce you back in different ways. Many people who have begun the journey of awakening have reported feeling "scared back to the mind" or "bored back to the mind." Sitting with not-knowing and non-ego can trigger strong fear signals and corresponding responses from ego defenses. As strange as it may seem, you must be willing to feel bored by peace at first. Because we're used to a lot of stimuli from emotional drama and mental fascination, getting accustomed to peace and wellbeing can be a big transition—even though that's what we truly want. (We just don't want to be seduced along the way and remain in the eddy of peace, stillness, and calm.) There can be a pull back up to ego-identification to "be somebody" right after we let go of our old identity. We may be "overwhelmed back to the mind" if we cannot bear the detox and the slow transition of rewiring. Being is able to bear the fears and protests of the old programs and know that our emotions are real, but what they are saying is not true.

As we establish an ability to abide in the ground of being, the fabric of love we sense leads us to engage in compassionate, creative action and expression. When awake awareness meets our humanity, four qualities interweave; these are *loving-kindness, compassion, sympathetic joy,* and *equanimity.* These essential qualities allow awake awareness to incarnate as the love and interconnection that permeate our body. The four qualities of love are known in Pali as *brahma viharas,* "houses of the Divine" or "highest dwellings." When formless awareness comes into forms of consciousness, these four qualities manifest, revealing themselves to be essential structures and natural capacities of love.

Doing from Being

There is a Chinese term called *wu wei,* which can be translated as "spontaneity" or "effortless action." Wu wei does not mean passively waiting around, but actively recognizing that spontaneous action is already occurring, without being conducted by an ego-identified "doer." Being is always already naturally here, but we aren't yet wired to function from Being. Functioning from Being means interacting, responding, and

Free Gifts!

Visit **SoundsTrue.com/Free** to download these **3 free gifts**

The Self-Acceptance Project
Twenty-three respected authors and spiritual teachers discuss the power of self-compassion, especially during challenging times.

The Practice of Mindfulness
Guided practices from six leading teachers to open us to the depths of the present moment.

Meditation Music
Nine inspiring tracks for healing, relaxation, and releasing stress.

SOUNDS TRUE
many voices, one journey   800.333.9185

Free Gifts!

Visit **SoundsTrue.com/Free** to download these **3 free gifts**

The Self-Acceptance Project
Twenty-three respected authors and spiritual teachers discuss the power of self-compassion, especially during challenging times.

The Practice of Mindfulness
Guided practices from six leading teachers to open us to the depths of the present moment.

Meditation Music
Nine inspiring tracks for healing, relaxation, and releasing stress.

sounds true
many voices, one journey   800.333.9185

creating from a panoramic flow state where we feel free of self-centeredness and ego-identification, yet retain full access to our memory and learned skills. Most of us who aren't living in a monastery or cave—or who aren't meditating most of the day—must find a balance between doing and letting be. Therefore, we need to learn how to function in the world without going back to the doer. Awake awareness as the ground of Being has intentionality and the ability to choose.

The discovery of local awareness and the intentionality of open-hearted awareness enable us to trust the spontaneous action that arises from Being. In order to move from abiding to stabilizing, and from stabilizing to expressing, we need to learn the paradoxical dance of doing from Being. Ultimately, doing from Being is much easier and more comfortable than acting from our overwhelmed and frightened ego-identification. The more we act from the ground of Being instead of ego-identification, the easier it gets. Eventually, acting from Being becomes the new habit and happens by itself.

Not doing, in the sense of effortlessness, doesn't mean doing nothing; wu wei is about not identifying with the old "doer." However, holding the fixed belief "there is nothing to do" can mistakenly reinforce inertia. Compared to wu wei, the old doer program of ego-identification may feel compulsive, like a dog digging obsessively for a bone. In shifting out of willful, ego-identified subpersonalities, we begin to experience effortless action as we connect with a spontaneous, alive intelligence that is a hallmark of the awakened life. We may feel supported and contented, like a child on a summer day, enjoying a liberated sense of playfulness and curiosity. Additionally, we can feel the power to act and the freedom of choice. Paradoxically, we are sur-rendering our personal will to a power greater than our ego; yet in so doing, we gain true freedom and response-ability.

When living from open-hearted awareness is our new normal, our motivation, intention, willingness, and dedication spring forth from a new place. The ground of Being is not limited to our individual identity; it sees itself in others. As a result, a sense of communion and communication arises on many levels between people and within groups. When we see others as ourselves, we are free to live from a new ethic based on the common good, instead of being driven by fear of deficiency or a list of "shoulds."

A student who was doing a series of phone sessions with me reported that she'd begun to access a felt sense of Being. "It's incredible, the openness I feel," she said. "But I'm a little afraid to continue with this awakening because I don't want to lose my passion for creating art, which has always been the love of my life."

"What thoughts are making you believe you might lose your passion?" I asked.

"If I think that everything's okay the way it is, I worry I'll lose all my motivation and drive. I won't create. It's almost like, 'Why bother?' My thoughts are telling me that satisfaction will lead to lethargy."

"You're describing the first stage of discovering Being: resting as Being," I said. "Being does not rely on doing or thinking. In order to *be* who you are, you don't need to *do* anything." I concluded, "As Being becomes the source of your identity, a new rewiring occurs that allows life energy to bubble up. If you can wait and trust, you'll be freshly inspired to act and to do in a new way."

I suggested my student inquire: "What would it be like right now if your primary motivation for creating art were based upon your sense of wellbeing, curiosity, and energy?" My student took this inquiry to heart. Three months later, she phoned me to report that her artwork had taken a new direction, and that she'd been commissioned to create an installation in a public park.

As we go through rewiring and detoxification, some people take the opportunity to change aspects of their lives. But many continue with the same relationships, professions, and outer lives. The initial time of rest, non-doing, or unhooking from the drive of will is important to recognize, and this process is often necessary before the new doing kicks in. Just as adolescents often sleep more than children, undergoing growth spurts can make us sleepy. The dropping away of our old motivations may briefly reduce our active drive as we rewire and transition to our new operating system. Some people's minds become quiet during this time. Others start to energetically thaw out, perhaps experiencing necessary grief as they unfreeze their emotional lives. For some people, thawing out feels like the unclenching of emotional and physical knots in their bodies. It's important to remember that the same ego defenses that protect against emotional pain also depress our natural life force. When these knots of emotion (and defenses against emotion) finally untangle, more spiritual, emotional, and physical energy becomes available to us than ever before.

As we allow defenses to arise, run through our bodies, and dissolve, some of our old belief systems call us back with threats and ancient tapes, such as: "You're lazy!" or, "You'll end up a no-good bum!" Because the big ocean liner of your life has been steaming along in one direction up to this point, it must come to a full stop before it can pivot and start in another direction. It may seem as though you're slowing down and going nowhere, when, in fact, you're in the midst of making the extremely important transition toward living from Being.

Living from Being

One of the reasons we don't remain as Being is that the "new knowing" and development of "doing from Being" need both nurturing and practice. It's easy to pause and get lost in transitional states like subtle-body bliss or meditative witnessing, because these states are free of the intense energies of life. It's essential that we inhabit the next stage of open-hearted awareness and nonconceptual knowing. Without this foundation, we'll find ourselves unable to function in the world without regressing back to ego-identification in order to get through the day. The new knowing from awake awareness can eventually rewire us so that ego function and memory are linked to Being.

After shifting into awake awareness and embodying it for a while, doing something new—like giving a presentation—may make you feel nervous, but there's no underlying worry about failure. You will make mistakes as you experiment with doing from Being during this transitional stage, but you'll be able to laugh about these mistakes and feel compassion for yourself. When you face a difficult task, you will not have to shut down or return to ego-identification because another quality of heart is available to you: a sense of courage and honesty. Being open-hearted and vulnerable is possible when you have the support of awake awareness. You can meet adversity or challenge without collapsing.

A couple, who owned their own business and had been involved in decades of different kinds of spiritual work, attended a week-long retreat that I led. They found that the open-hearted awareness approach immediately brought together everything they'd experienced before. After practicing a few months, they began to make important changes. They had previously felt trapped in a mandate to "always be positive," which they reported had led them toward codependence and wishy-washy indecisiveness, especially with their employees. They had formerly let deadlines slide and allowed projects to fall off track for fear of hurting people's feelings. They now realized that, because they'd previously been unable to communicate clearly and take appropriate risks, they'd sabotaged themselves.

The couple reported finding new courage, clarity, and willingness to act. One year later, their company was voted the Top Green Business in their state. The husband said: "We were freed to get out of our own way and communicate our needs to our employees. We had the courage to be honest and decisive."

The wellbeing we're talking about here is not just a physical, mental, emotional, or even psychological wellbeing; this is the wellbeing of your very essence—a true safety that cannot be hurt and a basic trust that is the foundation of the new identity. Because the identity is not based on ideas, actions, or anticipation, there's a feeling of openness and a deep sense that all is well. The feeling of wellbeing is not limited to your own internal experience; it extends itself horizontally to the way you perceive other people and the world. This wellbeing isn't based on belief or positive thinking but comes from a core realization that you and others are not separate.

As the unfolding of awakening continues down and in—to the well of Being—we reach a depth that brings refreshing waters of life to the darkest hidden parts of ourselves. Permeating all conscious and unconscious dimensions, it knows that feelings of shame, worthlessness, and being unlovable are not true. This extends to the root energy of survival. This vertical dimension of Being connects us to the subtle channels and energy centers of our body from top to bottom and back up again. There is an ability to feel at home in and with our own body and flesh.

Living from Being gives the rest and love we've all longed for. We know awake awareness, which has the pristine clarity of a vast, stunning morning sky. The ground of Being brings the balance of the night sky, where there's a feeling of stillness deeper than sleep, yet wide awake, a primordial peace. As a student phrased it: "The ground of Being is the only thing that made the terror go away." The fear of the fear of death is finally seen through. For the first time, we are able to feel two important truths simultaneously: that awake awareness as our ground of Being is unborn and cannot die or even be harmed; and that our precious human body is born, changes, and feels pain and love until one day it passes on. From the Now, we can feel both truths and know that all is well.

The Lines of Love

Open-hearted awareness establishes a new foundation of compassion and ethics in the way we treat other people. As we progress through the levels of mind, at every stage we gain benefits, such as the ability to make more rational choices and be considerate and mindful of others; however, there remain limitations if we don't continue to grow. If we remain in the very subtle mind of the pure witness, we can be detached and may do a spiritual bypass of our emotions and those of others. We can end up in a state of ethical relativism where everything seems the same to us and we end up minimizing the pain and suffering in people's everyday lives.

By contrast, when we shift into living from open-hearted awareness, we're able to feel others' pain without shutting down or being overwhelmed by it because we also see the vast awakeness at the same time. Love is a unifying force. Open-hearted awareness sees from the unconditional love of our true nature that we are all interconnected.

At some point, we begin to feel liberated from habitual patterns of ego-identification. We begin experiencing the boundless ground of the infinite, invisible life source. Directly experiencing our interconnectedness, we begin to awaken to our heart's intention and learn to put contemplation and action together. Our foundation at that point is unconditioned awareness and unconditional love. From open-hearted awareness, we also see the uniqueness and individuality of others. While feeling boundless, we also respect personal boundaries. We see other people's strengths and weaknesses, and we learn to relate from respect and integrity.

Unconditional love flows through specific channels of respect, integrity, purpose, meaning, value, response-ability, forgiveness, kindness, and compassion—and these form the foundation of our new, naturally ethical lives. As awakening unfolds, we start to see that there are different types of love and respect, and each follows its own line, like different-colored electrical wires. There is friendship love, romantic love, brotherly love, sisterly love, parent-child love, child-parent love, student-teacher love, collegial or collaborative love, and employee-employer love. Each type of love has its own wire, and when unconditional love flows through the wire it can be full and strong, like a river to the sea. When the types of love stay inside respectful boundaries, and the lines don't cross, there's usually not any kind of confusion, seduction, or abuse.

From our conventional sense of self, our ethics are often imposed on us from outside, perhaps from a set of commandments, laws, or rules that we're told we disobey under threat of punishment or guilt. How easily people will follow the ethics of a mob or a state that asserts an intellectual "right way" and defines dissenters or cultural subgroups as "wrong" and "other."

From open-hearted awareness, we begin from a very different position; our potential to see compassionately and act spontaneously, and even courageously—both personally and socially—is a whole new dynamic. This is not something we can think about or can only create with effort. This new capacity helps us deal with external difficulties as well as the inner process of rewiring and detoxing our emotional lives. Once we've shifted levels of mind and heart, we begin to feel at home wherever we go.

Shifting allows us to step back to a new view that can profoundly change us. A lot of people experience something similar when they first see a picture of our precious blue planet taken from outer space. By each discovering our own inner truth and then joining together while respecting diversity in our unity, we can apply our hearts to act from unconditional love and transform the way we live together.

GLIMPSE **Welcoming Shadow Parts**

You can do this glimpse at the end of any practice session or at any time during your day when you feel you need some love and awareness or that part of you has re-created ego-identification. People who have had an initial awakening often deny or do not see these shadow parts because they think they've gone beyond their ego-identity for good. However, facing and including our shadow parts within our ground of Being is the way to stabilization and expression.

Begin by checking within and around your body to see if there are any subpersonalities or parts of you that you're aware of. From open-hearted awareness, become curious about these parts of you. See if you can allow yourself to feel one of these parts clearly and distinctly.

1. Feel that who you are is seeing from Being. Ask yourself: "Am I aware of this part? What does this part look, sound, or feel like?" Let this part, inner child, persona, or commentator show itself fully—not just as a passing thought, belief, or attitude but as a personified pattern organized within you. Often this is a part that speaks as if it is you.

2. While you're seeing this part more clearly, ask these questions: "Am I aware of this part from my head or my heart? From open-hearted awareness, how do I feel toward this part?" Feel that you are seeing from Being.

3. Then ask this part, "Are you aware of me? How do you feel about me being here and seeing you? Are you aware of my compassion toward you?"

4. Wait until you distinctly experience this separate part communicating with you.

5. Next, ask this part directly: "What do you want me to know about you?" and, "Is there something you are afraid of that has kept you hidden?" One part might say, "I feel alone. I don't feel like anybody listens to me. I am afraid of being rejected." If you are accepting of this part within you, if you're listening from open-hearted awareness, then everything begins to change.

The first aim of this process is to see and relate to these parts as they arise so that they don't take over the central seat of your identity and speak through you. The second aim of this process is to connect to the subpersonalities so they realize that they are unconditionally loved. "Unconditional" means *no* conditions at all. The subpersonalities are patterns just like ego-identification, which will often subconsciously take over our identity on the journey of awakening if they're ignored or reduced to mere thoughts and feelings. A hidden part that is met with unconditional love can let go of its agenda. The shadow parts can then be seen, liberated, and their life energies returned so we can live from Being.

CONCLUSION

DANCING STILLNESS

Sometimes you have to play a long time to be able to play like yourself.
MILES DAVIS

I magine what our world would be like if more and more people began to awaken. What if awakening became available to us as a normal stage of development? It can happen, and I am hopeful it will.

In these contemporary times with so many choices, we can become distracted and end up living on the surface. I designed this book and these practices to encourage experiences of the simplest and deepest dimensions of our human experience in the midst of our daily life. We all have the potential to recognize awake awareness, which brings true peace of mind and an open heart. I do not know enough about evolution to say our species will evolve, but I *can* say that this stage of growth can be intentionally developed. Perhaps this evolution requires us to show up and consistently participate, the way we do when we learn to read and write. Awakening is one of the greatest gifts we can give to our fellow human beings and our planet.

Like changing any habit, awakening requires making your practice a priority. It takes as much unlearning as learning. Starting your day with a short sitting or a tuning-in practice of ten to twenty minutes is as important as eating breakfast. You can skip it, but your whole day will be different.

Learn the principles of glimpsing and abiding. Do one of the glimpse practices in the book that works best for you. Make it your own. Shift awareness, tune in, marinate, then open your eyes and begin to see and do from Being until you become reidentified. Then do a small glimpse to re-recognize. You can do this anywhere. I do it at home, on the subway, standing in line at a store, walking on the street, and while talking to someone. The inner silence, the dancing stillness, and the awareness are always available.

Ultimately, my hope is that by beginning with small glimpses, you will fall in love with love. When you fall in love with your own true nature and its natural qualities, you will want to return. Like romantic love, when you're in love with your true self, you have a natural interest, motivation, and devotion. Then the next step is no longer seeking in the spiritual marketplace but making a commitment. The love you've been seeking is already who you are—so you're already living together! You may have been worried that there was going to be a funeral for your ego, but instead it's a wedding celebration.

Once you develop the habit of small glimpses, you'll begin to see changes in your day-to-day life. You'll discover a wellbeing and ease with things that used to upset you. You'll also begin to recognize this awareness and basic goodness, as well as the pain of ignorance, within other people around you. When you're grounded in the awareness that knows it cannot be harmed, you can respond, rather than react, to other people in pain.

Life is a teacher, and we can learn as much from mistakes, difficulties, and disappointments as successes. During this process, it's important to recognize that doubt is a discriminating tool of thought. For instance: "I'm not sure that awareness is unhooked from thought. Let me try again." We don't want to suspend this kind of doubt, open-minded investigation, or curiosity. But we do want to be aware of another kind of doubt that can become an identity, often making people abandon their awakening process. This doubt whispers: "Everyone else seems to be getting this. I never will. I might as well not even try." This sort of doubt is a sign you're back in ego-identification or a "doubter" subpersonality. From open-hearted awareness, you begin to hear this doubter voice and respond with "Thanks for sharing." Then all thoughts, feelings, and parts of yourself are welcomed.

The glimpse practices in this book will lead you to discover the natural love and wisdom within you. Kindness and awareness become your life. It's easier to find forgiveness and let go of resentments toward others. If you take away nothing else, remember that in difficult situations the first step is to shift your level of mind. No advice can be given ahead of time about how you should act, there is no guarantee about how you will respond or what it will look like. Simply shift and you will know. If you have experienced great pain, awake awareness is the ultimate medicine. Your heart can heal. Change, loss, and death are always part of life. Even people like me who have experienced the tragic loss of loved ones can open to something bigger than the grip of grief.

You can choose any time of the day to step off the train of thought and into awake awareness. Once you've done this, you will naturally find new motivation, creativity, kindness, and passion for life. Please don't wait until you're stable in your awakening to enjoy the journey.

Here are a few things to do along the way: Do what you love. Do your ethical, psychological, and relational development, and continue to grow in all areas of your life. Walk in nature, dance, play with animals, be by the water, connect with friends, do something silly, laugh out loud. Sing in the shower. Go to a museum or a concert. Spend time with children and have tea with their invisible friends and stuffed animals. Perform a random act of kindness, like paying for someone's coffee (do some of these kind acts boldly and others anonymously). Explore fun activities by yourself and enjoy your own company, but also take the initiative to invite a friend to join you in some fun. Shift into awake awareness. Accept whatever is happening as it is. Don't react to reactivity. Don't judge judgment. Just allow everything to move through.

Give someone a compliment; make a gratitude list and count your blessings. Ask for a hug and receive it; ask someone else if they want a hug and give it. Wear bright colors one day (or most days); walk around with an inner smile. Be kind to your inner voices and say, "I hear you, sweetheart; it's okay." Send heartfelt good wishes to someone you know, and then say a prayer for a stranger who seems down and out. Receive the support of the universe. Pause before sending important emails.

Dedicate your practice to all people, animals, the earth, and the universe. Make a list of all people who have helped you or been kind to you, even in small ways, and feel that they are here now as your support team through your day and night. Examine your own prejudices. Forgive someone unconditionally. Try to see someone who is mean as someone in pain; don't hate them and don't back down, but talk to them with love. Call someone you haven't talked to for a long while and tell them you're thinking about them. Smile and take a slow, cool breath of air and enjoy the now. Send a small check to a charity. Listen to someone without giving advice or thinking about how this relates to you—just listen and be with him or her fully. Resource with your Source first, and then feel vulnerable about what hurts now in life. Feel your feelings from Being without creating a story or going to the future. Write a sentence or two in your journal to honestly communicate what you know, think, and feel. Be the dancing stillness.

Say thanks.

Ask, "Please help me," to the universe.

Say "no" to something you don't want to do; then say "yes" to life.

Shift into awake awareness and embrace life.

Breathe and smile.

NOTES

Introduction

1. Mary Oliver, "The Summer Day," in *House of Light* (Boston: Beacon Press, 1990), 60.
2. Dzogchen Ponlop Rinpoche, *Wild Awakening: The Heart of Mahamudra and Dzogchen,* Second Impression edition (Boston: Shambhala Publications, 2003), 30–31.

Chapter 1: Being Home While Returning Home

1. Lama Gendun Rinpoche, from a popular spontaneous song known as, "Free and Easy."
2. This ancient wisdom saying is a commonly known idiom, possibly from the Zen tradition. It's published without attribution in Anthony de Mello, *One Minute Wisdom* (New York: Bantam Doubleday Dell, 1985), 126.
3. Hsin-Hsin Ming, *Verses on the Faith-Mind by Seng-ts'an, Third Zen Patriarch,* trans. Richard B. Clarke (Buffalo, NY: White Pine Press, 2001), 11.

Chapter 2: Direct Recognition, Gradual Unfolding

1. Tulku Urgyen Rinpoche, *Rainbow Painting,* trans. Erik Pema Kunsang (Hong Kong: Ranjung Yeshe Publications, 1995), 121.
2. Eugen Herrigel, *Zen in the Art of Archery,* trans. R. F. C. Hull (New York: Vintage Books, 1999), viii.
3. Ibid.
4. Sam Harris, *Waking Up: A Guide to Spirituality Without Religion* (New York: Simon & Schuster, Kindle Edition), 137.
5. B. Alan Wallace, *The Attention Revolution: Unlocking the Power of the Focused Mind* (Somerville, MA: Wisdom Publications, 2006), 7.
6. Ibid., 7.

7. The Tennyson quote is from an 1874 letter. The excerpt appears in footnote 228 of William James's *The Varieties of Religious Experience: A Study in Human Nature* (Rockville, MD: Arc Manor, 2008), 280. The same excerpt is also reported in William T. Stead, "Tennyson the Man: A Character Sketch," in *The Review of Reviews,* vol. 6, 1893 (American Edition, edit. Albert Shaw), 569.

8. "True Meditation," Adyashanti's website (Adyashanti.org), accessed February 11, 2015, adyashanti.org/index.php?file=writings_inner&writingid=12.

9. Saint Francis of Assisi "What we are looking for is what is looking." Ken Wilber, *The Holographic Paradigm* (Boston: Shambhala, 1982), 20.

10. Sri Ramana Maharshi, *Who Am I?,* trans. T. M. P. Mahadevan (Tiruvannamalai, India: Sri Ramanasramam, 2013), 9.

11. Ibid., 8

Chapter 3: Local Awareness

1. *The Secret of the Golden Flower: The Classic Chinese Book of Life,* trans. Thomas Cleary (New York: Harper Collins, 1996), 11.

2. Wang-Ch'ug Dorje, the Ninth Karmapa, *The Mahamudra: Eliminating the Darkness of Ignorance,* trans. Alexader Berzin (Dharamsala: Library of Tibetan Works & Archives, 1978), 71.

3. Dudjom Rinpoche's quote is cited in: Sogyal Rinpoche, Patrick Gaffney, and Andrew Harvey, *The Tibetan Book of Living and Dying* (New York: HarperCollins, 1994), 161.

4. *Merriam-Webster OnLine,* s.v. "attention," accessed March 6, 2015, merriam-webster.com/dictionary/attention.

5. William James, *The Principles of Psychology, Vol. 1* (New York: Henry Holt, 1890), 420.

Chapter 4: Location, Location, Location

1. Ken Wilber, *The Fourth Turning: Imagining the Evolution of an Integral Buddhism* (Boston: Shambhala Publications, 2014, Kindle Edition [Kindle Locations 481–486]).

2. Tulku Urgyen Rinpoche, *Rainbow Painting,* trans. Erik Pema Kunsang (Hong Kong: Ranjung Yeshe Publications, 1995), 204.

3. Stephan L. Franzoi, *Social Psychology, Fifth Edition* (New York: McGraw-Hill Humanities/Social Sciences/Languages, 2008), 61.

4. *Merriam-Webster OnLine,* s.v. "moment," accessed February 15, 2015, merriam-webster.com/dictionary/moment.

5. Mingyur Rinpoche's words are quoted in: Tony Duff, *A Complete Session of Meditation* (Katmandu, Nepal: Padma Karpo Translation Committee, 2014), 108.

6. Gampopa is quoted in Ken McLeod, *Wake Up to Your Life: Discovering the Buddhist Path of Attention* (New York: Harper Collins, 2001), 415.

7. George Santayana, *Reason in Common Sense* (New York: Charles Scribner's Sons, 1905), 284.

8. Tulku Urgyen Rinpoche, *As It Is: Volume 1* (Hong Kong: Rangjung Yeshe Publications, 1999), 17.

Chapter 5: The Art and Science of Awakening

1. Blaise Pascal, *Pensées 48, 1651,* trans. W. F. Trotter and Thomas M'Cric (Dover, 1941).

2. Britta K. Hölzel, et al., "How Does Mindfulness Meditation Work? Proposing Mechanisms of Action from a Conceptual and Neural Perspective," *Perspectives on Psychological Science,* 6, no. 6 (November 2011): 537–559.

3. Donald O. Hebb, PhD, *The Organization of Behavior,* (New York: John Wiley & Sons, 1949), 5.

4. Rich McManus, "PET Pioneer Raichle Intrigued by Brain's Default Mode," *NIH Record,* 59, no. 9 (May 4, 2007): 2.

5. Matthew A. Killingsworth and Daniel T. Gilbert, "A Wandering Mind Is an Unhappy Mind," *Science,* 330, no. 6006 (November 12, 2010): 932.

6. Ibid.

7. Ibid.

8. Samantha J. Broyd, et al., (2009), "Default-mode brain dysfunction in mental disorders: A systematic review,"

Neuroscience and Biobehavioral Reviews, 33 (2009): 279–96, doi:10.1016/j.neubiorev.2008.09.002. PMID 18824195.

9. Kathleen A. Garrison, et al., "Effortless awareness: using real-time neurofeedback to investigate correlates of posterior cingulate cortex activity in meditators' self-report," *Frontiers in Human Neuroscience,* 7 (August 2013): 440.

10. Zoran Josipovic, et al., "Influence of meditation on anti-correlated networks in the brain," *Frontiers in Human Neuroscience,* 5 (January 2012): 11.

11. Andrew Newberg and Mark Robert Waldman, *Why We Believe What We Believe: Uncovering Our Biological Need for Meaning, Spirituality, and Truth* (New York: Free Press, 2006), 176.

12. Andrew Newberg, Eugene D'Aquili, and Vince Rause, *Why God Won't Go Away* (New York: Ballantine Books, 2008), 2.

13. Ibid., 7.

14. David Bohm's quote is cited by Anna F. Lemkow, "Reflections on Our Common Lifelong Learning Journey" in *Holistic Learning and Spirituality in Education,* ed. J. P. Miller, et al. (Albany, NY: State University of New York Press, 2005), 24.

15. Thrangu Rinpoche, *Essentials of Mahamudra: Looking Directly at the Mind* (Somerville, MA: Wisdom Publications, 2004), Kindle locations 99–102.

16. Adyashanti, interview by Oprah Winfrey, *Super Soul Sunday,* Oprah Winfrey Network, episode 510, April 20, 2014.

17. Jill Bolte Taylor, "My stroke of insight," filmed February 2008, TED video, 18:44, posted on March 13, 2008, ted.com/speakers/jill_bolte_taylor.

18. "Cortical Visual Impairment, Traumatic Brain Injury, and Neurological Vision Loss," American Foundation for the Blind website, accessed May 5, 2014: afb.org/info/living-with-vision-loss/eye-conditions/cortical-visual-impairment-traumatic-brain-injury-and-neurological-vision-loss/123.

Chapter 6: Thinking as the Sixth Sense

1. Yogi Berra's quote is cited in: Patrick Goold, ed., *Sailing—Philosophy for Everyone: Catching the Drift of Why We Sail* (Malden, MA: Wiley-Blackwell, 2012), 31.

2. *Merriam-Webster OnLine,* s.v. "concept," accessed February 11, 2015, merriam-webster.com/dictionary/concept.

3. Adam S. Radomsky, et al., "Part 1—You can run but you can't hide: Intrusive thoughts on six continents" in *Journal of Obsessive-Compulsive and Related Disorders* 3, no. 2 (July 2014): 269–279. Available at: hdl.handle.net/1959.3/369325.

4. From the abstract: Patricia Sharp, "Meditation-induced bliss viewed as release from conditioned neural (thought) patterns that block reward signals in the brain pleasure center" in *Religion, Brain & Behavior* 4, no. 3 (2014): 202–229, accessed March 8, 2015: tandfonline.com/doi/abs/10.1080/2153599X.2013.826717#. VPyXnUs-7KN.

5. Ibid.

Chapter 7: Nonconceptual Awareness

1. Tulku Urgyen Rinpoche, *Rainbow Painting,* trans. Erik Pema Kunsang (Hong Kong: Ranjung Yeshe Publications, 1995), 119.

2. Howard Gardner, *Frames of Mind: The Theory of Multiple Intelligences* (New York: Basic Books, 2011).

3. Mihaly Csikszentmihalyi, "Flow, the secret to happiness," filmed February 2004, TED video, 18:56, posted on October 24, 2008, ted.com/talks/mihaly_csikszentmihalyi_on_flow?language=en.

4. Lao Tsu, *Tao Te Ching,* trans. Gia-fu Feng and Jane English (New York: Vintage, 1989), 51.

5. Mark Leary, Claire Adams, and Eleanor Tate, "Hypo-egoic self-regulation: exercising self-control by diminishing the influence of the self," in *Journal of Personality* 74, no. 6 (December 2006): 1804. DOI: 10.1111/j.1467-6494.2006.00429.x.

6. Malcolm Gladwell, *Blink: The Power of Thinking Without Thinking* (New York: Back Bay Books, 2007), 11.

7. William Shakespeare, *Hamlet,* Act 1, scene 5, lines 166–167.

8. Jill Bolte Taylor, *My Stroke of Insight: A Brain Scientist's Personal Journey* (New York: Viking, 2006), 146.

Chapter 8: A Simple Case of Mistaken Identity

1. Dōgen, *Shōbōgenzō: Zen Essays by Dōgen,* trans. Thomas Cleary (Honolulu: University of Hawaii Press, 1986), 2.

2. Luke 9:23–24 (New International Version).

3. Rick Hanson and Rick Mendius, "Train Your Brain #6: Mindful Presence" (July 10, 2007) from the Wellspring Institute for Neuroscience and Contemplative Wisdom website: wisebrain.org/ MindfulPresence.pdf. Accessed February 15, 2015.

4. This quote is from an uncredited editorial: "In Search of Self" in *Nature Neuroscience* 5, no. 11 (November 2002): 1099. DOI:10.1038/nn1102-1099.

5. Joshua Fields Millburn, "Waking Up: Sam Harris Discusses the Benefits of Mindfulness" on The Minimalists website: theminimalists.com/sam/.

6. *Oxford Dictionaries,* s.v. "ego," accessed February 15, 2015, oxforddictionaries.com/definition/english/ego.

7. The example of the evolution of a microorganism is from: Christian de Quincey, *Radical Nature: Rediscovering the Soul of Matter* (Rochester, VT: Park Street Press, 2010), 273–4.

8. Ibid.

9. Eckhart Tolle, as cited in John W. Parker, *Dialogues with Emerging Spiritual Teachers* (Fort Collins, CO: Sagewood Press, 2009), 101–2.

Chapter 9: The Anatomy of Awareness

1. Shunryu Suzuki, *Zen Mind, Beginner's Mind,* ed. Trudy Dixon (Boston: Shambhala Publications, 2011), 24.

2. Patanjali, *The Yoga-Sutra of Patanjali: A New Translation with Commentary,* trans. Chip Hartranft (Boston: Shambhala Classics, 2003), 68, line 4.25.

3. William Blake, *The Marriage of Heaven and Hell: A Facsimile in Full Color* (Mineola, NY: Dover Publications, 1994), 36.

4. Tsoknyi Rinpoche, "Two Truths—Indivisible" on *Lion's Roar* (online magazine), August 12, 2014, lionsroar.com/two-truths-indivisible-2/.

5. Stephen Hawking, *Curiosity: Did God Create the Universe?* The Discovery Channel, August 7, 2011.

Chapter 10: Open-Hearted Awareness

1. Sri Nisargadatta Maharaj quote from "Stream of Life" blog on the Gaiam website, accessed February 16, 2015, blog.gaiam.com/quotes/authors/nisargadatta.

2. Jiddu Krishnamurti, *Intelligence, Love and Compassion: Sixth Public Talk at Saanen,* online video and transcript, filmed July 1979, posted on the J. Krishnamurti website, jkrishnamurti.org/krishnamurti-teachings/view-video/intelligence--love-and-compassion-full-version.php.

3. Anam Thubten, *The Magic of Awareness* (Boston: Snow Lion, 2012), 15.

4. G. K. Chesterton, from the essay "A Defence of Heraldry" in *The Defendant,* reprint of the 1901 edition, Project Gutenberg, 2004. gutenberg.org/files/12245/12245-h/12245-h.htm.

5. Daniel J. Siegel, MD (2014) talk at the Education of the Heart symposium in the Netherlands, garrisoninstitute.org/about-us/thegarrison-institute-blog/1950-educating-the-heart.

Chapter 11: The Next Stage of Human Development

1. Pierre Teilhard de Chardin, as cited in Robert J. Furey, *The Joy of Kindness* (Crossroads, 1993), 138.

2. Stephen Ilardi, "Depression Is a Disease of Civilization," filmed April 2013, TEDxEmory video, 22:20, posted on May 23, 2013, youtube.com/watch?v=drv3BP0Fdi8. Accessed February 16, 2015.

3. Vijay Rana, "The Future of Spirituality: An Interview with Ken Wilber," on *Watkins Mind Body Spirit* (online magazine), posted July 8, 2014, watkinsmagazine.com/the-future-of-spirituality-an-interview-with-ken-wilber. First published: *Watkins Mind Body Spirit* 35, Autumn 2013.

4. John Welwood, *Toward a Psychology of Awakening* (Boston: Shambhala, 2002), 11.

Chapter 12: Effortless Mindfulness

1. Tulku Urgyen Rinpoche, *Rainbow Painting,* trans. Erik Pema Kunsang (Hong Kong: Ranjung Yeshe Publications, 1995), 155.

2. Ibid., 110.

3. Jon Kabat-Zinn, *Wherever You Go, There You Are: Mindfulness Meditation in Everyday Life* (New York: Hyperion, 1994), 4.

4. Tulku Urgyen Rinpoche, *Rainbow Painting,* 120.

5. Joseph Goldstein, *Mindfulness: A Practical Guide to Awakening* (Boulder, CO: Sounds True, 2013).

6. Yongey Mingyur Rinpoche with Helen Tworkov, *Turning Confusion into Clarity: A Guide to the Foundation Practices of Tibetan Buddhism* (Boston: Snow Lion, 2014), Kindle locations 329–336.

7. Stephany Tlalka, "Willoughby Britton: 'The Messy Truth about Mindfulness,'" on Mindful.org, July 4, 2014, mindful.org/mindfulness-practice/willoughby-britton-the-messy-truth-about-mindfulness.

Chapter 13: Living from Being

1. Rumi, *The Essential Rumi,* trans. Coleman Barks with John Moyne (New York: Harper Collins, 1995), 109.

2. Richard Schwartz, PhD, "The Larger Self," an essay on The Center for Self Leadership website, accessed February 16, 2015, selfleadership.org/the-larger-self.html.

ACKNOWLEDGMENTS

Every book is a creation with many influences. I may have written it down, but I had tremendous help—this has been a collaboration with a growing, changing, supportive community.

These are some teachers who helped me along the way: Tulku Urgyen Rinpoche, Tsoknyi Rinpoche, Godwin Samaratne, Kosuke Koyama, Coleman Brown, Ann Ulanov, Fr. Bede Griffiths, Dan Brown, Anthony DeMello, Traleg Rinpoche, Namkhai Norbu, Khenchen Thrangu Rinpoche, and particularly Adyashanti and Mingyur Rinpoche.

I want to especially thank my editors: Robin Reinarch, Amy Rost, Naomi Rosenblatt, Stephanie Gunning, Ann McNeal, and Jenny Tufts.

There are people who have helped me in innumerable ways who I feel I want to acknowledge: Maggi Kelly, Melissa Kerr, Nick Herron, Alice McLelland, John Irwin, Dick and Susan Roth, John Slicker, James Brosnan, Robin Rose, Katy Perlman, Nick Herron, Scott McBride, Paige Kelly, Carrington Morris, Satja Khalsa, Zach Hodges, Amy Gross, Susan and Scott Anderson, Lalita Devi, Nancy Schaub, Dawn Legere, Yoga Science Foundation, Nick Rutherford, Dorothy Lichtenstein, Kurt Johnson, and my agent Bill Gladstone.

I am not able to thank everyone who has helped me by name; know your support has helped this book become available to many people.

And finally, I want to thank all my clients and students over the years who have allowed me to share their journeys and have given me the great feedback that has helped me be able to help others.

INDEX

ABOUT THE AUTHOR

L och Kelly, MDiv, LCSW, is the director of the nonprofit Open-Hearted Awareness Institute. He is an educator, licensed psychotherapist, and recognized leader in the field of meditation who was asked to teach Sutra Mahamudra by Mingyur Rinpoche and nondual realization by Adyashanti.

Loch has graduate degrees in psychology and spirituality from Columbia University and Union Theological Seminary, where he was awarded a fellowship to study meditation traditions in Sri Lanka, India, and Nepal. He has helped establish homeless shelters and community lunch programs, and worked in an outpatient mental health clinic in Brooklyn, New York.

Loch collaborates with neuroscientists at Yale, the University of Pennsylvania, and New York University in the study of meditation to discover ways to improve compassion and wellbeing. He currently resides in New York City with his wife, Paige, and their cat, Duffy. For more, please visit the Open-Hearted Awareness Institute website at lochkelly.org.

ABOUT SOUNDS TRUE

Sounds True is a multimedia publisher whose mission is to inspire and support personal transformation and spiritual awakening. Founded in 1985 and located in Boulder, Colorado, we work with many of the leading spiritual teachers, thinkers, healers, and visionary artists of our time. We strive with every title to preserve the essential "living wisdom" of the author or artist. It is our goal to create products that not only provide information to a reader or listener, but that also embody the quality of a wisdom transmission.

For those seeking genuine transformation, Sounds True is your trusted partner. At SoundsTrue.com you will find a wealth of free resources to support your journey, including exclusive weekly audio interviews, free downloads, interactive learning tools, and other special savings on all our titles.

To learn more, please visit SoundsTrue.com/freegifts or call us toll free at 800-333-9185.

sounds True
many voices, one journey